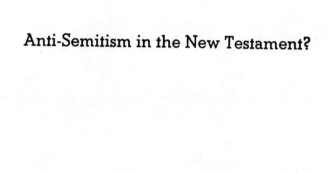

Anti-Semitism in the New Testament?

Anti-Semitism in the New Testament?

SAMUEL SANDMEL

FORTRESS PRESS   PHILADELPHIA

Library of Congress Cataloging in Publication Data

Sandmel, Samuel.
    Anti-Semitism in the New Testament?

    1. Jews in the New Testament.   2. Christianity and antisemitism. I. Title.
BS2545.J44S26   225.6   77-15245
ISBN 0-8006-0521-7

6523L77   Printed in the United States of America 1–521

Contents

Contents

*In memory of my parents,
refugees from persecution,
who bequeathed much to me,
but no bitterness*

Preface

Why a book on this topic? And why does a Jew write such a book? A focused study of the straightforward question that comprises the title has become increasingly imperative. It has been forced upon our time by the searching desire for a basic understanding of anti-Semitism that has been the unabated concern of religious communities since the Holocaust—the destruction of the Jews of Europe by Hitler —though the need for objective inquiry of course predates our present decades.

My embarking on this book is not the result of my own initiation, nor a response to timeliness, but rather a response to urgent proposals and suggestions coming even more frequently from Christians than from Jews. In writing it, I have two primary loyalties. One is to objective scholarship, the other is to my Jewish background. I am a rabbi. My life's work has been the study of early Christianity; in this study my teachers have been not Jews but Christians. I have written books in some abundance: for example, *A Jewish Understanding of the New Testament* (New York: KTAV, 1968), *The Genius of Paul: A Study in History* (New York: Schocken Books, 1970), *We Jews and Jesus* (New York: Oxford University Press, 1965), *The First Christian Century in Judaism and Christianity: Certainties and Uncertainties* (New York: Oxford University Press, 1969), and *Judaism and Christian Beginnings* (New York: Oxford University Press, 1978). In all these books, and in others, I have sought to understand and thus portray Christianity with the measure of sympathy and critical admiration that is my genuine conviction.

This book is published by a Christian firm, a Lutheran publishing house. The director, upon learning that I was giving a series of lectures entitled "Anti-Semitism in the New Testament?" to a national meeting of Reform rabbis, became interested in publishing a book on the subject. A few years earlier I had been invited to contribute an

ix

article, "New Testament Attitudes to Jews," to the supplementary volume of *The Interpreter's Bible Dictionary*. After I accepted the assignment the editor said, "Do tell it straight. Pull no punches." I attributed those words to the admirable intellectual honesty that I had already discovered to be widespread among Christian scholars.

These two examples of Christian concern surely call, on the one hand, for a treatment of the topic in as candid and academically sound a way as possible. Surely each editor was reasonably entitled to a manuscript that would be honest in its content. On the other hand, the present book, however honest its content, ought not to be ugly in tone, for it would be the height of churlishness for me to respond to sincere concern in an antagonistic, deliberately recriminating manner that might cloud understanding. It has never been my intention or purpose to disparage Christianity or Christians. But how can one succeed in writing a book in an area of great sensitivity and totally avoid the inadvertent offensive phrase or sentiment? How can one in an academic fashion assemble materials the sum total of which could seem to be a deliberately unfriendly stacking of the cards?

Accordingly, I confess to constant trepidation throughout the writing of this book. I am acutely conscious of the deep emotions that can be aroused merely by the words of the title, "Anti-Semitism in the New Testament?" I have feared that I will inadvertently offend both some fellow Jews and some Christians—the Christians through assertions that will seem to asperse their sacred Scripture, the Jews through not seeming to asperse Christian Scripture enough. How academically impartial can I be? I do not know; I can only make the effort. What kind of book is this? I hope it is a solid, substantial study.

I wish to record my gratitude to Justin Friedman, a friend, for his critical and helpful reading of the manuscript. And I record especially the assistance of my wife, Frances, and her invaluable help in matters of style and clarity.

Introduction

Some words of historical orientation must lead us back from the present to the New Testament itself. The basic presupposition is that in the Western world of modern times the trespasses of religious bigotry, religious intolerance, and religious persecution came to be acknowledged as evil and that they were largely repudiated from the eighteenth century on. This is not to suggest that all forms and manifestations of such bigotry, intolerance, and persecution have by any means disappeared, that there have not been repeated instances of intense animosity, or that deeds of violence or revived aspects of the worst of premodern bigotry have not occurred. When these have occurred, however, it is significant that the instances have been completely out of accord with the major suppositions of the modern age. They have gone against its grain, whereas before, deeds of bigotry or violence were all too often direct expressions of the essence of their age. When Protestants and Catholics warred with each other, when the disestablished sects of England were persecuted by the Church of England, when German pietists were harassed by Lutherans or the Huguenots massacred in and expelled from France, the misdeeds of organized religions rested on the premise that they were sanctioned by the societies in which they occurred.

It was in the eighteenth century that religious persecution began to lose the social sanction it had once possessed. The transition—slow and painful—was from that premise of approval to the newer conviction that overt persecution was not only devoid of sanction but out of keeping with the enlightenment modern man was achieving. Religious liberty implied that men had the right to express their religious adherences and to cultivate their legacy in fullest freedom from all external influences or restraints. Accordingly the First Amendment to the American Constitution provided for religious liberty. And in Britain in the nineteenth century Roman Catholics and thereafter

Jews were accorded full civil rights. Here and there, of course, restrictions persisted (sometimes against aspects of Christianity, sometimes against Jews), but such persistence was clearly against the constantly growing and spreading conviction that religious freedom was a cornerstone of the modern spirit.

New nations, like the United States and Canada, fostered a multiplicity of denominations, some owing their origin to European national churches, others to an emphasis on some aspect of inherited doctrine. Some (like the Church of Jesus Christ of the Latter-Day Saints, usually called the Mormons, and the Christian Science church) were entirely new. In this multiplicity there arose a kind of paradox: on the one hand an intensified loyalty by adherents to their own particular denomination and, on the other hand, the subordination of denominationalism to a general sense of Christian identification. Thus, however intensely a Baptist or Methodist identified with the Baptist or the Methodist church, the primary identification was not with the denomination but with Christianity. While denominationalism might obstruct an intermarriage between adherents of diverse Protestant churches, it became common for an Episcopalian to marry a Presbyterian, or a Congregationalist to marry a Methodist, without any sense of rupture of one's Christian identification. The migrations within the country as the frontier was extended added to the decline of denominationalism; men went into business partnerships without regard to shades of sect. Religious affiliation became a private matter; moreover, all denominations—indeed, all religions— were deemed to be good, and equal in value, being a person's own choice by conscience.

The theological bases for denominationalism became largely forgotten. Indeed, the subtle shift took place wherein for the most part Christians came to view Christianity not as a set of theological convictions but as a set of virtues. While the creeds continued to be recited in worship services, it was the virtues of caring for the sick, the poor, the widow, and the orphan, and the education of the young, that seemed most completely to define what Christianity had come to be. Being a Christian was no longer essentially theological but rather synonymous with the highest of human decencies. It was widely held that if these virtues had prevailed in the past there would never have arisen the inner hostilities and persecutions. Now at last Christianity had emerged as a way of decency, as the life of virtue. The exemplar of these virtues was Jesus.

This Jesus was found in the Gospels, but there his figure was at times obscured, either by miracle stories that might or might not be credible or by mystifying (and irrelevant) theological ideas. Nevertheless, Jesus was easy to understand, for he personified all human goodness. On the other hand, Paul was not easy to understand and, indeed, as the philosopher Whitehead had written, Paul had done more than anyone to distort the clear and appealing teachings of the Christ. The complexities of Pauline thought and doctrine were not worth the effort. For most Christians there was a "simple gospel" in the New Testament, dealing with the ideal teacher and ideal example for modern man, Jesus of Nazareth.

However much the professional theologians protested against the "simple gospel" as being either superficial or untenable, or both, the usual American Christian nevertheless clung to the view of Christianity as an aggregate of virtues and of Jesus as the epitome of all of them. He had taught the Golden Rule and the Golden Rule was theology enough. Even in the denominations wherein traditional theology was perpetuated with some zeal, the "simple gospel" was often deemed an adequate summary and Jesus as the good and wise and decent and humble teacher stood for the epitome of what the theologically minded were saying so laboriously.

As for Jews and Judaism, consistent with the view that all religions were good and of equal value, Judaism too was good, and equal in value to Christianity. After all, Jesus himself was a Jew, and his teachings were Jewish. Alas, as happened so often, Jesus had run afoul of some of his fellow Jews: the self-righteous hypocrites, the Pharisees, who opposed him, and the usual trustees of the establishment—the high priests and the Sanhedrin[1]—who resented his just criticism of them and who, as establishments will, conspired against him so that the Romans executed him. But Jesus was a Jew and what he taught was the highest version of Judaism; hence Judaism was a good and noble religion. As for the Pharisees, the high priests, and the Sanhedrin, there were universal types with ample counterpart in the various forms of historic Christianity.

With the ghetto walls fallen, Jews and Christians came to know each other. They cooperated in public endeavors. Here and there a business partnership arose, here and there an intermarriage took place. Just as Christianity was an aggregate of virtues, so Judaism

---

1. While I prefer to use "Sanhedrin," the RSV uses "the council" in its translation. Both terms are used interchangeably in this book.

also was a way of comparable virtuous living. There were of course ignoble Jews, but there were ignoble Christians too. Decency demanded an end to bigotry, and Christianity could not be decent so long as it fostered bigotry against Jews. Only among unenlightened Christians could bigotry persist; enlightened Christians could not countenance any disrespect for the ancient and worldly religion, the religion of Jesus, which Judaism represented.

In the nineteenth and early twentieth centuries there arose in eastern Europe and in Asia pogroms against Jews. Both Western Christian leaders and ordinary Christians deplored and denounced these residues of medievalism, for modern men and modern Christians could not countenance trespasses. Such acts violated the spirit of Christianity as fully as they violated the spirit of modern man. The Dreyfus affair at the turn of the century had been the last gasp of bigotry against Jews. Dreyfus had been innocent and was at last vindicated of the charges against him; Europe and Western Christianity had purged itself of animosity toward Jews. Whatever residual hostility might abide would continue to decrease and in time disappear—so it was believed in the early twentieth century.

Then in the 1930s Hitler came to power in Germany. Nazism unleashed an unprecedented assault on Jews, whether they were practicing Jews or Christians with a single Jewish grandparent. Beyond the ravages of the "total warfare," as in the German attacks on Poland, Holland, and Belgium with their attendant unprecedented horrors, the Nazis carried out the ultimate ravage of "the final solution," the extermination of innocent and defenseless Jews. Why this special bestiality? The Nazis were, if not Christian, at least by birth Christians; how could nominal Christians have done these things to Jews? Indeed, what was there in Christian Germany that enabled Hitler to gain the assent of the best-educated country in the world to the anti-Jewish sentiments he preached? What had happened to Christianity as an aggregate of virtues if anti-Jewish preachments and practices could be tolerated or endorsed or even glorified?

Or was the conception of Christianity as an aggregate of virtues merely sentimental self-deception on the part of comfortable, middle-class people, the reality being that Christianity represented also intolerance, arrogance, and cruelty? Was the Nazi unprovoked war against Jews out of keeping with the reality of Christianity or was it instead the direct and logical result of the very nature of Christianity? If the latter, when and how did hostility to Jews enter into Christianity? One answer was to ascribe the origin of anti-Jewish motifs to the second or even the third Christian century, to a time after the age of the New Testament, in order to exempt the New Testament itself. After all, Jesus and his disciples were Jews and some, perhaps most, of the New Testament literature was written by Jews; hence the New Testament could not have been anti-Jewish. But perhaps it is the New Testament itself that is, or at least can be, the source of and sanction for Christian hostility and contempt for the Jews.

Decent, noble Christians, free of all bigotry, have been asking such basic questions, especially since Hitler's time, out of genuine, heart-felt concerns. Such Christians and their Jewish counterparts in the quest for understanding are the audience of this book. The book is an effort to set forth the facts. We shall see that some matters are complex and that the "simple gospel" is scarcely a reality. Why try to set forth the facts? To accuse? Hardly! To arouse Jewish suspicion of even worthy Christians? Hardly! There can be only one purpose: One cures a disease only by recognizing its full medical implications, only by understanding the disease.

The paramount problem concerning this study is that it treads not only on uncertain ground but on holy ground as well. There is a wide range within Christendom respecting the implication of the word *sacred* in the phrase *sacred Scripture*. One conviction is that *sacred* means eternally authoritative and that sacred Scripture is necessarily free of every kind of blemish, whether in matters of history and fact or in matters of attitude. Another conviction is that although Scripture is indeed sacred it is not exempt from some bondage to time and circumstance, nor is it fully free from a human element, namely, that men preserved this literature and that men wrote it.

The Hebrew Bible is in these respects no different from the New Testament. There exists an immense modern scholarly literature on the Hebrew Bible, in which the writings have been studied, analyzed, and dated. One conclusion from all this study is that the writings in the Hebrew Bible come from a time span of almost a thousand years and that they reflect distinct historical epochs, such as the Wilderness Period; the Settlement in Canaan; the Monarchy, including the conquests by the Assyrians in 722 B.C. and the Babylonians in 597–587 B.C.; the Exile, including the Persian conquest; the Restoration of the Temple, and, thereafter, the conquest by Alexander the Great. Many minds and hearts contributed to the thinking behind the writings and to the ideas expressed within them. Did all these minds represent only one view? Or did these minds at times reflect a range and variety of views? Are all the views of the same lofty idealism or are some influenced by the historical events within the thousand-year span? If out of disaster, warfare, tension, disappointment, or even a sense of betrayal there were those who wrote in anger or bitterness, is this to be wondered at?

How shall one assess the last lines of Psalm 137? Here are the words:

> Remember, O Lord, against the Edomites
> the day of Jerusalem,
> how they said, "Rase it, rase it!
> Down to its foundations!"
> O daughter of Babylon, you devastator!
> Happy shall he be who requites you
> with what you have done to us!
> Happy shall he be who takes your little ones
> and dashes them against the rock!

When the Babylonians destroyed Jerusalem in 587 B.C. the Edomites were allied with them. The Edomites were a kindred people to the Hebrews. Scripture ascribed their origin to an ancestor, Esau-Edom, who was a son of Isaac and a grandson of Abraham (Gen. 25:21–26). Was not the Edomite alliance with the Babylonians all the more a source of understandable bitterness on the part of the Judeans? Can we not grasp why the author of these lines in Psalm 137 wrote with a desire for vengeance? More difficult, yet still within our capacity to understand, is the last sentence, which sanctions and praises the killing of Edomite babies by throwing them down from the Edomite capital located high on some rocky crags.

Let us assume that we can understand and even sympathize with the cruel and vindictive bitterness. Need we share it today? Is the tone of these sentences one we would appropriate for ourselves? And are there not attitudes and sentiments in the Hebrew Bible that are exactly the opposite? For example, Deuteronomy 23:7 reads: "You shall not abhor an Edomite, for he is your brother." The reasonable conclusion from widest study is that the affirmative, noble sentiments in the Hebrew Bible outnumber and outweigh the negative and the ignoble. But the fact remains that negative and ignoble sentiments are there.

Should one expect otherwise of the New Testament? I do not think so. We shall see certain New Testament materials on Jews and Judaism that are not easy to assess with respect to our topic. Thus, in the Hebrew Bible the prophets of the age before the Babylonian Exile provide variations of a similar theme, that the Hebrew people had in their actions proved false to the religious-ethical standards expressed in a covenant with God and expected of a holy people. Accordingly, an Amos, an Isaiah, and a Jeremiah each speak with wondrous poetic eloquence about the shortcomings of the people, whether monarchs or priests or ordinary folk. Clearly these words by the prophets are denunciations from within; surely no one would ascribe to Amos, Isaiah, or Jeremiah that form of hostility which we call anti-Semitism (to use for the moment the word that I shall later speak of as wrong). It was out of the loyalty to and identification with the people and their religion that the Hebrew prophets spoke their sharp criticisms. When in the Gospels the Jew Jesus speaks in criticism of Jews, is it not reasonable that he too speaks out of loyalty and identification? But is it not also possible that words which Jesus spoke as a loyal insider came to be put into a context in which they appeared to be those of an outsider, no longer identifiable with his people? These are matters we need to look into.

Indeed, these matters can be quite complex. Let us look in a preliminary way into the reason for the basic complexity: Jesus was a Jew. He became central in a religion with obvious Jewish roots that became a different religion, the adherents of which were preeminently Gentiles, that is, non-Jews. If Jesus had not been a Jew and if Christianity had not derived from Judaism, the New Testament writings would not have contained those passages that are the concern of this book.

Or if the Jews, like the Edomites, had vanished from the face of the earth, there would exist no more direct concern in our time about the Jews in the New Testament than about the Edomites in the Hebrew Bible. After the New Testament age it became normal for Christians in their unfolding ascendancy to fashion political and economic restrictions on the Jews because of the import of New Testament sentiments about them. Limitations in rights and various forms of oppression, such as forced conversion or expulsion, were frequent experiences of Jews at the hands of Christians in the Middle Ages. The matter of the Edomites is essentially antiquated, quite unrelated to today. Not so with the Jews.

Christians have wanted and Jews have needed urgently to understand the *why* of it all, why Christianity became a source and mandate for Christians to express unreserved hostility to Jews and Judaism. Is the hostility part and parcel of sacred Christian Scripture, potentially or actually, perpetuated in ordinary Christian worship still today when the Christian Scripture is read? But the crucial question, the ultimate one, is this: Is hostility to Jews something merely ancient, something merely transient in Christianity? Is its renewal in every generation through the use of Christian Scripture in a chapel, church, or cathedral no more than an unfortunate carry-over from the past? Or is hostility to Jews, as some—Christians as well as Jews—have charged, a basic, permanent, unremovable aspect of Christianity?

Our concern is to see precisely what is in the New Testament and to try to understand why the hostility is there, and thereafter to try to answer this question: Is or is not anti-Semitism a permanent, unremovable aspect of Christianity?

Christianity became a religion separate from Judaism primarily out of convictions about Jesus, about who and what he was. As to who he was, the brief answer is that he was a Jew of Galilee, the leader of some kind of a movement—its teacher as well as its leader. He was considered by his followers to be the long-awaited Jewish "Messiah," a term we shall need to define. He was executed by the Romans. His followers became convinced that he was resurrected and on being resurrected appeared to some of these followers.

This conviction of resurrection prompted the natural questions: What kind of figure was he—only human or more than human? What was the meaning of his career? For whom did this career have meaning—for his followers alone or for all humanity? Out of the answers that his followers gave to such questions the new movement fashioned its outlooks and doctrines, became an entity of its own, and spread and grew.

The writings in the New Testament came from his followers, for either Jesus himself never wrote anything, or else nothing that he wrote was preserved. Our procedure is to follow the writings in their chronological order. We need to be prepared to encounter in this literature reflections of differing Christian viewpoints. Although the new movement was based on the conviction that Jesus was resurrected from the dead, we shall see, for example, that there were some Christians in the earliest times who did not believe Jesus had truly been resurrected. We shall see too that even those who believed in his resurrection did not agree on what resurrection meant, and they quarreled bitterly with each other. Indeed, within the new movement acute controversies arose, and some of these controversies became quite nasty, pitting not Christian against Jew but Christian against Christian.

We shall also see in the New Testament writings quarrels and controversies between Christians and Jews, and controversies between Christians advocating certain Jewish practices and other Christians denying the necessity for these practices. The inner Christian controversies arose out of differing viewpoints that centered in such questions as: How Jewish should Christianity be? What was there in the legacy from the ancient past that Christianity needed to preserve, what in the legacy could be abandoned, and on what basis could it be abandoned? To say this another way, the issue arose as to what of Judaism was permanent and valid in Christianity and what could be appropriately discarded.

Those who advocated discarding certain elements of Judaism were in effect raising the question What is the essential nature of Judaism? That facets of Judaism appeared to merit discarding involved a criticism—whether fair or unfair—of the very nature of Judaism. Accordingly, Christianity in its very nature implies a criticism of Judaism. That is, side by side with controversies between Christians and Jews (over questions about whether or not Jesus was resurrected) there were controversies about *Judaism.* It became a Christian conviction that Christianity is a better—the word *better* must suffice here—religion than Judaism. We shall see as we proceed that at times it is Judaism that Christian writings denigrate and at other times it is Jews. Granted that Jews and Judaism are intertwined, we shall go astray if we are not alert to the valid distinction between Christian criticism of Judaism and Christian bitterness against Jews.

The term *Christian* has been used in the above paragraphs somewhat inaccurately. It came into being after the new movement had already been under way for some time. The Acts of the Apostles (11:26) tells that "in Antioch the disciples were for the first time called Christians." That is, a Jewish movement had spread beyond the borders of its native Judea and after attracting Gentiles came to bear the name "Christian." Often the author of Acts uses as the name for the movement the term *the Way.* Obviously in the time prior to the rise of the term *Christian* the new movement was simply a grouping deemed to be within Judaism, however much it differed from other groupings within Judaism. It is technically wrong to speak of the movement in its earliest phases as Christianity; I shall nevertheless do so.

It is also technically wrong to use *anti-Semitism* in connection with the New Testament. That term arose in the nineteenth century, appearing for the first time in the writings of a Wilhelm Marr around 1878. At that time it was not used in relation to matters of religion or to Christian sentiments. It had emerged as a result of a mingling of notions about race and nationalism. Out of nationalism there arose theories about the need for a nation to have a homogeneous population. The implication in the theories was that certain peoples, Jews and gypsies, for example, could not be part of such a homogeneous national population. Homogeneity was a matter of race. Germans were by race Aryan (a term central in later Nazism) and Germans were a superior, indeed the supreme, race; on the other hand, Jews were of the Semitic race, an inferior one. Anti-Semitism was the avowed intention of racists to bar Jews from legitimate membership in the body politic in Germany or in other European states.

The terms *Aryan* and *Semite* were borrowed from the study of languages. The Semitic languages include Hebrew, Syriac, Arabic, and a number of others; all these related to each other in vocabulary and syntax. As a family of languages they are different from the family that includes Sanskrit (a language of India), Greek, Latin, and German, and some others. At one time students of language spoke of this latter family as Indo-European, since the languages stretched westward from India into Europe (but German scholars preferred the term *Indo-Germanic!*). Then the term *Aryan* arose for this family of languages.

Relative to languages these terms make sense, but they were transferred to peoples, where they make no sense. Americans of Turkish, Basque, Chinese, or Hawaiian extraction all speak English; the language of a person or of a people in no way defines the race, for throughout the ages given languages have been replaced by other languages through migration or conquest. For example, throughout the eastern Mediterranean basin in the age of Jesus the language of Jews in Grecian lands had changed from the Semitic Aramaic to Greek.

Not only did the "racists" incongruously borrow these linguistic terms, but they ascribed value judgments in relation to peoples. The Aryan race was superior, the Semitic inferior. To be light-complexioned (like a Swede or a Norwegian) was to possess better innate traits than to be dark-complexioned (like a Greek or a Spaniard). Complexion suggested race and race meant quality.

Prior to 1880 whatever hostility existed toward Jews in western Europe was religious, not racial. Racial animosity could be aimed by nominal Christians at dark-skinned Christians of Spain or Italy quite as readily as at Jews, even at blond, blue-eyed Jews. While in

Spain in the sixteenth and seventeenth centuries there had existed a somewhat similar distinction between "pure" Spaniards and those who were of "impure" blood through having Jewish or Moorish forebears, it was in France and Germany in the nineteenth century that the distinction among races was declared to rest on some "scientific" basis. That "scientific" basis was pure hogwash, but advocates nevertheless succeeded in persuading those who wanted to be persuaded, especially if the pseudoscience could be used for political manipulations. Christianity also came under attack from racists of that time simply because it had Jewish roots; there were those racists who scorned Jesus as preaching a religion of weakness that was out of keeping with the manly heroism of the German legendary characters of mythology and of the operas of Richard Wagner. On the other hand, some German racists, because medieval artists had painted Jesus with red hair, declared him an Aryan and not a Jew! Racism thoroughly permeated Nazism, and when the Nazis came to power they slaughtered Jews and others who were deemed non-Aryans.

During Christian persecutions of Jews, a Jew could escape by converting to Christianity. Not so with the Nazis. A Jew could escape Nazi persecution only by succeeding in fleeing. Religious affiliation ceased to have direct bearing, for anti-Semitism was focused on race, not religion. Accordingly, the nineteenth- and twentieth-century word *anti-Semitism* is a completely wrong term when transferred to the first and second Christian centuries. Yet wrong as it is, it has been and continues to be used in connection with Christian hostility to Jews. Scholars have proposed other terms: *Anti-Jewish* or *Anti-Judaism*. These terms are better because they are correct; they simply have not caught on. In this book we use "anti-Semitism" consciously, aware of how wrong the term is.

1. Pagan Anti-Semitism

Hostility to Jews in the Greco-Roman world predates Christianity. Was this anti-Semitism a legacy to Gentile Christians from pagans? We might for convenience speak of two different types of pagan anti-Semitism. One type was the vulgar social frictions that arose between Jews and pagans in part of the Greco-Roman world, like that among immigrants to America in a common urban neighborhood. Jews had been granted first by Hellenistic and then by Roman kings the right to live under Jewish law and to be exempted from aspects of imperial law. In such circumstances the frictions between Jews and pagans were chronic and much less than acute, at least as compared with specific acute events, which we will presently turn to.

Such chronic static social friction in some given locality in the Greco-Roman world stemmed from the separatism—religious, political, and social. In accord with the religious separatism, Jews ate food in accordance with their dietary laws. They abstained from intermarriage. Jews scorned idolatry and refused to worship imperial idols and imperial personalities. To pagans, the Jews appeared to be atheists. Reports about the Temple in Jerusalem come to be reflected among pagans in two ways. One such report was that in the most foolish of ways the Jews maintained a completely empty chamber in the holy of holies of the Temple. But along with this "foolishness" there arose a logically contradictory view that there was actually something contained in the Temple, namely, the head of an ass! The two allegations have in common only that they express a pagan scorn. As for the contradictory nature of the allegations, the Roman historian Tacitus in one passage (*History* 5. 3–4) sets forth this matter of the head of the ass, even explaining its origin as going back to Moses in the wilderness; water was lacking (as in Exod. 17:1–7), but the Hebrews, by following a herd of wild asses

1

that knew of an oasis, obtained the necessary water. Moses thereupon enjoined the dedication within the sacred shrine of the head of the animal through whose guidance water was discovered.[1] Yet Tacitus writes, directly after the matter of the ass's head, that Jews, *unlike* Egyptians who worship many animals and images, conceive of only one God and do so with mind alone, regarding as sinful those who make representations of deities in the image of man. He adds that Jews do not erect statues, not only not in their sacred places but nowhere in their cities. In the following section (*History* 5. 5) Tacitus tells that through the entrance of the Roman Pompey, the conqueror of Judea in 63 B.C., into the Temple, it became a matter of common knowledge that the shrine was totally empty.

But quite different from reserved, spontaneous neighborhood frictions were incidents of consequence both within Judea and also in Alexandria and North Africa. Such incidents were not trivial or detached items. Among those incidents in Judea were the deeds of Pontius Pilate that outraged the populace.[2] Pilate brought into Jerusalem busts of the emperor Tiberius, used Temple funds to pay for building an aqueduct, and apparently set up decorated shields in Jerusalem in the name of the emperor. Such incidents, involving a Roman official presumably acting on behalf of the emperor, are quite different from a spontaneous physical fight between an individual Jew and a pagan in some unimportant town in Asia Minor.[3]

The Jewish community of Alexandria, Egypt, experienced a full-fledged pogrom in A.D. 38 with the acquiescence of the Roman governor Flaccus. Not only was the pogrom a concerted mob action, but its way had been prepared for by literary propaganda. This propaganda has been preserved, through the quotation of its contentions, and a refutation of them, by the Jewish historian Josephus (A.D. 37–100) in his essay "Against Apion." In the Alexandrian setting there was an immense Jewish community, more numerous indeed than the population of Judea. Alexandria, a cosmopolitan

---

1. This matter of an ass's head in the Temple was widespread among pagan writers, e.g., Plutarch *Quaestiones Convivales* 4. 5. The same allegation was later made against Christians; see Tertullian *Apologeticum* 16. 1–3.

2. See *Antiquities* 18. 55–62; *War* 2. 169–77; Philo *Legation to Gaius* 299–305.

3. Cicero, defending in 62 B.C. an official named L. Valerius Flaccus, in *Pro Flacco* 28. 68–90, does not deny that Flaccus appropriated large sums of money that Jews of Asia Minor had received permission to send to Jerusalem. Cicero contends that what Flaccus had done was not theft, but something quite open and for which there was precedent in a variety of places in Asia Minor. (This Flaccus is different from the Roman governor of Egypt a century later.)

city, contained Greeks and native Egyptians, as well as other transplanted peoples. The anti-Jewish allegations took the form of countering the account in the book of Exodus by asserting that instead of the Hebrews having escaped from slavery in Egypt they had been ignobly expelled from it. Josephus cites an Egyptian priest, Manetho, who wrote a history of Egypt around 250–200 B.C. Manetho had spoken of a people whom he calls the Hyksos, an eastern people who had invaded Egypt and ruled it cruelly for half a millennium. The Egyptians had revolted and had expelled the invaders; these had then returned to their place of origin, Syria, and on the way there founded the city of Jerusalem.

There is still another account in Manetho. It speaks of an enslaved people in Egypt who had revolted against the Egyptian king; the leaders of the rebelling slaves appealed to those people, earlier expelled and now living in Jerusalem, to help them. These came, drove the Egyptian king into Ethiopia, pillaged and polluted the land, and did unspeakable acts of violence; they were lepers. But in due time the Egyptian king rallied the forces necessary to expel them and drive them back into Syria. Some modern scholars contend that Manetho is not speaking about the Jews at all and that Josephus is mistaken in his interpreting Manetho's account as directed against them, for Manetho does not specifically mention the Jews. But subsequent writings that directly or passingly denigrated the Jews came to view Manetho's assertions against the Hyksos as being against the Jews. That is, in Alexandria (and in the rest of Egypt) the clashes were not limited to the minor local or individual frictions but entailed what one might call entire communities. Involved in the clashes also were matters of economic and political concern. The Jewish community of Egypt was by no means passive, but rather quite aggressive, and in due time there arose a notable revolt against the Romans in Egypt, North Africa, and Cyprus in A.D. 115–17.[4]

So too in Judea events such as the Roman conquest in 63 B.C.

---

4. Accounts of Jewish history usually focus so much on Judea that in ordinary religious schools, both Jewish and Christian, the events outside Judea receive little or no attention. Whatever attention is paid is normally based on materials assembled in the nineteenth century and does not utilize the nonliterary papyri, assembled in V. A. Tcherikover and A. Fuks, *Corpus Papyrorum Judaicarum,* 3 vols. (Cambridge, Mass.: Harvard University Press, 1957–64). These papyri greatly amplify our knowledge and in certain instances considerably alter the previous understanding. For example, the letter of Claudius (2:38–43) is a document of the highest importance for understanding the situation of the Alexandrian Jewish community; this letter of Claudius shows that the Jews did not possess as many rights as earlier believed.

and the inner strife between the partisans of Herod (reigned 37–4 B.C.), abetted by Romans and by his foes, the remnants of the Maccabeans, were matters of broad and corporate action. Insensitive or arbitrary Roman governors, at times spurred by distant emperors unaware of the response by the populace to their caprices, elicited Jewish animosities that erupted into the independence movements of A.D. 66–70 and A.D. 130–32.

In his study *The Roots of Anti-Semitism in the Ancient World,* J. N. Sevenster inquires into the question Did this pagan anti-Semitism rest on a "social" basis such as wealth and vocational pursuits, or did it not?[5]   His answer is that clearly it did not. The hostility was only indirectly religious; directly it was not so at all. Instead, it essentially rested on the separatism of the Jews, the latter a result of the religious convictions. The separatism, to repeat, resulted in ascribing a "strangeness" to Jews, which included such elements as their abstention from idol worship, the Sabbath regulations, their practice of circumcision, and, in short, their *amixia,* their disinclination to mix. The Roman satirists such as Juvenal and Horace aspersed the Sabbath. The emperor Caligula suddenly asked the delegation of Jews sent to protest the pogroms in Alexandria why Jews do not eat pork. This sort of thing is usual in human friction between differing groups.

Sevenster makes two important points. One, the scorn of Jews by Roman writers is only a single facet of the scorn felt by them toward a broad variety of other non-Romans. Second, alongside the scorn there are to be found, especially among Greek writers, statements that express admiration, sometimes for Jews, sometimes for Judaism. Since these are quoted by such writers as Josephus, they may be suspect as Jewish inventions. But the fact of pagan converts to Judaism (this a .token of some admiration) is attested to even in writers scornful of Jews such as Horace and Tacitus.[6]   In the period after 70 B.C. a number of emperors (Vespasian, Domitian, Hadrian, and Antoninus Pius) tooks steps to curtail or end such Jewish proselyting. There existed besides proselytes those pagan sympathizers who did not take the final steps of conversion. More women converted than men, the latter presumably deterred by the pain involved in circumcision.[7]

---

5. J. N. Sevenster, *The Roots of Anti-Semitism in the Ancient World* (Leiden: E. J. Brill, 1975).

6. See the summaries in ibid., p. 195.

7. Ibid., pp. 198–99.

It is at times said, as if to excuse or condone Christian anti-Semitism, that it is merely a legacy left to Christendom from the pagan world. My opinion needs to be made as emphatic as possible: there is no relationship between the pagan anti-Semitism and the Christian anti-Semitism. Pagan anti-Semitism was an expression by total outsiders to Judaism and Jewish people; Christian anti-Semitism has its basis in what one might call quasi-insiders. Pagan anti-Semites did not know sacred Scripture; Christians did. Pagans scorned the Sabbath; Christians scorned not the Sabbath itself but what they regarded as a Jewish distortion of a day meriting respect. We shall see the fuller bill of particulars. Pagans scorned Jews as possessed by a heritage that pagans had no respect for; Christians contended that the Jewish heritage no longer belonged to the Jews, but had passed into Christian possession. To equate Christian anti-Semitism with the earlier pagan anti-Semitism is grossly to misunderstand Christian anti-Semitism.

2. Paul

We turn first in the New Testament to the Epistles of Paul, universally held to be the earliest writings in the New Testament. The dates of the various Epistles can be set as roughly between A.D. 40 and 55. If the date of the death of Jesus is taken to be around the years 29 to 31 or 32—as scholars seem to agree—Paul's activity begins just about a decade later. It is to be recalled that there were still alive in the year 40 those who had been followers of Jesus in his lifetime, these apparently living in Jerusalem and under the leadership of James, the brother of Jesus, who is mentioned in the Gospels but there has no role at all in relation to the movement led by Jesus.

Paul, of course, had not been one of these followers. Thus, early as was the time when Paul came into the movement, from the perspective of those already in it he was a newcomer to it. When he came into the movement it was still within Judaism; its adherents were Jews who seemingly lived a normal Judaism to which had been added convictions about Jesus, but without affecting the observance of the usual Jewish practices. Through Paul the movement began to become Gentile. Paul conceived himself as designated by God to be the "apostle to the Gentiles," with the divine mandate to bring them into the movement. The sphere of Paul's activity was outside Judea, that is, in the vast reaches of the Greek world that had long before been conquered and were still ruled over by the Romans. One needs to think, accordingly, of a Judean aspect of the new movement and, through Paul, of an aspect outside Judea, that is, in the lands that Jews spoke of as the Dispersion. There were emerging, then, both Judean and Dispersion geographical aspects of Christianity, and also Jewish and Gentile ideological aspects. Presumably in Judea the adherents were all Jews. In the Dispersion at an early time there were both Jews and Gentiles in the movement;

in the course of an apparently short time the movement in the Dispersion became dominantly Gentile and thereafter it became virtually exclusively Gentile.

Others besides Paul sought to bring Dispersion Gentiles into the movement, as we know from Paul's mention of them. These others seem to have required that such Gentiles in effect must become Jews, that is, observers of the practices and regulations customary among Jews. But it was, or else quickly became, Paul's conviction that Gentiles could be welcomed into the movement without being obliged to observe the Jewish practices and regulations. As Paul's missionary activities expressed this conviction in practical terms, he came into conflict with the other missionaries who were working among the Gentiles. Moreover, representatives of the Jerusalem "Christians" visited Dispersion areas where Paul had worked and at places tried to impose on Paul's converts a new demand for the Jewish observances. Paul, accordingly, was in sharp and direct conflict with fellow missionaries in the Dispersion areas, and in indirect conflict with the church in Jerusalem. These conflicts, beyond the personal frictions, were both practical and theoretical. The practical issue was Should new converts be compelled to observe the Jewish practices? The theoretical, theological issue was What was the "true nature" of Judaism, and in the light of that true nature, what place, if any, was there for Jewish observances *in Judaism?*

So far as we know, Paul's missionary opponents did not raise the theoretical, theological question; they simply carried on the usual Jewish observances as if their validity were automatically to be assumed. Paul, however, did raise this question, and he did so as a central issue and with immense vigor and eloquence. In support of his view that Gentiles need not conform to Jewish observances, he came to argue that these observances were not the primary element in Judaism; that is, he went beyond merely exempting Gentiles from the observances and even proceeded to contend that Judaism, properly understood, did not any longer need to preserve its inherited regulations. In other words, Paul provides what is in effect an evaluation, a criticism, of the essence of Judaism. That criticism of Judaism became, and remains, a rather constant factor in the Christian assessment of Judaism.

At the heart of Paul's criticism of Judaism is the place of the laws of Moses, the primary source for the Jewish regulations. First Pharisees, and then later the ancient rabbis, extended these regulations, these extensions being known as the *halacha* ("way of walking"); by *halacha* we mean the post–Old Testament regulations and observances derived by interpreting Scripture. But the issue between Paul and his ancestral religion was centered in the laws of Moses.

To begin to grasp Paul's attitude it is necessary for us to distinguish between Scripture (more precisely the Pentateuch) and the laws contained in the Pentateuch, these beginning in Exodus 20. For Paul the sanctity of the Pentateuch abided in fullest force and he in no way ever turned his back on it. It was the laws in the Pentateuch that he questioned. He repudiated them as obsolete and annulled. Indeed, he proceeded beyond annulment to an attitude that can be described as one of contempt.

The attitude of Paul in deeming that the Laws were annulled is without direct precedent or parallel in any other literature produced by Jews. Indeed, the usual Jewish premise is that the revelation of God at Sinai, and the laws thereafter ascribed to Moses, has constituted the central core of Judaism in all its diverse versions then and later.[1] The Jewish premise is that God, through and to Moses, revealed the laws by which his divine will and demands could be known and obeyed. Obedience to the laws meant righteous living. Disobedience or nonconformity meant unrighteousness, sin. Two aspects of sin were in theory possible. One was the inadvertent failure to observe the laws through such normal human weaknesses as forgetting or through some other explainable inability or unintentional failure to observe. Thus, if a person forgot that it was the Sabbath and violated the injunctions, or if one wrongly assumed that a stew was made of permitted meat, clearly such a person had no deliberate intention to disobey the Law. On the other hand, there could conceivably be someone who knowingly and deliberately violated the Sabbath law or knowingly and deliberately ate forbidden food. In Scripture it is asserted that deliberate violation was an affront to the Deity and that such affront was unforgivable; the Deity himself would punish such a transgressor by "cutting off that soul from the midst of his people."

For unintentional sin, divine forgiveness and restoration to innocency was attainable through penitence. The biblical penitential system presupposed that the inadvertent sinner could go through rituals and the offering of sacrifices whereby he could shed his guilt.

---

1. In context, neither the Karaites (who arose in the eighth Christian century) nor Reform Jews (who arose in the nineteenth) ever expressed an attitude toward the Laws in any way similar to Paul's.

The prime occasion for penitence was the period from the New Year (which falls on Tishri 1) through the Yom Kippur, the Day of Atonement (Tishri 10). The period came to be known as the Ten Days of Repentance. The underlying theory was that there was maintained in heaven an account book with a record of the deeds of all humans. A divine court convened on the New Year, the annual judgment day. The Deity opened the account book and, on the basis of the record, made his decision for every human for the ensuing year, whether he would live or die, be exalted or lowered. That decision, if unfavorable, was subject to divine reconsideration and even revision or total cancellation, this through the period of the ten days, depending on the earnestness of the penitence. The original decision, or its subsequent revision, was "sealed" on the Day of Atonement.[2]

Inadvertent trespass, then, was forgivable, if God so willed it, provided that sincere human repentance took place.[3] In a word, man could inadvertently sin, intentionally repent so as to effect his atonement, and God could forgive. There is a noticeable inherent coherence in these related views. From the thought of Paul this pattern of sin and repentance is entirely missing; perhaps it was deliberately abandoned. Indeed, though the words *sin* and *atonement* do appear in Paul, they have senses markedly different from what these words have in the usual Judaism. It is especially striking that the idea of repentance is singularly missing from Paul, with the word itself appearing in his Epistles very rarely. Moreover, in Paul's thought, sin and atonement are linked with the Messiah, the Christ; such linking is not found in any other version of Judaism.

For our present purposes, we might set forth briefly the main aspects of Paul's views, not to present an exposition for its own sake but to relate these views to our topic of anti-Semitism. Paul's basic assumption about sin is quite unrelated to the inadvertent acts in violation of the laws in Scripture, whether of commission or omission. Instead, sin is viewed as a power that holds man in its control.

2. The New Year greeting among Jews—found on commercial greeting cards—reads, "May you be *inscribed* for a good year," inscribed, that is, in the account book. The Day of Atonement greeting is, "May you be *sealed* for a good year."

3. While the New Year–Day of Atonement period was considered the preeminent occasion for repentance, it was also assumed that repentance could take place and be effective at any time. Moreover, the advice was offered that a man should repent the day before his death—and since that day is unknown, one should repent every day!

Sin, indeed, so permeates man (this by the very nature of man) that man is innately a sinner. Man is universally under the power of sin, whether he is a Jew or a Gentile.

Man on his own is powerless to cope with, let alone overcome, this bondage to sin. We might here express this idea by saying that man cannot work his own atonement. Rather, atonement, if man is to gain it, must be wrought outside of man on his behalf by a supernatural power greater than he. That supernatural power is the Christ. It was Paul's view that the Christ, having become the man Jesus, underwent the experience of death and thereby brought atonement to mankind, releasing man from his bondage to sin. Man, in Paul's thought, does not and cannot work his own atonement. (One notices how differently the word *atonement* rings in Pauline and in usual Jewish thought.)

If we set two over-simple statements side by side we can see most readily the contrast between Paul's views and those in other aspects of Judaism. The Jewish view: man sins, man can atone, God can forgive. The view of Paul: man is under bondage to sin, the divine Christ atones for man, and then man is "forgiven."

Consistent with such views is Paul's uniquely negative attitude toward the laws of Scripture. These laws, in his view, were by no means eternal as Jews have contended; rather, they had a beginning (through Moses) and for a span of time were operative, but that span of time had ended. The advent of the Christ had marked the end of that span of time and now the laws were superseded and accordingly nullified.

Paul provides a range of statements that are consistent with this view. One of these, Galatians 3:19, is in part enigmatic. In context, Paul is asserting that the basic relationship between God and his people rested on *promises* made to Abraham (in Gen. 12:3) and that that relationship based on promises could not properly become altered into one based on laws (as Jews by implication contended). Galatians 3:19 concludes by saying that the Mosaic law was "ordained by angels through an intermediary." Precisely what Paul means is debatable, as for example whether or not angels should be understood as demons. What is clear in Paul's thought is that the Mosaic laws associated in biblical thought with the revelation to Moses at Sinai are of secondary, not primary, significance, and the role of the man Moses hardly more than that of an intermediary between the angels (whatever they are) and mankind. To Paul's age, Moses is not the giver of an eternal law, nor is Moses of any crucial significance.

Paul has two related views about possible fidelity to the Laws. One view is that man is innately incapable of observing the Laws simply because bondage to sin impedes man's capacity to observe them. The accompanying second view is that fidelity to the Laws, even were it possible, is of no consequence at all because he who successfully or unsuccessfully observes the Laws is relying on himself and is thereby relying on mere man. It is God, rather than man, on whom man should rely.

This reliance on God is reached through Paul's view of Abraham in Scripture. The patriarch lived before the Mosaic laws came into existence. Yet Scripture (Gen. 15:6) says of Abraham that "he believed the Lord; and he reckoned it to him as righteousness," meaning that Abraham through his faith in God achieved righteousness and that accordingly the Laws, which came only later, were not and are not needed for such an achievement.

Consistent with his view that righteousness, whether by Abraham or by Paul's contemporaries, was attainable without the Laws, Paul sets forth a doctrine uniquely his own: that man is justified by faith and, indeed, only by faith. My understanding of this view is as follows: Paul's premise is that all men, Jews and Gentiles, are under bondage to sin. This bondage to sin inevitably and universally results in deeds of trespass; hence all men become guilty of trespass. Guilty mankind can achieve a transition from sinful guilt to innocence, that is, to righteousness, through *faith,* a man's total reliance on God. Paul's phrase for the transition from such past universal guilt into a present state of guiltlessness is "justification by faith." The basic supposition in justification rests on the conviction of the universal nature of man's past guilt.

Faithful obedience to the Mosaic law is in Paul's view unyielding and of no spiritual gain. Indeed, according to Paul, the Mosaic laws and efforts to observe them are an impediment to the attainment of righteousness. He provides a series of synonymous expressions that, though different, have in common the inadequacies or deficiencies that Paul ascribes to the Laws. He uses phrases such as the "law kills" (contrasted with the Holy Spirit which "gives life") and "the law is a curse"; and he also contends that "law" is responsible for the introduction of sin into the experience of the human race.

Shall we classify these convictions and expressions that denigrate the laws of Moses as anti-Semitism? Or, since Paul is a Jew, is he, like an Amos or an Isaiah, a loyal critic of his inherited Judaism

from within? Paul states that God appointed him as the "apostle
to the Gentiles." In his activity in the spread of the new movement
he founded local churches, such as that in Galatia, on the basis that
his Gentile converts were exempt from the need to observe the
Mosaic laws. The occasion for his angry, eloquent Epistle to the
Galatians was his learning that the Galatians had been induced by
certain unnamed visitors to observe the Mosaic laws. Paul not only
felt that a basic principle, precious to him, had been violated, but
also that he personally, as their founder, had been repudiated and
betrayed.

This personal sense of betrayal was all the deeper because of certain previous incidents that for him were decisive in character. Thus,
earlier at Antioch the church had been primarily Gentile and the
Mosaic laws were there not observed, not even by the Jew Cephas.
But after certain men from Jerusalem had come to Antioch, Cephas
and other Christian Jews who had been eating with Gentiles—without concern for Jewish food laws—now ceased such eating. Paul
had confronted Cephas with the accusation that he who had lived
as the Gentiles did was now compelling Gentile Christians to live
like Jews.

Paul was all the more aggrieved because he had even earlier received a sanction from leaders in Jerusalem for his "mission to the
Gentiles." They had asked only one thing of him, that he remember the poor in Judea and send funds for them. He had gone to
Jerusalem not to be subordinate to the leaders there but to avert
their interfering with his activities. (He could not be subordinate
for he was an apostle designated by God, not by the leaders in
Jerusalem; in fact, he was long personally unknown in Jerusalem.)
The Epistle to the Galatians reveals Paul in controversy, both on
the basic issue of the need of Christians to observe the Mosaic laws
and also his outrage at what seems to him a personal betrayal.

Paul's opponents in Galatia are not Jews as such but rather Christians, possibly or probably of Jewish birth, who are advocating the
necessity for observance of the Mosaic laws by all Christians. The
name for such advocates is "judaizers." While a judaizer may have
been of Jewish ancestry, he is no longer a Jew; a judaizer is a Christian. Paul's recurring controversies are inner Christian; it is with
rival apostles, with judaizers within the movement, not with Jews
who are outside it. Paul is very bitter against judaizers; we shall
presently see how relatively little he says about Jews as such.

His bitterness, his basic convictions, and his special concern for

Gentiles lead him in Galatians to a contrast between observers of the Mosaic laws and nonobservers; he speaks of nonobservance as marked by "freedom" and of observance as "slavery." Genesis 16 speaks of Hagar, the Egyptian slave of childless Sarah, through whom Abraham begot a son, Ishmael, prior to his begetting Isaac through Sarah. Paul asserts that observers of the Law are descended from the slave Hagar, who, he says, symbolizes Sinai and the city of Jerusalem. Those who are "free" of the Law are descendants of Abraham through Sarah, related to the "heavenly" Jerusalem.

In Romans, Paul defines a Jew as someone who is one inwardly, not by outward matters such as circumcision (Rom. 2:25–29). What Paul has in mind is that the "Jews" are not the true Jews; he means that the "true Jews" are the Christian nonobservers of the laws of Moses. Nevertheless, Paul, in several passages, speaks of the priority of the Jews in God's scheme of things. Such priority might, in principle, have been only that of time: the Jews had long been on the historical scene before Christianity had arisen. But a second kind of priority was part of the Jewish heritage of the past; the Jews had been, and up to Paul's time were, first in God's favor in that they were God's chosen people.

Priority in both of these senses was part of Paul's own heritage as a Jew. Yet while Jesus and his first followers were Jews the particular assertions that the followers of Jesus were making were either not accepted by the Jews or, indeed, were even contradicted by them. (Overwhelmingly, Jews of that age, dispersed throughout the Greco-Roman world, were unaware of Jesus and his followers; a very tiny fraction of Jews were involved in either the assertions about Jesus or the denial of them.) The Jews in contact with the early "Christians" denied the assertions that Jesus was the Messiah and that a special resurrection had been granted to him. These denials were explained by Paul and other Christians through ascribing to "the Jews" a blindness that led to a lack of perception and comprehension.

Though Paul accepts the priority of the Jews in time, he feels, despite his Jewish heritage, that he must reject the priority of Jews in divine favor. In his view the priority in God's favor has now passed from the Jews to "the Christians," indeed to Gentile Christians. Yet Paul is reluctant totally to dissolve the Jewish priority. His way out of the dilemma is to consider the blindness of the Jews as only temporary. Since it is only temporary, Gentile Christians need constantly to remember that Jews are the first true "tree" and that Gentiles are newcomers, the "branches" engrafted onto that tree.

Concerned for his fellow Jews despite their blindness (Rom. 9:1–6), Paul has both the hope and expectation that in due course Israel will be saved. He expresses this hope through allusion (Rom. 9:27, which cites Isa. 10:22–23; Rom. 11:2–3, which cites 1 Kings 19:10–14) to a "remnant" of Israel that had remained in divine favor when the total Israel had been "rejected." In the age of Isaiah, God had not cast the totality of Israel aside, for there was a righteous remnant on hand. The present blindness of Israel had brought about the salvation of the Gentiles (Rom. 11:11). Now, if the fall of Jews from God's favor—a fall on the part of all but a remnant of Israel—had brought riches to the Gentiles, how much richer would matters be if all Israel were to be saved. Accordingly, Paul looks forward to that time. Just as all Gentiles were enabled to become saved, so too would all Israel be. The enmity of the Jews to the gospel (Rom. 11:28) had indeed worked on behalf of Gentiles, but the Jews nevertheless remained the beloved of God for the sake of the patriarchs.

It is to be noticed that Paul ascribes to Jews a hostility to Christian belief and to Christian contentions about Jesus. He does not ascribe to them hostility to Jesus the man, except in a single passage, 1 Thessalonians 2:14–16. In that passage there appears a motif also present in Romans 11:2–3, namely, the citation of Elijah's lament in 1 Kings 19:10–14, wherein Elijah charges the Israelites with infidelity to the divine covenant and (for our purposes important) the slaying of the prophets. In 1 Thessalonians 2:14–16, in a context in which Paul is encouraging the Thessalonians, he urges them to imitate the constancy of the "churches of God . . . in Judea." The Thessalonians are suffering from their countrymen what the Judean churches have suffered from theirs, namely, the enmity of the Jews, "who killed both the Lord Jesus and the prophets, and drove us out . . . and [hinder] us from speaking to the Gentiles. . . . But God's wrath has come upon them at last."

Here and here alone in the Epistles of Paul is the allegation that "the Jews" were guilty of killing Jesus. Because this theme does not appear elsewhere in Paul, there are modern scholars who regard 1 Thessalonians 2:14–16 as an interpolation by a later hand; such scholars tend to view the words "the wrath has come upon them at last" as an allusion to the destruction of the Temple in the year 70, a time quite a bit after Paul. Whether or not this passage is a late insertion is a matter of scholarly speculation; but it is clear that only here in Paul's Epistles is there the specific accusation that the Jews had killed Jesus.

Moreover, it is in the Gospels (written a generation after Paul) and not in Paul's Epistles that betrayal is a recurring motif. In 1 Corinthians 11:23–26 Paul speaks of the inauguration by Jesus of the eating of bread, symbolic of his body, and the drinking of wine, symbolic of his blood. He begins with these words: "For I have received [literally, "taken over"] of the Lord what I transmitted to you, that on the night on which Jesus was taken over . . ." (my translation). The words *taken over* are from the same Greek word from which the word *received* comes. The translation "on the night on which [Jesus] was betrayed" (RSV) may be right; on the other hand, an equally good translation could read, "on the night on which Jesus was arrested. . . ." In the Gospels the betrayer is Judas Iscariot. Paul at no time mentions Judas; at no time does he mention the trial of Jesus before the council; these items never appear in Paul's Epistles.

Paul speaks of his own experiences with his fellow Jews, not of any experience of Jesus with them. In 2 Corinthians 11:24–25, in a context of speaking of his sufferings in pursuit of his missionary activities, he tells of receiving from the Jews the thirty-nine stripes (Deut. 25:3) five times, of being beaten with rods three times, of being stoned once, and of being shipwrecked three times. Whether the beatings and the stonings were from Jews or from pagans is not clear. The Jewish sacred days are of no concern to Paul. He is totally silent about the Sabbath. He does not at any point directly mention the New Year and the Day of Atonement or the Ten Days of Repentance. In Galatians 4:9–10 he chides the Galatians for subjection to the elements of this world and for observing "days, and months, and seasons, and years." It is likely that by the latter Paul means days of a sacred calendar, but whether of the Jewish or the pagan calendar is uncertain.

Paul does not directly speak in annulment of Jewish dietary restrictions; he does speak specifically about food offered to idols, saying that such food is without any meaning, whether it is eaten or not (1 Cor. 8:4–13). In denying that there is anything basically wrong in such food, he is indirectly dissolving the Jewish food laws. Nevertheless, solicitous for unity, he recommends abstention from food set before idols, lest those who eat it offend others in the community.

Paul's significant controversies, we have said, are not with non-

Christian Jews but with Christian judaizers.   Yet in contending
against the latter he speaks with scorn of such matters as circumcision (Phil. 3:2); elsewhere he says angrily that he wishes that advocates of circumcision would fully mutilate themselves (Gal. 5:12).
That is to say, there is a note in Paul's Epistles that calls for some
attention.   His tone toward his rivals and opponents is one of denunciation and name-calling, scarcely matched by the love of which,
in another context, he speaks in 1 Corinthians 13.   Paul is bitter at
his opponents to the point of unrelieved invective.[4]   If in defense
of Paul's tone it is said that he has been the target of comparable
personal attacks and is only replying in kind, the fact remains that
there is a tenor to his writings that is considerably less than chari-
table.   If his difference with his inherited Judaism is essentially
theological, there is also some clear evidence that he is not free of
recurrent scorn of it to the point of contempt.

The new movement, Christianity, is in Paul's view an entity separate both from the Jews and the pagans.   Though the exact bound-
aries of the new movement are not given,[5] he scolds those Christians
who go to courts outside the "church" (1 Cor. 6:1–6).   Opposed
to divorce, Paul is quite content for the non-Christian spouse of a
Christian to leave his or her mate (1 Cor. 7:15).   Paul uses for
Christendom the figure of the body, a single body (1 Cor. 12:12–
27); while those in the church may antecedently have been either
Jews or pagans, they are now all united within Christendom.

Accordingly, it is Paul's view that a new entity, Christendom—a
term he does not use—has come into being.   It breaks from Judaism
in offering a new, dramatically different penitential system, replacing
the function of the New Year or the Day of Atonement.   Further,
the Mosaic laws, whether of circumcision or of food or of the sacred
calendar, are no longer binding.   Sinai, Paul indicates, was a mis-
direction, a regrettable enslavement.   Paul's criticism, if we may use
that word, is directed not so much toward Jews as it is toward
Judaism.   It is against Jews only indirectly in that since no religion
exists in a vacuum Judaism is the religion of the people called Jews.
It is thus essentially Judaism that Paul denigrates.

Are Paul's assessments, judgments, and contentions fair, and are
they valid?   This double question cannot be answered impartially.

4. See, e.g., Phil. 1:15–16; 3:18–19; Gal. 1:7–8; 2 Cor. 2:17; 11:12–15;
Rom. 16:18.

5. The evidence of Colossians and Ephesians is not here adduced because
there are numerous Christian views that Paul is not truly their author.

Christians would tend toward the view that since Paul is an apostle, a person with divine credentials, his views are in effect God's views and hence are right and valid. Jews would hold to the view, against Paul, that the Mosaic laws, being God-given, are in no way a source of sin, in no way a source of death, not an enslavement, nor are they superseded and annulled. Nor would Jews hold that fidelity to the Laws is of no account.

As to Paul's allegation of blindness, we may ask, What were the Jews blind to? If to the resurrection of Jesus, then Paul attests that there were so-called Christians who also denied the Resurrection (1 Cor. 15:12). If the blindness was a failure to recognize Jesus as the Messiah, did there ensue from the "coming" of Jesus what Jews expected of the Messiah, namely, the end of Roman domination, the inauguration of a Jewish kingship, the ingathering of the exiles? Did not the new movement instead alter what the Messiah was expected to accomplish and in effect retain only the term without the expected Jewish content? (Is not this sharp distinction in the meaning of Messiah a barrier to Jewish-Christian communication in our time? Failing to notice that the terms so usual in religion, such as sin, righteousness, and atonement, have one meaning for Christians and another for Jews, Christians and Jews often speak past each other instead of to each other.)

Is Paul's aggregate of religious views something superior to the aggregate of Jewish views? Paul both thinks so and says so. Is Paul's view one of objective truth or one of subjective partisanship? Or are those Jews right who have joined certain modern Gentiles in denigrating Paul[6] and who assert that Judaism is superior to Pauline doctrine and to Christianity? Is not the situation that, through Paul, something was fashioned that was *different* and therefore not subject to comparison? Only partisans speak of superior and inferior in dealing with the phenomena of religious entities. Is Protestantism superior to Catholicism, and Islam superior to Christianity? Such questions cannot be answered objectively.

We can notice that Paul has repudiated doctrines central to Judaism and exceedingly precious to Jews. He has charged "the

---

6. In my *The Genius of Paul: A Study in History* (New York: Schocken, 1970), pp. 61–62, I cite two examples, one the Harvard philosopher Alfred North Whitehead, who said, "The man who, I suppose, did more than anybody else to distort and subvert Christ's teaching was Paul. I wonder what the other disciples thought of him—if they thought anything. Probably they didn't understand what he was up to, and it may well be doubted whether he did himself. . . ." I also quoted the jingle "A man named Saul, later called Paul, came and spoiled it all."

Jews" with "blindness."   But in his Epistles there is an almost complete lack of ascription to the Jews of those unedifying traits that the Gospels ascribe to them.   If modern Christians can infer aspersions against historic Judaism from the Epistles of Paul, they could not readily and easily infer from him the same kind and measure of aspersions of Jews that can arise from the Gospels.

3. A Preface to the Gospel Materials

These prefatory words are for those readers who have little or no knowledge of the Gospels. Like all ancient literature, written in a language many centuries ago and thousands of miles away, the Gospels present the usual problem involved in a modern person's need to put himself in tune with a form of composition so different from our day. The special problem about the Gospels rotates about their manner. For example, each Gospel is a chain of short items, some of them very short. Transition from one item to the next is often abrupt. Due to the brevity of the items we are not provided with rounded characters or fully described incidents and therefore many items are not in themselves completely clear. In my presentation I have (by adding parenthetical explanations and footnotes) tried to clarify what the Gospel writers assumed the readers would promptly understand but which often eludes the modern reader.

The Gospels express, in deceptively simple narrative, ideas that are elsewhere abstractly or theologically stated. For example, while Paul states that Jews were blind to the Christian message, the Gospels relate narrative incidents in which the Jews are portrayed as acting out the blindness. Again, there is a theme in several of the New Testament writings that Jesus came to his own people and they did not know him for what he was; a narrative vignette in the Gospel of Mark shows that friends of Jesus thought him insane.

Several episodes presented depict Jesus in controversy with other Jews over Sabbath observance. The Jews are depicted as being over-rigorous or mechanically observant, to the point of forgetting or ignoring humanitarian concerns. The issue is not the validity of the Sabbath observance but the propriety of the observance as practiced. That is to say, at stake in the narratives is something more than the episodes themselves. The Gospels are filled with anecdotal illustrations of miracles performed by Jesus; elsewhere in the New Testament his divinity is alluded to without examples.

Thus, the narratives in the Gospels are much more than simple episodes. All have meaning beyond the event being narrated and most have nuances which, if they escape the reader, will obstruct his grasping what the Gospels are saying. As one reads an episode in the Gospels, one must always ask, What is the meaning of this passage and what are its overtones? In many places in my exposition I try to clarify these matters. On the one hand, some materials, such as the controversies over Sabbath healings, are repeated, and I do not always repeat the explanation. On the other hand, there is little explicit to add to a statement such as Mark 14:50 that at his arrest the disciples all forsook Jesus and fled. Surely the reader can infer how tremendously significant in meaning and emotional impact this very short statement is.

Mark, Matthew, and Luke recurrently give us as many as three accounts of the same incident. It is often my procedure in commenting on the incident in one of the Gospels to allude to the differences found in the other two in these common matters. The purpose of this cross-referring is to help concentrate on the unique aspect of the Gospel I am discussing by showing that the other Gospels handle the same matter differently and how they do so. The changes introduced by Matthew and Luke in their Gospels in their respective uses of Mark as a source help us to see what is singular to each of the Gospels. It is out of such helpful notice that one best assesses the way in which each of the Gospels treats the Jews.

Neither the Gospels nor the Gospel material that I present should be read rapidly. Rather, it needs to be pondered if it is to be absorbed. This is especially the case in view of the fact that I present only those excerpts that relate to our topic. The reader is encouraged, prior to reading each of the four chapters on the Gospels, to read each of the Gospels as a totality. For such reading I recommend a translation into modern English, especially editions with explanatory footnotes. Three such editions can be useful: The Oxford Annotated Bible, *using the Revised Standard Version; or the* Oxford Study Edition, *using* The New English Bible; *or the* Jerusalem Bible. *Let me strongly recommend that those who are without previous exposure to the Gospels read as a further preface Chapter 10 of this book, which is in reality set forth as a summary. Quite possibly to read that summary first can clarify for the uninitiated what the narratives in the Gospels are all about.*

Finally, the chronological presentation of the so abundant, seemingly unfocused material admittedly runs the risk of confusing or dis-

couraging the reader. I have felt it necessary to run this risk. The Gospel content itself, rather than mere summary or passing allusion, seems to be the obligation of the book. In the chapters on the Gospels the reader is encountering what is actually present in the Gospels, and he can make his own assessment rather than relying solely on a modern interpreter.

4. The Gospels: A Brief Introduction

The Gospels are a form of composition different from the Epistles of Paul. Information about Jesus in the Epistles is both scant and indirect; the Gospels, on the other hand, focus on him. Most of the contents of the Gospels are absent from the Epistles. But since the Epistles appear to have been written a generation or so before the Gospels, the question can arise as to whether or not ideas or viewpoints found in the Epistles are in any way reflected in the Gospels. In general, Christian scholarship denies that there is any substantial influence of Paul on some or all of the Gospels. This denial is based primarily on the surprising absence from the Gospels of that doctrine so distinctive in Paul's thought, justification by faith. If the absence of the doctrine from the Gospels is indeed decisive, Paul's influence on the Gospels may be properly dismissed. But a few comments are in order.

First, the Jewish high holy days, the penitential system of the New Year–Day of Atonement, are totally unmentioned in the Gospels, and atonement or forgiveness of sin is handled without reference to these days; the same is the case with the Epistles of Paul. Second, the blindness of the Jews, a theme in Paul, appears in intense form in the Gospels. Third, Christianity in the Gospels, as in Paul's Epistles, is normally viewed as having arisen in Judaism, but it is regarded as distinct from it. Fourth, though only very scattered vestiges of what Jews expected of the Messiah are to be found in the Gospels—and these are not fully identical with the view of Paul—this may again, perhaps, be a result not of content but of manner. Surely the Messiah in the Gospels is more akin to Paul (despite differences) than to the Messiah in Judaism. We need to be alert to the possibility of the Gospels presenting in narrative form facets of what are in Paul doctrines expressed in abstract or theological form.

In the ensuing exposition, our discussion will follow what the over-whelming majority of Christian scholars regard as the chronological sequence in which the Gospels were written, namely, Mark, Matthew, Luke, and John. The assumption is that Matthew and Luke utilized Mark as a literary source, and the non-Markan material common in content in Matthew and Luke is designated in the scholarship as Q.[1]

Certain other preliminary statements are necessary. First, our in-quiry is not into the full meaning of all facets of the Gospels but is restricted to the question of anti-Semitism. Only what is directly or indirectly related to that topic will come into view. Second, mod-ern Christian scholarship, after abundant concern with the question of the historical reliability of the Gospels, seems persuaded that much of the content reflects not Jesus himself but the church at the time that each Gospel was written. Some Christian scholars even doubt entirely the historical reliability of the Gospel accounts as they re-late to Jesus. The usual Christian layman assumes that the Gospels are both reliable and accurate historically; the usual Christian scholar would incline to the view that they are generally reliable but by no means completely accurate in all or most of the details. These issues are not of direct concern to our primary purposes; we will, however, need to give some attention to the fact that the Gospels differ from each other in presentation and, indeed, in content.

Third, in modern Gospel scholarship there have been efforts to explain by hypothesis the transition from oral materials in Aramaic to the full documents written in Greek. One tool has been "form criticism," which we might here describe as the effort to trace mate-rials back from the Gospels to the Judean scene and even possibly to Jesus himself. A second tool, "redaction-criticism," is the inquiry into how the writers of the Gospels shaped whatever inherited mate-rial they had; aspects of redaction-criticism need to be considered especially, for example, in comparing Mark and Luke. But for our purposes debates among the Christian scholars about the historical reliability of the Gospels will be of limited relevancy.[2] To be clear

1. Q, short for the German word *Quelle,* reflects a mid-nineteenth-century view that the non-Markan material found commonly in Matthew and Luke was drawn from a source that was lost. It is true that a few modern scholars deny there was ever a Q, holding that Luke utilized Matthew. That issue is largely irrelevant here.

2. My own position (see *The First Christian Century in Judaism and Chris-tianity: Certainties and Uncertainties* [New York: Oxford University Press, 1969], Lecture IV) is that there is indeed historical reliability within the Gos-pels and also undoubtedly the influence of the later church. Much of Christian

to the reader, I will recurrently speak about historical reliability, but only where the question will illuminate what in the Gospels is relevant to our topic.

Most important in my exposition is the governing conviction that the Gospels reflect one side, the Christian side, of a two-sided Jewish-Christian controversy. Only stray aspects of the Jewish side are known to us, partly from the Gospels, partly from material I will speak of found in the ancient rabbinic literature. It is likely that we have inherited this inequity because Christianity, as a younger and dissident movement, was considerably aggressive and very articulate, while Judaism may have been relatively much more passive, more reactive than active, and not as much impelled to overt expression. And since the Gospels in part reflect controversy, we must be prepared for a minimum of gentility, forbearance, and courtesy, characteristics that do not ordinarily mark controversy, particularly religious controversy of the age with which we deal.

Again, the views presented will primarily echo the Christian scholarship in which I was trained and the frames of reference in which I have consistently worked. I do set forth some opinions of my own respecting the Gospels, each as an entity. But I want to avert being misunderstood. It is not at all my opinion that anti-Semitism is the single motif that animated the writers of the Gospels. I will try to do some limited justice to the motifs in the Gospels that are unrelated to anti-Semitism, but anti-Semitism is our topic. I shall therefore isolate certain facets of each of the Gospels as these relate to anti-Semitism. I trust that I shall be setting this factor adequately into the total context.

I begin the inquiry into each Gospel with some general statements about its character and purpose as found in the usual Christian scholarship. Then I set forth my view as to the nature of anti-Semitism in the particular Gospel.

Gospel scholarship has tried in various ways to distinguish between the two. In particular, form criticism was deemed to be a usable tool by which one might, as it were, go from the Gospels, written at least forty years after Jesus and far away from Judea, back to Judea and to Jesus himself. I wrote that I cannot participate in this sort of endeavor, for I know no objective way of deciding what in the Gospels is historical and what is not. I have hunches and accumulated biases, but try not to confuse these with academic impartiality. My view has been correctly called "historical agnosticism" by Father Gerard Sloyan (*Jesus on Trial* [Philadelphia: Fortress Press, 1973], p. 6). This simply means that I have no simple "solution" to what is historical and what is not; my "agnosticism" is that I do not know. See also Chapter 12, n. 1.

5. The Gospel According to Mark

Two recurrent motifs in Mark have frequently been used as the basis for characterizing the purpose and import of this Gospel. One motif relates to the fact that there are three passages in which Jesus is presented as predicting to his disciples the death that awaits him when he will have reached Jerusalem, to which he is to go from his native Galilee. It has been suggested that the purpose of this motif is to answer the question Why did the supernatural Jesus allow himself, as it were, to experience that death? The answer implicit in Mark is that the death of Jesus was no surprise, for Jesus knew in advance what would happen; moreover, his death was in no way a defeat but rather a fulfillment of a divine plan.

The second motif long noticed in the scholarship is that of secrecy. When Jesus has worked a miraculous cure or exorcism, he frequently enjoins secrecy and silence on his beneficiary. It has been suggested that the purpose of this motif is to explain why it was necessary for the message of Jesus to be proclaimed and taught, why the world at large did not know about it without requiring that the message be preached to them. The silence-secrecy[1] motif in Mark is interpreted to mean that as part of a divine plan the significance of Jesus was at first concealed so that it could be unfolded at the appropriate time. (Radical scholars have interpreted the

1. In the history of Gospel scholarship, the view of William Wrede in *The Messianic Secret* (Naperville, Ill.: Allenson, 1972; originally published in German in 1901) became influential among scholars. At the turn of the century Wrede explained the secrecy motif by saying that Jesus never claimed to be the Messiah, nor was the claim made on his behalf in his own lifetime. Rather, only after people became convinced of his resurrection was he regarded as the Messiah. In the subsequent scholarship some derived views arose, for example, that Jesus was too modest to claim the messiahship or that the inner "psychological" development of Jesus can be traced as the conviction slowly dawned on him that he was the Messiah.

25

secrecy motif as reflecting the fact that the view that Jesus was the Messiah arose only after the Resurrection.)

Assuming that such interpretation of the two motifs is reasonably correct, we need to inquire into the way in which Jews fit into the presentation. First and foremost for our attention is the matter of the relationship of the Jews to the death of Jesus. Though Mark sets forth that the death was part of a divine plan, he also sets forth that it was Jews who caused and were responsible for the death. Indeed, the death of Jesus was only the culmination of an antecedent Jewish hostility to him and an early wish to kill him. That hostility is portrayed as having arisen from a series of encounters and controversies between Jesus and a variety of Jews.

The initial encounter is presented in Mark 1:21–28. Earlier, Mark begins with the person of John the Baptist, who is identified as the forerunner of the Messiah. John preached repentance and baptized many in the Jordan, these confessing their sins; he predicted that after him there would come "he who is mightier than I, the thong of whose sandals I am not worthy to stoop down and untie. I have baptized you with water; but he will baptize you with the Holy Spirit" (1:7–8). Jesus came from Nazareth of Galilee and was baptized by John. Promptly the Holy Spirit descended on Jesus in the form of a dove and a heavenly voice identified Jesus as "my beloved Son; with thee I am well pleased" (1:11).[2] Jesus was then driven into the wilderness by Satan, who for forty days tempted him. (The point is to assert that Jesus was in no way subordinate to or acting for Satan; allegations of this kind on the lips of Jewish adversaries will shortly occur in Mark.) Jesus was with wild beasts in the wilderness; angels ministered to him. Now[3] he came to Galilee, where he preached the gospel of God: "The time is fulfilled, and the kingdom of God is [now] at hand; repent, and believe in the gospel" (1:15). Jesus gathered disciples, the brothers Simon and Andrew and the brothers James and John, sons of Zebedee. Now the initial encounter takes place in the synagogue at Capernaum

2. There are textual variants in manuscripts of Mark 1:11 with reference to the words spoken, these apparently derived from Isa. 42:1 and 44:2. Thus the words are also given as: "You are my Son; today I have begotten you." This version greatly emphasizes the significance of the baptism of Jesus. The view in these words is called "adoptionism."

3. The time of his coming is "after John [the Baptist] was arrested" (Mark 1:14).

on a Sabbath. Jesus taught there, and those present were "astonished at his teaching, for he taught them as one who had authority, and not as the scribes" (1:22). (This difference probably means that Jesus had supernatural authority but the scribes did not.) A man with an unclean spirit was present and that unclean spirit recognized who Jesus was. Jesus exorcised it. Those in the synagogue, witnessing the exorcism, were amazed and marveled that Jesus commanded the spirits with authority and that they obeyed him. That is, Mark sets forth that the Jews in the synagogue at Capernaum did not understand who or what Jesus was.

Next, some cures of the sick and of the demon-possessed brought Jesus some considerable renown; he went throughout Galilee, preaching in the synagogues and casting out demons (1:29–45). The healing of a paralytic took place in the presence of some scribes (2:1–12). They heard Jesus say, "My son, your sins are forgiven." The scribes "questioned in their hearts" whether Jesus was guilty of blasphemy, for "who can forgive sins but God alone?" Jesus, however, knew what they were thinking. He affirmed his possession of the authority on earth to forgive sins. He then cured the paralytic to the amazement of all; they glorified God, saying, "We never saw anything like this!" For our purposes there is here ascribed to the scribes for the first time their view that Jesus may be guilty of blasphemy; this matter of blasphemy will reappear emphatically.

Among the disciples whom Jesus called was a tax collector,[4] Levi the son of Alphaeus. Jesus ate at a table with "many tax collectors and sinners." Scribes and Pharisees asked the disciples why Jesus ate with sinners and tax collectors. Jesus, learning of this question, replied that he had come to call not the righteous but sinners (2:13–17). Now questioning came from "the people." They asked Jesus why his disciples observed no fasts but the disciples of John the Baptist and of the Pharisees did (2:18–22).

Next comes an encounter with Pharisees (2:23–28). These saw the disciples of Jesus violate the Sabbath by plucking ears of grain and asked Jesus why the disciples were doing what was not lawful on the Sabbath. In reply Jesus alluded to an incident in which David, being in need and hungry, ate the sacred shewbread that lawfully only priests could eat (1 Sam. 21:1–6). He proceeded to say

---

4. Tax collectors were notoriously corrupt, being dishonest and readily amenable to bribery.

that "the sabbath was made for man, not man for the sabbath" and that he ("the Son of man") had authority over even the Sabbath. There is no presentation here of the Pharisees' reaction to these words. (In general, the controversies over the Sabbath might be described not as a challenge of the Sabbath itself but as a criticism of the over-rigorous practices and demands of the Jews. Jewish scholars have noted that the Gospel passages present a Jewish rigor about the Sabbath which greatly exceeds that found in rabbinic literature.)

Immediately after the encounter over the plucking of grain there comes another controversy over a healing in a synagogue on the Sabbath (3:1-6). It is the manner of the presentation here that should concern us. In the synagogue those present watched Jesus to see if he would heal a man who had a withered hand, "so that they might accuse him." Mark does not specify what the accusation is to be or to whom it is to be made. Jesus said to "them": "Is it lawful on the sabbath to do good or to do harm, to save life or to kill?" The people were silent. Jesus looked at them in anger, grieved at the hardness of their hearts; then he healed the man. Now the Pharisees—not previously mentioned in this episode—went out and "immediately held counsel with the Herodians" on how to destroy Jesus.

One needs to notice the anger ascribed to Jesus and the hardness of heart ascribed to the people in the synagogue. Is this in proportion to what we are told has taken place? One wonders too at the violent response ascribed to the Pharisees who suddenly appear here. Why should the Pharisees want to destroy Jesus? For Sabbath violation? Again, who are the Herodians with whom the Pharisees take counsel? Are they certain partisans of the supplanted line of Herod?[5] "Herodians" as such are quite unknown to us from any other literature; in the versions of this episode in Matthew and Luke (Matt. 12:14; Luke 14:5) the Herodians go unmentioned, as if by deliberate omission.[6] For our purposes, however, one notices that here, relatively early in the Gospel, there is ascribed to the

5. Herod died in 4 B.C. Archelaus inherited Judea but was deposed by the Romans in A.D. 6, and thereafter until the year 66, except for an interval (about the years 39–42 when Herod's grandson Agrippa was given the throne), Rome ruled Judea through procurators. Herod Antipas received Galilee, as tetrarch, in 4 B.C.; he was deposed by the Romans in A.D. 39.

6. Later (8:15) the "leaven of Herod" is mentioned; in Luke's version (Luke 12:1) "Herod" does not appear; in Matt. 16:6 "Sadducees" replaces Herod.

Pharisees a desire to destroy Jesus, but the reason for this desire is left unexplained.

It might be noted that Jewish law and practice sanctioned Sabbath violation in matters of illness, provided the illness was critical. The general Jewish position was to forbid on the Sabbath what did not need to be done on that day. That is, a healing that was not urgent and could wait until the Sabbath was over would have been forbidden, an urgent healing would not.

Mark then tells that Jesus healed an abundance of people who came to him from all over. Unclean spirits knew who he was; he ordered them not to make this known (3:7–12). Jesus then appointed twelve "to be with him, and to be sent out to preach and have authority to cast out demons" (3:13–19). The twelve are named. The last is "Judas Iscariot, who betrayed him." One notes how early in the Gospel the betrayal is mentioned. Yet no explanation is given as to what it is that Jesus is presumed to have done that could be betrayed. Is it something more than Sabbath violations? Since these acts have taken place openly in synagogues, in what way can betrayal be involved?

Immediately after the mention of Judas, Mark relates that Jesus went home, where a crowd gathered. Then "his family . . . went out to seize him," because his friends were saying that Jesus was "beside himself," that is, insane (3:21). Scribes who had come from Jerusalem said, "He is possessed by Beelzebul [Satan]" and through this "prince of the demons he casts out the demons." In the first item, the friends—Jews—do not understand who Jesus is and they attribute his actions to insanity. In the second item, the scribes from Jerusalem are not portrayed as denying that Jesus has exorcised demons but rather as saying that in doing so Jesus was controlled by Satan (something already refuted in the "temptation," above). That is, the scribes from Jerusalem also did not understand who and what Jesus was.

Mark presents Jesus as refuting the allegation of the scribes by reducing things to a logical absurdity: "How can Satan cast out Satan? . . . Truly, I say to you, all sins will be forgiven the sons of men, and whatever blasphemies they utter; but whoever blasphemes against the Holy Spirit never has forgiveness" (3:28–29). What seems to be presented here is not only a further rejection of the allegation that Jesus was possessed by Satan but also a countering of the matter of blasphemy. In Mark 2:7 it is the scribes who impute blasphemy to Jesus; here, Jesus is imputing blasphemy to the scribes, a blasphemy that is unforgivable[7] in that the scribes deny that it is through the Holy Spirit that Jesus has cast out the demons.

In a brief episode (Mark 3:31–35) Jesus is portrayed as identifying as his mother and brothers only those who do the will of God. Before, the over-againstness is in the form of friends ascribing insanity to Jesus; here it is in the form of Jesus rejecting his own family. (Jewish blindness and God's "rejection" of the Jews as his people seem intended in the two items.)

The parables (4:1–34) will not here concern us, but we will return to them presently.

In the account of the Gerasene demoniac (5:1–20) the setting is Gentile territory and the people involved are Gentiles. Among Gentiles in the Decapolis the fame of Jesus had spread widely. Jesus, when he had exorcised the demon from the Gentile, said to him, "Go home to your friends, and tell them how much the Lord has done for you, and how he has had mercy on you." The immediate sequel to this incident is a set of intertwined miracles. One is about the daughter of a synagogue leader who was deemed dead but whom Jesus enabled to rise and to walk. Between the request to Jesus to heal this dying girl and his actually doing so is the other miracle, that of a woman with "a flow of blood for twelve years, and who had suffered much under many physicians, and had spent all she had" (5:25–26); she touched Jesus' garment and was immediately healed. Jesus told her that her faith had made her well.

Immediately Jesus was back in "his own country" with his disciples. He taught in the synagogue in Nazareth on the Sabbath, to the astonishment of many. They asked, "Where did this man get all this? What is the wisdom given to him? What mighty works are wrought by his hands! Is not this the carpenter, the son of Mary and brother of James and Joses and Judas and Simon, and are not his sisters here with us?" (6:2–3). The astonishment led to many taking offense at him. Jesus said, "A prophet is not without honor,

---

7. One wonders whether the accusations and counteraccusations of blasphemy reflect episodes in the lifetime of Jesus or in the later church. In the later time the range of affirmations by Christians about Jesus and the denials of these by Jews could well have raised the reciprocal allegations of blasphemy. The way in which blasphemy appears in the Gospels is, on the other hand, rather enigmatic, for the Gospels do not clearly specify in what way blasphemy is manifest. That the blasphemy is here described as unforgivable is presented as if "the Holy Spirit" is in some way involved, but the mention of the Holy Spirit seems abrupt and intrusive; hence the explanation suggested in the text.

except in his own country, and among his own kin, and in his own house." He "marveled because of their unbelief" among his own people in his own area. Mark rounds out the episode in Nazareth with the words that Jesus "could do no mighty work there, except that he laid his hands upon a few sick people and healed them" (6:5). One notices the sequence: a miraculous exorcism in the area of Decapolis, the intertwined account of the young girl and the old woman, followed by the "rejection" at Nazareth. This arrangement of materials seems hardly accidental. The sequel to the Nazareth incident is the sending out of the Twelve and their accomplishment of the missionary charge laid on them (6:6b–13).

In 1:14 Mark had alluded to the arrest of John the Baptist. Now (6:14–29) he tells that Herod Antipas, tetrarch of Galilee, having heard of the fame of Jesus, wondered who he was. John the Baptist has already been put to death by Antipas, without Mark's relating it.[8] Antipas now believes that Jesus is John, raised from the dead. In a digression Mark gives the account of the execution of John: Antipas had imprisoned John for his having denounced Antipas for illegally marrying Herodias, the wife of his brother. She was unable to influence Antipas to kill John. But when at a banquet on his birthday the daughter of Herodias (her name, Salome, does not appear in the Gospels) danced and pleased Antipas, he offered her any gift she wanted. She asked for, and received, the head of John on a platter. After the beheading of John, his disciples came for his body and laid it in a tomb. Why this attention to Antipas? Why this rather long digression on the death of John? It is to show that Antipas, the Jewish tetrarch, had no understanding of who Jesus was. The story of the execution of John by "Jews" foreshadows the execution of Jesus, for which also "the Jews" are to be held responsible.

The miraculous feeding of the five thousand (6:30–44) portrays the disciples as requesting Jesus to send the multitude of people away so that they can procure food. Jesus told the disciples to give the people food. They replied that they had only 200 dinars with which to buy bread. They had, however, five loaves of bread and two fishes. Jesus miraculously fed five thousand people with these, and there was even a residue. (One notes here how little the disciples appear to know about who or what Jesus is.) The direct

---

8. Josephus *Antiquities of the Jews* 18. 116–19 gives an account of the death of John; that account is free of all mention of the material in Mark 6:14–29.

sequel tells that Jesus walked on the water. The disciples thought he was a ghost and were terrified. At the conclusion of this episode Jesus commented on the opaqueness of the disciples, especially in their not having understood about the loaves in the earlier episode. The next controversy (7:1–23) is with Pharisees and scribes who have come from Jerusalem. The chief issue is "defilement." "The Pharisees, and all the Jews, do not eat unless they wash their hands, observing the tradition of the elders. . . ." The Pharisees and scribes asked Jesus why his disciples did not walk (live) according to "the tradition of the elders" but ate with defiled hands. To the issue of defilement there is added a second issue, the validity of "the tradition of the elders." The latter is an allusion to what in the Jewish tradition is known as the "oral Torah." In the Jewish view, the revelation to Moses at Sinai was twofold, the "written Torah," or Pentateuch, and inherent in this revelation, the subsequent oral Torah, or extension, by learned elders, of the Law. The oral Torah was deemed every bit as valid and quite as authentically the result of divine revelation as the written. Here the response ascribed to Jesus denies the authentic validity of the oral Torah.[9] This is done by alleging that an indiscreet oath to give an animal for sacrifice to God prevails over the same man's obligation to honor his father and mother. The supposed inviolability of an oath is a topic found in the oral Torah; the honoring of one's father and mother stems from the written Torah. For a person to follow the oral Torah and thereby to violate the written one in effect makes "void the word of God which you hand on." The essence of the response by Jesus to his opponents is in Mark 7:8: "You leave the commandment of God, and hold fast the tradition of men." Does Mark know that oral Torah is never viewed as merely the tradition of men? Or does he, knowing how Jews regarded the two Torahs, simply brush aside the Jewish view of the divine nature of the oral Torah?

As to ritual defilement, on which Scripture has a great deal to say both respecting defilement and rites of purification and respecting foods prohibited in Scripture, the attitude on such matters ascribed

9. In the Jewish tradition a scriptural "law" is known as a commandment (mitzvah); a postbiblical law is a *halacha,* a "way of walking." When in the postbiblical era a sage proposed some law derived from but not explicit in Scripture he justified its validity in that he was not in any way innovating but only articulating something revealed earlier to Moses at Sinai. In due course the oral Torah came to be written down; such works as the Midrash, the Mishna, and the Gemara (the latter two comprising the Talmud) have continued to be known as oral Torah even after having been recorded in writing.

to Jesus (7:14–15) is expressed in the words "There is nothing outside a man which by going into him can defile him; but the things which come out of a man are what defile him." The intent is surely to denigrate the Jewish food laws, both the scriptural and the later Jewish expansion of them. (That ritual defilement is involved in connection with prohibited foods is an inference, not something explicit in Jewish law.) Mark 7:19b declares that Jesus "declared all foods clean." The implication is that even the foods prohibited in Scripture (pork, crustaceans, and others) are permitted in Christianity. If this encounter is historically within the career of Jesus, then one is puzzled as to why this dissolution of the food laws is not cited by Paul in the food controversy at Antioch recorded in Galatians. Is it historically reliable that Jesus annulled Jewish food laws? The washing of the hands and of utensils, with which the episode begins, strangely does not reappear in the account. The criticism here, though pointed at Jews, is in reality directed at Judaism. (In this controversy it is ritual defilement, not hygiene, that is at stake, though these Jewish laws involving food and cleanliness are popularly defended on the basis of hygiene. In the Middle Ages, during the Black Plagues, fewer Jews than Christians died directly due to washing or not washing. The consequence was that the contention arose among Christians that Jews had poisoned the Christian wells.)

The matter of food leads directly into the next episode, allocated to the Gentile region of Tyre and Sidon (7:24–30). There a Gentile ("a Greek, a Syrophoenician") woman asked Jesus to cure a little daughter possessed by a demon. His reply, using the figure of food, was: "Let the children [the Jews] first be fed, for it is not right to take [their] bread and throw it to the dogs [Gentiles]." Her answer, "Even the dogs under the table eat the children's crumbs," led him to cure the daughter. The narrative is very curious as written in that Jesus speaks narrow, parochial words. Possibly Mark has inadvertently slipped in the art of writing. The point of the incident as an entity is to affirm that the benefit of Jesus was not limited to Jews but extended to Gentiles. The next item (7:31–37) is not explicitly about Gentiles but it again takes place in the region of the Decapolis; Jesus there healed a deaf mute, presumably a Gentile.

The account of the feeding of the four thousand (8:1–10) is not of significant concern beyond our noting that the disciples are again devoid of knowledge of the supernatural nature of Jesus. A sequel (8:11–13) tells of the Pharisees asking for a sign from heaven, to test Jesus. (The feeding, if known to the Pharisees, might have been such a sign.) Jesus replied that "no sign shall be given to this generation." (Elsewhere in the Gospels the "sign of Jonah" is indeed given; see Matt. 12:39.) One notes the emphasis on "this generation" in a number of Gospel passages.[10] We will speak of "the discourse on leaven" (8:14–21) later; so too the "confession at Caesarea Philippi" (8:27–33). The discourse in 8:34—9:1 on discipleship is not of concern to our topic.

The Transfiguration (9:2–8) is not of direct relevance, but its sequel (9:9–13) is. The disciples asked Jesus why the scribes said that Elijah must come before the Messiah. Jesus replied: "Elijah does come first to restore all things; and how is it written of the Son of man, that he should suffer many things and be treated with contempt? But I tell you that Elijah has come, and they did to him whatever they pleased, as it is written of him." The allusion to things "done" to Elijah is possibly 1 Kings 19:2, 10, though these verses do not bear out that "they did to him whatever they pleased." That John, identified at the beginning of the Gospels with Elijah, was put to death seems here ascribed to the Jews, that is, "they." As to where in Scripture it is written that the Son of man is to suffer many things and be treated with contempt, there is no ready answer. Some scholars point to Psalm 22:6 and Isaiah 53:3; neither of these verses mentions "the Son of man." We shall return to Mark 9:9–13. So, also, we shall return to the healing of the epileptic boy (9:14–29) and to 9:30–32.

In Mark 10:1–12 the Pharisees asked Jesus if it was lawful for a man to divorce his wife. They told him that Scripture (Deut. 24:1) permits this. Jesus, granting that this was the case, nevertheless prohibited divorce. Above, Jesus deviated from the Mosaic regulations by permitting what was prohibited; now he prohibited what the regulations permitted.[11] (The theme that Jesus is greater than Moses is found in the Gospels.)

In the matter of the rich young man (10:17–31) the point appears to be that there is an obligation greater than even faithful observance

10. In Matthew it is often called a "generation of vipers." Occasional Christians infer from the allusions to "this generation" that there was a low spot in the time of Jesus in an otherwise exalted Judaism.

11. In 1 Cor. 7:10–11 Paul, after speaking for himself, adds, "Not I but the Lord." The passage imposes on a married woman the rule that she not separate from her husband but that if she nevertheless does so, she should either remain single or else be reconciled with her husband; a husband should not divorce his wife.

of the commandments, namely, that the young man should sell his possessions, give the proceeds to the poor, and come follow Jesus. To this account we shall return. We shall also return to Mark 10:32–45.

After his entry into Jerusalem (11:1–10) Jesus visited the Temple, apparently very briefly. He then went back to Bethany. The next day he returned to the Temple, where he drove out those who sold and bought in the Temple and would not allow anyone to carry anything through it. (Something is amiss here, for Mark seems not to distinguish between the large compound where the Temple stood and the Temple itself. Christian scholars have noted that Mark seems to have some tiny Greek temple in mind. The Temple had an antechamber and an inner holy of holies. Into the latter only the high priest ever entered, and he only on the Day of Atonement. That people would carry things through the Temple makes no sense.)

Jesus is now portrayed as teaching, "Is it not written, 'My house shall be called a house of prayer for all the nations'? But you have made it a den of robbers" (11:17). The reaction of the chief priests and the scribes on hearing this was to seek a way to destroy Jesus. Above (3:6) it was the Pharisees who held counsel with the Herodians about how to destroy Jesus. The import of *how* to destroy was not explained there; the "seek a way" here is explained, namely, that the chief priests and the scribes "feared him, because all the multitude was astonished at his teaching." The implication is clear that some *plot* against Jesus was needed because of his popular following.

An enigmatic episode (11:12–14, 20–25) is found in two parts in Mark. On Jesus' way to the Temple, before the cleansing, he cursed a fig tree; the next day the fig tree was found withered to its roots. The episode serves as a point of departure for words about the power of faith. Precisely what the cursing of the fig tree means is elusive, especially since Mark says that "it was not the season for figs." Since vineyards and fig trees appear to have been used as symbols for Israel (as is the case of the vineyard in Isa. 5), there are those who view the cursing of the fig tree as a cursing of Israel; this interpretation goes well beyond direct evidence.

In Mark 11:27–33 the chief priests and scribes demanded to know the source of Jesus' authority. (It is to be recalled that he has worked miraculous exorcisms, permitted what Scripture prohibits, prohibited what Scripture permits, and "cleansed" the Temple.) In reply Jesus asked a counterquestion about the authority of John the

Baptist: "Was the baptism of John from heaven or from men?"   The chief priests and scribes argued with each other:

> "If we say, 'From heaven,' [Jesus] will say, 'Why then did you not believe [John]?'   But shall we say, 'From men'?"—they were afraid of the people, for all held that John was a real prophet.   So they answered Jesus, "We do not know."   And Jesus said to them, "Neither will I tell you by what authority I do these things."

The point of the episode is to underline the hostility and blindness of the Jews and to emphasize the skill with which Jesus dealt with his opponents.

Now there appears a symbolic story (12:1–12).   A man rented a vineyard to tenants and went away into another country.   He sent a servant to collect some of the fruit due him.   The tenants beat the servant and sent him away empty-handed.   The owner sent another servant whom the tenants wounded in the head and treated shamefully.   He sent another whom the tenants killed; so, too, with many other servants.   Then he sent his beloved son, thinking that the tenants would respect him.   But they killed him and threw him out of the vineyard.   In this "parable" the tenants are the Jews, the owner is God, the servants are the prophets, the vineyard is God's favor and grace, and the beloved son is Jesus.   In the "parable" it is the Jews who kill Jesus; Roman participation in the death does not appear at all.   The item ends with the statement that the chief priests and scribes "perceived that he had told the parable against them."   They "tried to arrest him, but feared the multitude" (as in 11:18, 32).

Jesus adroitly avoided the effort of "Pharisees and some of the Herodians to entrap him in his talk," asking him if it is lawful to pay taxes to Caesar or not.[12]   The point of the episode (12:13–34) appears to be that Christianity was always a law-abiding movement respecting Roman authority.   With similar skill Jesus handled the effort of Sadducees to reduce the doctrine of resurrection to a logical absurdity.   Still another effort to entrap him presents a scribe asking Jesus which is the "first" of the commandments.   Jesus gave not only the "first" but also the "second," eliciting praise by the scribe for Jesus and by Jesus for this scribe.   "After that no one dared ask him any question."

Next, Jesus spoke about the scribes, rather than to them, in refuting them (12:35–37a).   The subject is the nature of the Christ (or

---

12. The question is curious.   I know of no instance in Jewish literature in which the *lawfulness* of paying such taxes is raised.

Messiah) who, in the view of the scribes, ought to be a descendant of David (as, indeed, Jesus is presumed to be in 10:48 and 11:10, as well as repeatedly in Matthew and Luke). Here the contention is that the Christ is eternal and hence not a descendant of David.[13] (See also John 8:56–58, where the eternal Christ existed in the time of Abraham.) The point of the brief item is to show the lack of understanding on the part of the scribes. A great throng heard Jesus gladly (12:37b). He warned them against the scribes "who like to go about in long robes ..." but "who devour widows' houses and for a pretense make long prayers" (12:38–40).

Next (Mark 13) Jesus predicted the destruction of the Temple and the adjacent buildings. Four of the disciples asked him two questions: When will that destruction take place? And what miraculous signs will herald the event? The reply is preceded by a word of caution against being led astray by many who "will come in my name." Wars and rumors of war are indeed a prelude, but the climax will not then come directly; rather, a period of sufferings will take place. In that period Christians, especially leaders, will be brought before "councils; and you will be beaten in synagogues; and you will stand before governors and kings for my sake. . . . You will be hated by all for my name's sake." As the reply proceeds, there is a further allusion to "false Christs and false prophets" who will wish, if possible, "to lead astray . . . the elect." After heavenly signs, the sun being darkened, the moon giving none of its light, and stars falling from heaven, the Son of man will come "in clouds with great power and glory. And then he will send out the angels, and gather his elect from . . . the ends of the earth to the ends of heaven." The assurance is given that "this generation will not pass away before all these things take place. . . . But of that day or that hour no one knows. . . ." Therefore watchfulness is incumbent. For our purposes we need to note that the discourse predicts the destruction of the Temple. Whether this prediction authentically goes back to Jesus

---

13. There is surface inconsistency in that descent from David is recurrently affirmed but here denied. (Comparable inconsistencies characterize rabbinic thought.) That such inconsistency bothered the ancients as acutely as it has those of the modern age with its dedication to pure logic is to be doubted. Insofar as Jesus was a man, he was, in the view of the Gospels, a descendant of David; insofar as he was the eternal Christ, he had always existed. What is at stake is emphasis, not substance, and Mark, beyond aspersing the scribes, is here emphasizing an aspect of the Christ, namely, the eternal character. The surface inconsistency would be removed if the words attributed to the scribes had one more word, namely, if it read, "How can the scribe say that the Christ is *only* the son of David?"

or, as many Christian scholars hold, reflects a time after the destruction took place in the year 70, need not concern us; the strictures against the Temple here are possibly no more anti-Semitic than were the words of Jeremiah 7 against it.

There is no reason to doubt the historical reliability of Christians being brought before local Jewish councils and of being beaten in synagogues. We recall Paul's recollection in 2 Corinthians 11:23–26 (see above, p. 15). That "debates" between Jews and Christians were courteous and genteel seems improbable. That to Jews in synagogues interruptive contentions were combatted is readily understood, and that Jews utilized the autonomy granted to them to regulate internal matters and to punish troublemakers would have been normal; Christians after the triumph of Christianity also punished troublemakers. At times, in a local setting, spontaneous fistfights and beatings might well have occurred, followed by an action by a Jewish court. On the other hand, the allusion to governors and kings seems to be to Roman persecutions such as those in Rome in the time of Nero (and therefore is in the wrong chronology).

One must note two allusions to "the elect" (Mark 13:20, 27). The Christians are here viewed as a chosen entity, different from the Jews.

The "passion" narrative begins (14:1–2) with an allusion to the time, "two days before the Passover and the feast of the Unleavened Bread." Later in the Gospel the search by chief priests and the scribes for a way to arrest Jesus "by stealth" seems to be timed with the impending festival in mind; they wish to kill Jesus, but "not during the feast, lest there be a tumult of the people." But do the events remain in the prefestival period, as implied by these two references? They clearly seem rather to occur during the feast, not before it. To this matter we shall return.

It is related that Judas Iscariot,[14] one of the Twelve, "went to the chief priests in order to betray him to them. . . . [They] promised to give him money. And he sought an opportunity to betray him" (14:10–11). No explanation of "betrayal" is given, as none was given in 3:19. As matters proceed the betrayal would appear to be simply pointing out who Jesus is, as if Jesus were unknown. Yet in what has come before, it seems unmistakable that the chief priests know just who Jesus is. We are not told precisely what it is that

14. The question has been raised whether he really existed or whether the name Judas, suggesting both "Judea" and "Jews," is meant as a personification of Jewish hatred. No objective answer is possible.

Jesus has said or done that could lead to "betrayal." Out of this lack of precise information there has come a recurrent theory in the scholarship that Jesus was a political revolutionary engaged in secret plans against Rome, and that Judas was prepared to disclose these secret plans to Jewish collaborators with the Romans.[15] This theory rests more on logic than on abundant demonstrable evidence; only stray and uncertain clues are available. That Roman officials and Jewish collaborators would fear a popular revolutionary leader and take steps to nip his movement in the bud is reasonable. But Mark presents us with two more major puzzles: One, the chief priests and scribes encounter and know Jesus, but seem to need to have him identified. Two, the crowd is described as responsive to Jesus and approving of him, so that stealth is required; but, presently, without any explanation given, the crowd is against him and bitterly so.

The emphasis on "two days before" seems forgotten in Mark 14:12–16, for it is now "the first day of Unleavened Bread."[16] The disciples asked Jesus where he wished them to "go and prepare for you to eat the passover." When they were at the table eating, Jesus— knowing what would happen—said that one of those eating with him would betray him. A curious verse follows: "They began to be sorrowful, and to say to him one after another, 'Is it I?'" The answer of Jesus was that "it is one of the twelve, one who is dipping bread into the dish with me" (14:18–20). There ensues the institution of the Eucharist, that is, the eating of blessed bread and the drinking of wine "when he had given thanks." Thereafter they sang a hymn (14:26). (Is Mark here suggesting a Passover Seder? If so, very little of the ritual of the Seder, known to us from the Mishna Pesaḥim,[17] appears. Since nothing in Mark identifies this meal as a

15. The most thorough exposition of the theory of Jesus as a patriotic revolutionary is found in the late S. G. F. Brandon's *Jesus and the Zealots* (New York: Scribner's, 1967). Brandon proceeds to characterize the Gospel of Mark as a tissue of falsehoods and the "pacific Christ" as an unreliable Christian concoction designed to try to persuade Romans of the peaceful nature of the movement.

16. That Jewish days were reckoned from sunset to sunset seems here to be unknown or forgotten. The Passover Seder occurs at the sunset that ushers in the first of the seven days of the festival. As scholars have noted, something is greatly amiss here.

17. The Mishna is a collection of rabbinic regulations derived from Scripture, assembled from A.D. 175 to 200 from oral materials considerably older. Pesaḥim is the tractate in the Mishna that presents the Passover regulations; in its chapter 10 the Seder service is outlined virtually as it is still observed today.

Seder, and since so little of the Seder is presented, many, perhaps most, Christian scholars deny that this "last supper" in Mark was meant to be understood as a Seder. The enigma remains, therefore, as to why the time is given above as the first day of the feast.[18] But what is significant, whether that meal was meant as a Seder or not, is that the events are within the sacred festival time, not before it.)

At this point we must pause. Up to now we have looked at material dealing with non-Christian Jews in Mark. In what follows we encounter an intertwining of the alleged deficiencies, both in Jews and also in the disciples, Christians who are Jews. We now need to go back to some earlier materials about the disciples that we did not consider before.

The first disciples are spoken of as "called" in 1:16–20. The call continues in 2:13; the disciples are mentioned in 2:15 and 18. They pluck ears of grain on the Sabbath in 2:23. The appointment of the Twelve appears in 3:13–19. In these passages one might say that the Twelve are treated if not affirmatively then at least neutrally. But thereafter one finds a negative treatment. After the parable of the sower (4:1–9) the Twelve asked Jesus about parables. His reply seems to have a bit of sharpness in it: "Do you not understand this parable? How then will you understand all the parables?" It is stated that Jesus explained the parables to his disciples privately (4:11, 34).

In the stilling of the storm (4:35–41), as Jesus was asleep in the boat, the disciples woke him, saying, "Teacher, do you not care if we perish?" After Jesus stilled the storm, he said, "Why are you afraid?

18. In Lev. 23:5–6 there are recollections of a time when Passover was distinct from the Feast of Unleavened Bread, Passover coming on Nisan 14 and the feast on Nisan 15. In due course the two sacred occasions were welded into one; the Passover Seder took place at the beginning of Nisan 14, that is, in the evening (see above, n. 16). It is at times argued that the Gospels predate the coalescence of the two occasions, and that Nisan 14 was then not observed as the Feast of Unleavened Bread. In Mark, Matthew, and Luke the events of the arrest and the "trial" are on Nisan 15; in John they are on Nisan 14, that day being conceived of there as *prior* to the beginning of the sacred occasion. It is clear that John is providing a date one day earlier than that the other Gospels provide and that John intends that date to be in advance of the sacred occasion, being a day of preparation. In the settled Jewish practice, the day of preparation is Nisan 13. But precisely what the dates are here, and how they were observed before the Jewish practice became settled, is most uncertain. It is not impossible that in the time of Jesus the preparatory day was Nisan 14 and was deemed outside the Feast of Unleavened Bread.

Have you no faith?" Mark tells that the disciples "were filled with awe," saying to one another, "Who then is this, that even wind and sea obey him?" Is it not curious that the disciples are portrayed as without faith and without an understanding of who Jesus is? On the other hand the Twelve are presented in a favorable way when Jesus sends them out with authority over unclean spirits (6:6b–13). Yet, when the two accounts are joined together—the feeding of the five thousand (6:30–44) and the walking on the water (6:45–52)—the tone becomes different. When the disciples saw Jesus walking on the water they thought it was a ghost and were terrified. After Jesus got into the boat they were "utterly astounded, for they did not understand about the loaves, but their hearts were hardened."

In the controversy over the washing of the hands (7:1–23) the disciples did not understand what was meant by the words "nothing outside a man . . . can defile him"; this is called a parable (7:17). Jesus said, "Are you also without understanding?" At the feeding of the four thousand (8:1–10) the disciples (even after the earlier feeding of the five thousand) said to Jesus, "How can one feed these men with bread here in the desert?" (8:4). In 8:14–21 Jesus cautioned the Twelve to "take heed, beware of the leaven of the Pharisees and the leaven of Herod." Mark tells that "they discussed it with one another saying, 'We have no bread.' . . . Jesus said to them, 'Why do you discuss the fact that you have no bread? Do you not yet perceive or understand?' " The bulk of the episode, verses 17–21, is about the failure of the Twelve to understand.

At Caesarea Philippi (8:27–33), Jesus "began to teach them that the Son of man must suffer many things, and be rejected by the elders and the chief priests and the scribes, and be killed, and after three days rise again." Mark tells that Jesus "said this plainly." But Peter rebuked him, and in turn Jesus rebuked Peter, "Get behind me, Satan! For you are not on the side of God, but of men." Is this not a considerable denigration of the leading disciple?

After the Transfiguration (9:2–8), as Jesus and the three disciples descended from the mountain, Jesus charged them to keep silent about what they had seen "until the Son of man should have risen from the dead." Mark tells that they questioned what rising from the dead meant. As Jesus and the three came to the other disciples (9:14–29) there was a great crowd about these, with scribes arguing with them. A man had brought them his afflicted son, but the disciples had been unable to cast out the demon. The response of Jesus—whether to the disciples or to the crowd is unclear—is, "O faithless generation, how long am I to be with you? How long am I to bear with you?" Jesus then cast out the demon. The disciples asked him privately, "Why could we not cast it out?" His reply was, "This kind cannot be driven out by anything but prayer." In the episode the disciples are clearly deficient. They are even more so in the immediate sequel (9:30–32), the second prediction of his death. Mark tells that the disciples "did not understand . . . and were afraid to ask."

Jesus asked the disciples what they were discussing on the way. "They were silent, for on the way they had discussed with one another who was the greatest" (9:33–34). Next, Jesus indignantly rebuked the disciples for impeding the bringing of children to him (10:13–14). In connection with the rich young man (10:17–31) the sentence occurs, "But many that are first will be last, and the last first" (10:31). The exact meaning is far from clear. Is it possibly a contrast between the Twelve, the Jewish disciples, and the Gentiles who at a later time came into the movement?

A third time Jesus foretold his death (10:32–34). Mark tells that Jesus was walking ahead of the disciples and that they were amazed and those behind afraid; he does not give an explanation of the amazement and fear. In 10:35–41 the two sons of Zebedee asked Jesus for the privilege "to sit, one at your right hand and one at your left, in your glory." Jesus denied their request after asking, "Are you able to drink the cup that I drink, or to be baptized with the baptism with which I am baptized?" They affirmed that they were able. Jesus said, "To sit at my right hand or at my left is not mine to grant, but it is for those for whom it has been prepared." The other ten disciples heard this and were indignant at the sons of Zebedee.

So much for the material we have turned back to. Resuming at the Last Supper, there comes Mark 14:26–31, telling that as Jesus and the disciples went out to the Mount of Olives Jesus said to them, "You will all fall away. . . ." Peter said, "Even though they all fall away, I will not." Jesus said, "Truly, I say to you, this very night, before the cock crows twice, you will deny me three times." Peter said vehemently, "If I must die with you, I will not deny you." And they all said the same.

At Gethsemane (14:32–42) Jesus told the disciples to sit there while he prayed. To Peter, James, and John, he said he was greatly distressed and troubled, and sorrowful to the point of death. He asked them to remain with him and watch. He fell to the ground and prayed. After the prayer he found the disciples asleep. He said to Peter, "Could you not watch one hour?" Again Jesus went away and again he found them sleeping; then a third time too he came to them, saying, "Are you still sleeping and taking your rest?"

At this point (14:43–52) Judas came with "a crowd with swords and clubs." Judas had given the chief priests and other leaders a sign: "The one I shall kiss is the man." Judas came to Jesus, and said, "Master," and kissed him. "They" laid hands on Jesus and seized him. A bystander drew his sword and cut off the ear of the slave of the high priest. Jesus said to "them" (the crowd?): "Have you come out as against a robber, with swords and clubs to capture me? Day after day I was with you in the temple preaching, and you did not seize me." Is it not curious that on the one hand Judas must identify Jesus and on the other hand Jesus can allude to his frequent and open teaching in the Temple compound? At this point (14:50) the disciples all fled, abandoning Jesus (as he had predicted).

The crowd led Jesus to the high priest where all the chief priests, elders, and scribes were assembled (14:53–65). Peter had followed, entering the courtyard of the high priest, who was "sitting with the guards, and warming himself at the fire." The chief priests and the "whole council" (abruptly introduced) now "sought testimony against Jesus to put him to death; but they found none. For many bore false witness against him, and their witness did not agree." One false allegation was that Jesus had been heard to say, "I will destroy this temple that is made with hands, and in three days I will build another, not made with hands."[19]

The high priest, rising, asked Jesus to reply to the testimony, but Jesus was silent. To another question, "Are you the Christ, the Son of the Blessed?" the reply was, "I am; and you will see the Son of man seated at the right hand of Power [God], and coming with the clouds of heaven." In anger the high priest tore his mantle, alleging that the latter words of Jesus constituted blasphemy. "They all condemned him as deserving death. And some began to spit on him . . . and to strike him. . . . And the guards received him with blows."

In the courtyard below one of the maids of the high priest said to Peter, "You were also with the Nazarene, Jesus." Peter denied it, saying, "I neither know nor understand what you mean." The maid next spoke to bystanders, saying, "This man is one of them." Again

19. The Temple "not made with hands" is the body of Jesus. Cf. John 2:19, wherein Jesus is portrayed as saying, "Destroy this temple, and in three days I will raise it up"; John 2:21 reads, "He spoke of the temple of his body."

Peter denied it. Then bystanders said to Peter, "Certainly you are one of them; for you are a Galilean." Peter began to swear that he did not even know Jesus. Immediately the cock crowed. He broke down and wept (14:66–72).

One needs to note how very brief is the scene before the high priest and "all the council." Christian and Jewish scholars have noted the absence of the judicial procedures prescribed in the rabbinic treatise, the Mishna Sanhedrin; hence there are those who allude to this evening session as a hearing rather than a trial, especially since the session ends inconclusively. We should note that as much space is given to Peter's denial as to the "trial." Again, since the disciples have fled, how was it learned what took place in "the trial," at which no disciple was present?

Mark 15:1 tells that in the morning "the chief priests, with the elders and scribes, and the whole council held a consultation." Mark tells nothing of the content of the consultation; by inference it was about what to do with Jesus, with the decision to take him to the Roman authority. This they did. Pilate, the Roman governor, in Mark's very brief account (15:2–15), asked Jesus only two questions. One was, "Are you the King of the Jews?" The reply was, "You have said so"—an enigmatic answer. After the chief priests accused Jesus "of many things," these not specified, Pilate asked a second question: "Have you no answer to make?" But Jesus had no answer, and Pilate wondered.

The crowd, now portrayed as hostile to Jesus, asked Pilate to abide by his custom—something unknown outside the Gospels—of releasing a prisoner at the feast. They asked Pilate to release a certain Barabbas, who was "among the rebels in prison, who had committed murder in the insurrection." (Nothing is known of this insurrection.) Pilate asked, "Do you want me to release for you the King of the Jews?" for he had perceived that "it was out of envy that the chief priests had delivered" Jesus to him. The chief priests stirred up the crowd to ask for the release of Barabbas. Pilate asked, "What shall I do with the man whom you call the King of the Jews?" They cried out, "Crucify him." To Pilate's question about what Jesus had done "they shouted all the more, 'Crucify him!' " To satisfy the crowd, Pilate released Barabbas, had Jesus scourged, and then "delivered him to be crucified." One notes that the crowd has abruptly become hostile and that Pilate seems to know of no trespass on the part of Jesus; he acts as he does solely on the basis of Jewish hostility to Jesus. One notes too how the phrase "King of the Jews" has been introduced quite suddenly; nothing earlier in Mark prepares for the title "king."

The Roman soldiers mocked Jesus (15:16–20). They compelled a hitherto unmentioned man, Simon of Cyrene, to carry the cross. At Golgotha the soldiers offered him wine mingled with myrrh, which he refused, and they then crucified him. They divided his garments by lot. The inscription on the cross, containing the charge, was "The King of the Jews." Two robbers were crucified with him. Passersby mocked him, "Save yourself, and come down from the cross." Chief priests and scribes, and the two robbers crucified with him, mocked and reviled him.

At the death of Jesus, the curtain of the Temple (separating the antechamber from the inner holy of holies) was "torn in two, from top to bottom." A Roman centurion (we would say "sergeant") said, "Truly this man was the Son of God." That is, this Gentile saw and understood what the Jews, both disciples and opponents, were unable to see or understand.

In 16:40 Mark introduces some hitherto unmentioned women, Mary Magdalene, another Mary, and a Salome. These and other women had followed Jesus in Galilee. (The male disciples have all disappeared from the account.[20]) Joseph of Arimathea, "a respected member of the council, who was also himself looking for the kingdom of God," asked for and received Pilate's permission to bury Jesus after Pilate had verified from the centurion that Jesus was actually dead. (It can be presumed that in Jewish-Christian quarrels the resurrection of Jesus was denied on the basis that Jesus had not truly died. This passage is an affirmation of that death.)

Joseph wrapped the body of Jesus in a linen shroud he had bought, laid Jesus in a tomb hewn out of rock, and rolled a stone against the door of the tomb. The two Marys saw where Jesus was laid (15:42–47). After the Sabbath these two, along with Salome, went to the tomb early in the morning. They wondered who would roll the stone away, but found it already rolled back. They entered the tomb. A young man was sitting there, dressed in white. He told them, "You seek Jesus of Nazareth who was crucified. He has risen, he is not here; see the place where they laid him. But go, tell his disciples and Peter that he is going before you to Galilee; there you will see him, as he told you." The women fled the tomb, trembling and astonished. They said nothing to anyone, for they were afraid (16:1–8).

Is Mark anti-Semitic? For those who ascribe full historical reliability to the Gospel, the reply could be no. Such people could say

---

20. It has been suggested that the women are a device to denigrate the disciples further.

that Mark has portrayed accurately and reliably exactly what happened and that if Jews are portrayed in an unfavorable light, that is no more than the consequence of a valid report of the events as they took place. There exist Christians whose view is along that line. Such people explain that they are not anti-Semites. They assert that the Jews *of the generation of Jesus* had had the misfortune to go astray from good Judaism; they disown hostility to Jews of other generations such as ours.

But other Christians, accepting the judgment of the Christian scholars who hold that Gospels give neither a complete nor a completely accurate account, have not felt the need to subscribe to the anti-Semitism that they acknowledge is in the Gospel of Mark. Such Christian scholars have, rather, tried to understand the intent and purpose of the Gospels, and in the case of Mark, why he wrote as he did. Such scholars have offered the explanation that developing Christianity, spreading in the Roman Empire, was embarrassed that the tradition that the Romans had killed Jesus was central in its legacy. Developing Christianity handled this embarrassment by shifting the responsibility; it did not deny that the Romans had done the actual killing but rather blamed the Jews as responsible for what the Romans, through Pilate, had done.

There is a view among a minority of scholars along the following line: Jesus was a Galilean; in Mark it is said that scribes from Jerusalem came to Galilee and there opposed Jesus. The decisive hostility in Mark is allocated to Jerusalem. Moreover, it is in Galilee that the Resurrection appearance is to take place. Such scholars have concluded that the Gospel According to Mark is an attack from Galilean Christianity on Judea. Perhaps this judgment is partly right. But it scarcely is a full assessment of what is in Mark. According to Mark, Jews of every stripe—Pharisees, scribes, priests, Herodians, Herod Antipas, the Sadducees, the High Priest, the Sanhedrin, and abruptly in the passion narrative, the crowds—are virtually of a single mind in hating Jesus. I have elsewhere written that one gets an impression that Mark had a checklist, concerned that no portion of the Jewish community be omitted from his indictment.

The treatment of the Jewish disciples in Mark is scarcely less derogatory than that of the "Jews." The disciples do not understand Jesus; they do not know what he is, nor do they grasp what resurrection means; they vie for eminence; in the passion narrative they fall asleep; and three times Peter denies him. They flee and abandon Jesus, as he predicts they will. They are not present at the crucifixion; it is women, not the disciples, who come to the tomb and find it empty. Is the role of the disciples as described in Mark historical? We shall see that later Gospels, in a variety of ways, part company from Mark in the treatment of the disciples. If the role of the disciples is not historical, what can we reasonably infer that Mark is trying to say? In my judgment—with which some Christians agree— Mark is suggesting that both the Jews and the Jewish disciples were blind to what Jesus was. The Jews were blind and hostile; the Jewish disciples were blind and disloyal. The only clear sight is ascribed to the Gentile Roman centurion; he and he alone knew what Jesus was— the Son of God.

Does not Mark, in this light, present an attack on Palestinian-Jewish Christianity, this from the standpoint of Gentile Christianity? The inference from Mark is that the true Christianity was the Gentile, "Dispersion" version. Why such an assault on Jewish Christianity? Perhaps it is a reflection of one side of the inner Christian controversies that we noted in Paul's Epistles, between "the free" and judaizers.

But it seems that a more profound explanation is reasonable. Let us imagine a local church somewhere in Italy or Greece. The origin of the membership is entirely Gentile. There are Jews in the vicinity with whom debates take place over the validity of Christian contentions. To the Christian contentions (that Jesus was divine, the Son of God, who could forgive sins) such Jews reply, "Blasphemy." (The allegations of blasphemy were then read back into the lifetime and the career of Jesus.) The Jews further contended that the Christian Gentile community was rather ignorant; also, it abstained from observing Jewish laws and sacred days, even though it asserted that it was a legatee of Scripture. The curious passage "It was two days before the Passover" seems to me to be a reply to Jews who said to Christians, "Your account of the trial of Jesus is preposterous. No Jewish court would have sat on a sacred day like Passover, held a night trial, and a morning consultation." Besides, Jews would be in their homes observing Passover and would never leave the Passover Seder to attend even a meeting of the Sanhedrin. The Christian response to such Jewish assertions took the form of stating that the events took place two days before Passover.

But beyond all this the Christian community needed assurance of its own validity simply because it was outside Judea and composed of Gentiles. How could Gentiles be assured of their authenticity in a movement that began with Jews in Judea? In answer, the Gospel of

Mark was so shaped—probably reshaped—to assure the community that, though Gentile, it possessed full validity. In normal controversies the assertion of one's own validity is followed by denigrating one's opponents. Hence, Mark ascribes invalidity to all Jews and inauthenticity especially to the Jewish disciples of Jesus. "The last shall be first and the first shall be last."

In short, Mark is a tract on behalf of Gentile Christianity, contending that Christianity has only negative connections with the Judaism into which it had been born. Matthew and Luke seemed to disagree with this contention. In writing their Gospels they used Mark. But they were not reluctant to alter what they found in Mark to be uncongenial.

6. The Gospel According to Matthew

With respect to the relationship of Christianity to Judaism, the Gospel According to Mark presents some significant implications but abstains from making these fully explicit. Thus, while it is clear in Mark that Jesus is someone whose teaching is different from that of the scribes and the Pharisees in that Jesus teaches with supernatural authority, Mark does not delineate the particular ways in which religion as set forth by Jesus is different from Judaism. True, Jesus is portrayed as permitting what the laws of Moses prohibit and as prohibiting what those laws permit, but Mark abstains from a clear and inclusive statement of what Jesus taught. Matthew, however, presents a clear and in many ways precise statement of this kind.

Perhaps Matthew writes simply out of an understandable desire to make specific what in Mark (written in Rome) may have seemed too vague. Matthew's Gospel is held to be written in Antioch in Syria. Perhaps the fact that there were a great many Jews in Antioch lent a certain urgency to his writing. For example, Matthew appears to have encountered with some immediacy the thorny allegation that Jesus had not truly died. One can imagine that Jews, on hearing the Christian contentions that Jesus had been resurrected, made two allegations, either separate or joined together. One allegation was that Jesus had not truly died; thus Mark 15:37 had told explicitly that "Jesus uttered a loud cry, and breathed his last." Mark had also emphasized that Jesus really died, this in telling (15:44–45) that "Pilate wondered if he were already dead; and summoning the centurion, he asked him whether [Jesus] was already dead. And . . . he learned from the centurion that he was dead. . . ."[1] The Jewish con-

---

1. Some manuscripts of Mark read in 15:44: "whether he had been *some time* dead" in place of "already." Luke completely lacks a parallel to 15:44–45; then where Mark 15:45b reads, "[Pilate] granted the body to Joseph,"

49

tentions about the authenticity of the Resurrection, deflected at most in passing by Mark, may have been in Matthew's milieu occasions for acute confrontation.

Matthew deals with this more than just in passing. In his narrative the Jewish assertion that the emptiness of the tomb was not convincing takes the form of their contention that the disciples had stolen the body and that for that reason the tomb was empty. As if in reply, Matthew emphasizes in 27:54 that "the centurion and those who were with him" were "keeping watch over [the body of] Jesus. . . ." Matthew alone tells that chief priests and Pharisees gathered before Pilate requesting that the sepulchre "be made secure until the third day, lest his disciples go and steal him away, and tell people, 'He has risen from the dead' " (27:62–66). The reply of Pilate in Matthew is that a guard of soldiers should make the sepulchre secure. Thereupon they sealed the stone and set a guard. Next (28:11–15), after the account of the Resurrection, the chief priests and elders bribed the Roman soldiers to tell people, "His disciples came by night and stole him away while we were asleep." The soldiers "took the money and did as they were directed; and this story has been spread among the Jews to this day."

These statements in Matthew strongly seem to suggest a much more vivid controversy with Jews than that reflected in Mark. If this is indeed the case it would then be understandable that Matthew, if directly challenged by Jews as Mark may not have been, would be called on to give a more rounded depiction of the nature of Jesus' relation to the Jewish past than Mark has given. Such a depiction takes two related but different forms and could in part reflect the Christian answer to Jewish aspersions of Christians. One aspersion could well have been that Christians were ignorant. There is no evidence at all—beyond conjecture[2]—that even as late as the time

---

Matt. 27:58b reads, "Then Pilate ordered it [the body] to be given to him." Why no parallels to Mark 15:44? There is no answer. Perhaps Matthew and Luke thought Mark's passage disrespectful, or perhaps verses 44–45 were added to but not to the version that underlies Matthew and Luke. But, on the other hand, Matthew may be underscoring that Jesus has truly died by narrating (27:54) not only that the curtain of the Temple was torn in two but also that there was an earthquake, "tombs also were opened, and many bodies of the saints who had fallen asleep were raised. . . . When the centurion and those who were with him, *keeping* watch over Jesus, saw the earthquake and what took place, they were filled with awe. . . ."

2. As in Krister Stendahl, *The School of St. Matthew* (Philadelphia: Fortress Press, 1968).

of Matthew, Christian equivalents of the academies such as those of Hillel and Shammai (and their predecessors and successors) had arisen. If such an invidious comparison was being made by Jews, then one manner of Christian reply to the charge of ignorance was to demonstrate how much learning they possessed, and Matthew seems to do this by citing Scripture frequently. It is usual that where Mark is content to allude to or to paraphrase Scripture, Matthew quotes it. What has been described above as a certain vagueness in Mark about what Jesus taught is altered into the clear portrayal by Matthew of the teachings of Jesus and of Jesus himself as a teacher.

I have characterized Mark as being essentially negative. In distinguishing Christianity from Judaism, he tells primarily what Christianity is not, not what it is. It is conceivable that Jews in the vicinity of Matthew, more demanding because they are on the scene in greater abundance and in more direct confrontation than in Mark, contended to Christians, "You have abolished the binding validity of the laws of Moses; you have negated the Jewish sacred calendar, including the New Year and the Day of Atonement. You stand for nothing. You accompany your beliefs, in which we cannot share, with what amounts to chaos." Whether the depiction of Jesus by Matthew as a new and greater Moses arises directly from such Jewish challenges or from other circumstances cannot, of course, be determined. But it is unmistakable that the Gospel According to Matthew presents through the teachings of Jesus a clear program for an orderly church, with specific demands on and expectations from its communicants.

Matthew's determination to present Jesus as a new and greater Moses leads him, according to a view frequently found in Christian scholarship, actually to fashion his Jesus after the figure of Moses in Exodus. Like Moses, Jesus almost perished when a wicked king wanted to slaughter innocent babes. Like Moses, Jesus was for a time in Egypt. Like Moses at Sinai, Jesus gave his great teaching from a mountain (the Sermon on the Mount). Just as the teachings of Moses are recorded in five books, so there are in Matthew five blocks of teaching material, each terminating in a "colophon," a formal conclusion (Matt. 5:1—7:29; 10:5—11:1; 13:1-53; 18:1—19:1; 24:2—26:1).

There is a sense in which Matthew, in setting forth Jesus as the source of Christian law, is adopting the manner of Pharisees, for the Pharisees were also concerned with law. Matthew at times seems to steer a middle course between an approval of the Pharisaic manner and a disapproval of the Pharisees as persons. We shall presently see examples of both these attitudes, with the disapproval becoming quite hostile. We need to note that Matthew is totally different from Paul in that Matthew does not disdain law as such but, to the contrary, unqualifiedly endorses law,[3] even for Christians. But it must be equally clear that Matthew is not validating the laws of Moses, nor is he revalidating them after Christianity had already abandoned them. Rather, Matthew is validating a Christian law, a brand-new law designed to supplant and replace the laws of Moses. Matthew never revalidates circumcision, food laws, or the Jewish sacred calendar. In other places he provides a law more rigorous than that of Moses and in so doing reflects a desire to produce a righteousness which will exceed that of the scribes and the Pharisees (5:20). Matthew's double attitude can be summarized in these words: "The scribes and the Pharisees sit on Moses' seat; so practice and observe whatever they tell you, but not what they do . . ." (Matt. 23:2–3).

Matthew portrays Jesus as saying, "Think not that I have come to abolish the law and the prophets; I have come not to abolish them but to fulfil them. For truly, I say to you, till heaven and earth pass away, not an iota, not a dot, will pass from the law . . ." (5:17–19). One cannot know whether he is here speaking to Christians who in supposed imitation of Paul have denigrated and nullified the Law, or, instead, replying to Jews by asserting that they are wrong in deeming Christians lawless. Perhaps Matthew is speaking to both.

Matthew supplies a birth narrative about Jesus, something lacking in Mark. Matthew begins with a genealogy in three sets of fourteens. One needs to note the great frequency of the scriptural quotations. When Joseph learns that his fiancée, Mary, is pregnant, an angel informs him that she has conceived by the Holy Spirit. The name *Jesus* (which in Hebrew means "God delivers") is interpreted to mean "he will deliver people from their sins," in fulfillment of a compound prophetic passage, "a [virgin] shall conceive and bear a son" and "shall call his name Immanuel" (Isa. 7:14; 8:18). (The

3. This statement may offend certain Protestants who will insist that there is no essential difference between Paul and Matthew. Having read literature that harmonizes Paul and Matthew, I can only state that I have seen nothing in Paul like Matt. 5:17–19 and nothing in Matthew like Rom. 7:6 or Gal. 3:13 or 3:19. To such Protestants no form of religion is quite as reprehensible as legalism, and therefore Matthew, despite the plain and oft-repeated words about laws and commandments, is not to be classified as a legalism.

Hebrew text of Isa. 7:14 reads "young woman"; the reading "virgin" is from the Greek translation.) When King Herod has heard that wise men from the east have come to find the babe "born king of the Jews," he and all Jerusalem are troubled and he inquires of "all the chief priests and scribes of the people . . . where the Christ was to be born." They reply by quoting a prophet (Mic. 5:2) that the place is Bethlehem. An angel instructs Joseph to flee with Jesus and Mary to Egypt, in fulfillment of a prophetic passage, Hosea 11:1. The slaughter of innocent babes by the wicked Herod fulfills Jeremiah 31:15. That Joseph is to avoid Judea and go instead to Galilee, to Narazeth, fulfills another prophetic passage.[4]

In presenting John the Baptist (3:1–17), Matthew rewrites and expands the account in Mark (seemingly also correcting by omission Mark's citation of Mal. 3:1,[5] which in Mark is contained within a quotation wrongly ascribed to Isaiah). Matthew puts into the mouth of John the words "Repent, for the kingdom of heaven is at hand." He adds that John saw "many of the Pharisees and Sadducees coming for baptism" and called them a "brood of vipers." They were not to boast of their descent from Abraham, for "God is able from these stones to raise up children to Abraham." The intent here, presented as a narrative, is different in form but not in meaning from the contention of Paul that "the Christians" have supplanted the Jews as the true descendants of Abraham (Gal. 3: 7–9). In succeeding passages Matthew returns to this theme, expressing in his own way Paul's view that God had in Jesus turned first to the Jews and only on their rejection of Jesus had He turned to the Gentiles. Matthew's way is to depict Jesus as initially confining himself to Jews and only after his resurrection turning to Gentiles. In one passage (Matt. 10:5–6) Jesus restricts his disciples in the mission on which he sends them: "Go nowhere among the Gentiles, and enter no town of the Samaritans, but go rather to the lost sheep of the house of Israel." A second passage

---

4. But which passage is a puzzle, for the quoted words are not found in Scripture as given. It is conjectured that the intent is to cite Isa. 11:1, where in the Hebrew the word *rod* (*netzer*) could be the basis for a somewhat extreme instance of paronomasia ("pun"), linking *netzer* with Nazareth and Nazarene. A linguistic problem arises because the *tz* of *netzer* is a different consonant from the *z* of *Nazarene*. Also, scholars find little relationship between Nazarene, seemingly related to the *nazir* (Judg. 13:5 and Num. 6:1–21), and the career of Jesus. But it is probably wrong to ascribe to Matthew an intent beyond that of the desire to cite some prophetic passage.

5. The quotation from Malachi is used in Matt. 11:10.

is the incident of the Syrophoenician woman (Mark 7:24–30), here rewritten (15:21–28), with Jesus saying, "I was sent only to the lost sheep of the house of Israel."[6]   But at the end of Matthew, in what Christians call the Great Commission, Jesus instructs his disciples to "go therefore and make disciples of all nations . . ." (28:19).

The Sermon on the Mount (not found in Mark) begins with a series of "Beatitudes." The last of these (5:11) reads, "Blessed are you when men revile you and persecute you and utter all kinds of evil against you falsely on my account.   Rejoice and be glad, for your reward is great in heaven, for so men persecuted the prophets who were before you." This is a repeated charge against the Jews of Matthew's time, as if they were guilty for the deeds of their remote ancestors.   Yet the molestation of the prophets in Hebrew history was scarcely frequent; it was quite exceptional.   And the molesters were monarchs, hardly the people.

The words ascribed to Jesus that he has not come to abolish the Law and the prophets (5:17–20) now lead to a series of contrasts between the demands in the laws of Moses and a more rigorous demand by Jesus.   The contrasts are introduced, each by the formula "You have heard that it was said. . . . But I say to you. . . ." Thus, Moses prohibits murder, Jesus, murderous thoughts; Moses adultery, Jesus adulterous thoughts; Moses permits divorce, Jesus prohibits it (though Matthew adds to what is in Mark 10:11–12 the possibility of divorce for unchastity); Moses prohibits false oaths, Jesus forbids all oaths; Moses demands punishment equal to a crime, Jesus teaches against retaliation.

Matthew 5:43–48 is a puzzling passage.   Jesus is depicted as citing, presumably from the laws of Moses, "You shall love your neighbor *and hate your enemy.*" The puzzle is that no such verse is found in the Old Testament.   "Love your neighbor" is in Leviticus 19:18, but "hate your enemy" is not there or anywhere in Scripture in these precise words.

Presently Matthew presents the Lord's Prayer (6:9–15), preceded by comments about the giving of alms and praying:

> Beware of practicing your piety before men. . . .   When you give alms, sound no trumpet before you, as the hypocrites do in the synagogues and the streets. . . .   When you pray, you must not be like

6. Some scholars see a similar sentiment in 7:6: "Do not give dogs what is holy; and do not throw your pearls before swine."

the hypocrites; for they love to stand and pray in the synagogues and at the street corners, that they may be seen by men. . . .

One notes the accusation of hypocrisy, a theme later returned to. Christians are to pray after going into the privacy[7] of a room and shutting the door.[8] The Lord's Prayer is in content not at all alien to Jewish prayers; it is Christian by association, rather than by content. The motif of hypocrisy is returned to in the matter of fasting (6:16–18) and judging others (7:1–5). The Golden Rule (7:12) reflects a common Jewish sentiment.[9]

In Matthew 8:5–13 a Roman centurion asks the help of Jesus for his servant. Jesus offers to come and heal the servant. The centurion replies that he is not worthy that Jesus enter his home but let Jesus only say the word (from the distance) and the servant will be healed. Jesus says to his followers: "Truly, I say to you, not even in Israel have I found such faith. . . . Many will come from east and west and sit at table with Abraham, Isaac, and Jacob in the kingdom of heaven, while the sons of the kingdom will be thrown into the outer darkness. . . ." Are "the sons of the kingdom" the Jews? Possibly. But it is equally possible, and more probable, that unworthy Christians are here meant.[10]

There follows a passage the prologue of which states that "the harvest is plentiful, but the laborers are few" (9:37). Jesus therefore gathered the twelve disciples, gave them authority to cast out demons and to heal, and then sent them out. He restricted them to "the lost sheep of the house of Israel," as mentioned above; this restriction is found only in Matthew. The end of the long passage is followed by predictions of the possible vicissitudes that future missionaries will encounter:[11] "Beware of men; for they will deliver

7. Was it Matthew's intention to prohibit public prayer such as is found universally in Christianity?

8. A scorn of the way Gentiles pray is added (6:7–8). In 6:32 the Gentiles are again mentioned, this time in the context that God knows the universal anxieties of men and that Christians should therefore not be anxious.

9. There follow verses that reflect inner Christian tensions and controversies (7:13–27), with mention of false prophets and comparable Christian evildoers. A distinction is drawn between "doers" and mere "hearers" (7:24–27). Matthew, like Paul, can be very severe on fellow Christians. See also Matt. 13:36–43, 47–50; and 22:11–14.

10. See the preceding note. In 8:21–22 a disciple who must go and bury his father before obeying Jesus elicits the reply, "Follow me, and leave the dead to bury their own dead." Is this spoken against Jews or against deficient Christians? Either is possible.

11. Matt. 10:17–25 is possibly a recasting of Mark 13:9–13.

you up to councils, and flog you in their synagogues, and you will be dragged before governors and kings for my sake, to bear testimony before them and the Gentiles" (10:17–18). Though "governors and kings" may exaggerate the rank of the Roman officials who distressed missionaries, the "prediction" is a reflection of the actual experience of missionaries after the age of Jesus. The point of the passage is to encourage missionaries: "Do not be anxious how you are to speak . . . for it is not you who speak, but the Spirit of your Father speaking through you." Missionaries will be beaten and hated, as brother turns against brother, and father and children against each other, to the point of death. All this is clear. It is the ending that is puzzling: "Truly, I say to you, you will not have gone through all the towns of Israel, *before the Son of man comes.*" This assurance that the final events of history lie in the very near future is in the light of the realities of history most enigmatic. By the time Matthew was written, with its concluding Great Commission, Christianity had already spread beyond Judea, and Matthew knew that this was the case. How, then, can we explain this verse? What others have written has not enlightened me.[12]

In his version of Mark 2:23–28, Matthew (12:1–8) both slightly recasts (omitting Mark's error in identifying the priest as Abiathar, as is also the case in some manuscripts of Mark) and also adds, "Have you not read in the law how on the sabbath the priests in the temple profane the sabbath, and are guiltless? I tell you, something greater than the temple is here. . . ." It was never thought in Judaism that priests were profaning the Sabbath, but rather that they were properly observing the demands of worship. (Does a Christian clergyman, paid or supported by his church, profane his religion by holding worship services on the Christian Sabbath?)

The Sabbath controversy over the healing of the man with the withered hand (Mark 3:1–6) is expanded[13] in Matthew 12:11–14 and placed much later than in Mark. In the conclusion, whereas Mark writes that the Pharisees took counsel with the Herodians over how to destroy Jesus, Matthew omits mention of the Herodians,

12. My inclination is to view the verse as consistent with comparable exaggerations found in other literature of the time. The nub of the matter is encouragement; the matter of historical chronology is of little or no consequence. The same problem arises from 16:28.

13. Matthew writes that a Jew will rescue a sheep fallen into a pit on the Sabbath. The comment might be made respecting this verse (and Luke 13:15) that the principle existed in Judaism that concern for a helpless animal in distress abrogated the Sabbath regulations.

ascribing the intent to destroy Jesus to the Pharisees alone. In the sequel (12:15–21), a recasting of Mark 3:7–12, Matthew expands the instructions of Jesus to the people he has healed not to make him known as a fulfillment of Isaiah 42:1–4, quoted in a version at points containing significant differences from the inherited Hebrew text: "He shall proclaim *judgment* to the Gentiles" is altered to *justice.* "He will bring judgment *unto truth*" becomes "bring *justice to victory.*" "The isles shall wait for his *teaching [torah]*" becomes "and in his name will the *Gentiles hope.*" These alterations change entirely the tone of Isaiah 42:1–4, making it into a prediction of the passing of God's concern for his people from Jews to Gentiles.

Whereas in the accusations against Jesus in Mark 3:22 scribes "come down from Jerusalem" charged Jesus with casting out demons through the power of Beelzebul, in Matthew 12:22–24 the charge is stated as coming instead from Pharisees.[14] Matthew adds to his version (12:25–37) of the denunciation in Mark 3:23–30 a repetition of a "brood of vipers" and he proceeds to assert that "men of Nineveh" and "the queen of the South" will arise at Judgment Day and condemn the "evil and adulterous generation" (12:38–42). Indeed, that generation will experience a sharp increase in the number of evil spirits infecting it (12:43–45).

The explanation (13:51–52) of preceding parables includes these words: "Every scribe who has been trained for the kingdom of heaven is like a householder who brings out of his treasure what is new and what is old." While the passage is not completely clear, it seems to reflect praise for some Jewish Christians who combine Jewish and Christian teachings.

Matthew's version of the controversy over washing the hands (15:1–20; Mark 7:1–23) significantly omits Mark 7:19b, "Thus he declared all foods clean"; that would amount to removing jots and tittles from the Law. Matthew adds that the disciples informed Jesus that the Pharisees were offended by his words on defilement (15:12–14). The reply of Jesus was, "They are blind guides. . . . If a blind man leads a blind man, both will fall into a pit." The words, compared with some to follow, are relatively mild.

In the discourse on leaven (Mark 8:14–21) Matthew alters the warning to "beware of the leaven of the Pharisees and the leaven *of Herod*" into "beware of the leaven of the Pharisees and *Sadducees*"

---

14. Matthew omits Mark 3:21b, the accusation by friends that Jesus is "beside himself."

(Matt. 16:6). Matthew adds that the disciples did not understand "that he did not tell them to beware of the leaven of bread, but of the teaching of the Pharisees and Sadducees" (16:12). To Mark 9:9–13, about the coming of Elijah, Matthew makes specific the charge that the Jews did not recognize (through blindness) that John the Baptist was Elijah. The burden for the death of John, ascribed in Matthew 14:10 to Herod Antipas, is here put on all the Jews (in anticipation of the blame on them for the death of Jesus).[15]

The episode in 17:24–27 about paying the half-shekel tax for the support of the Temple is curious. It appears to concern the issue of whether Christianity is still within Judaism. The words "Then the sons are free" (17:26) would appear to mean that Christians are not obligated to make such payments. Yet the narrative tells about a shekel in the mouth of a fish by which Peter makes the payment for both himself and Jesus. Possibly the meaning is that though the Christians of Matthew's time, being outside Judaism, have no real obligation to this Temple tax, they should follow the example of Peter and Jesus and, by paying it, abstain from offending by not paying it.

That Christianity is conceived of as its own entity, different from Judaism, is to be inferred from 18:15–20. If a "brother" sins against another, the offended person should tell the offender his fault. If the offender does not listen, the offended may then take one or two brothers with him to inform the offender of his fault. If he still does not listen, "tell it to the church; and if he refuses to listen even to the church, let him be to you as a Gentile and a tax collector" (that is, outside the church). For Matthew, as for later Christians, humanity was divisible into three distinct entities: Jews, Christians, and Gentiles. To the Christians there is given authority to "bind and loose" on earth. In rabbinic terminology the word *bind* (*'asar*) means to prohibit, and *loosen* (from the root *natar*) means to permit. Clearly there is authority being conveyed here, but it is not clear whether it is authority given to disciples over the church or authority given to the church beyond its confines.

The dictum concerning divorce is given a second time (19:3–12; see 5:31–32), possibly because Matthew is here following the content of Mark 10:2–12. Like Mark, Matthew tells that the Pharisees tried to test Jesus. In Matthew 5:31–32 there is no reason given

15. Matthew does not shrink from portraying Jesus as rebuking his disciples for insufficient faith, as in 17:19–20.

for the prohibition of divorce; in 19:3–12, as in Mark 10:6–7, prohibition rests on the interpretation of Scripture, namely, Genesis 1:27 and 2:24. Matthew's presentation is more orderly than Mark's. In this passage Matthew again allows divorce in the case of unchastity. Matthew appends the comment of the disciples that "it is not expedient to marry." Jesus replied, "Not all men can receive this saying."[16]

In Matthew's version of the entry into Jerusalem (21:1–9) his combined quotation of Isaiah 62:11 and Zechariah 9:9 leads him into an error, for he misunderstands the parallelism in Zechariah 9:9 and consequently portrays Jesus as riding on two animals.[17] The words of the crowd are altered from what they are in Mark 11:9–10; Mark's words are, "Blessed is he who comes in the name of the Lord! Blessed is the kingdom of our father David that is coming!" They are changed into, "Hosanna to the Son of David!" followed by the sentence, unchanged from Mark, "Blessed is he who comes in the name of the Lord." Thus Mark's words "the kingdom of our father David," with their political overtones, are omitted in Matthew. In Matthew's account he writes that "all the city was stirred, saying, 'Who is this?'" The crowds, however, know the answer, for they say, "This is the prophet Jesus from Nazareth of Galilee."

Matthew has Jesus immediately enter the Temple and "cleanse" it; Mark defers the cleansing to the next day. Matthew adds to Mark's account of the cleansing that in the Temple Jesus healed the blind and the lame, and that the children there cried out, "Hosanna to the Son of David!" The chief priests and scribes become indignant at these things (21:10–17). (Is Matthew by these additions trying to minimize the significance of the cleansing itself and thus reduce the acute impression of Christianity's infidelity to the Temple of God?)

After the question about authority (21:23–27, based on Mark 11:27–33) Matthew adds a parable about two sons. One son, told to work in the vineyard, replied to his father he would not do so, but afterward repented and worked. The other told his father he would work and did not. Jesus asked his opponents, "Which of the two did the will of his father?" They said, "The first." Jesus

---

16. Compare 1 Cor. 7, esp. v. 7.

17. Ancient manuscripts reflect efforts to correct and reduce the two animals to one.

said (in application), "The tax collectors and harlots go into the kingdom of God before you." Other Jews had not believed John the Baptist when he came, but the tax collectors and the harlots had. Even when the Jews had seen this they had not afterward repented and believed him.

Matthew recasts the parable of the wicked tenants (Mark 12:1–12), especially in an addition (21:43): "Therefore I tell you, the kingdom of God [God's favor] will be taken away from you and given to a nation producing the fruits of it." In Mark this parable is addressed to chief priests, scribes, and elders (Mark 11:27); in Matthew 21:45 it is chief priests and Pharisees who hear the parable and understand that it is against them. When these tried to arrest Jesus, they feared the multitude that held Jesus to be a prophet (as in Matt. 21:11).

Matthew inserts at this place the parable of the marriage feast to illustrate the kingdom of heaven. A king, having invited the guests to a marriage feast in advance, sent his servants to summon them now that the feast was ready. The guests would not come. The king sent other servants with the message that the dinner was ready. Some of those invited made light of the summons, while the rest seized the servants, treated them shamefully, and killed them. The king was angry. He sent his troops and "destroyed those murderers and burned their city." He sent his servants into the thoroughfares to invite anyone at all to come to the feast; hence the wedding hall was filled with guests (22:1–10). The "story" in the parable is a series of symbols.[18] The king is God; the tenants are the Jews who are charged with having murdered the prophets; the city is Jerusalem, burned by the Romans in A.D. 70; the people brought in are the Christians. To this there is appended an item, that of a man who was present at the feast but was not dressed in a proper wedding garment. The king had him bound hand and foot and cast into the outer darkness. This section seems addressed to unworthy or unprepared Christians, not to Jews.

The question of tribute to Caesar (22:15–22) is only slightly altered from Mark 12:13–17. There "Pharisees and some of the Herodians" are sent by the chief priests, scribes, and elders to entrap Jesus; in Matthew Pharisees take counsel on how to entangle Jesus in his talk so that they send their disciples, along with the

18. Maybe, as scholars have suggested, a parable on preparedness underlies the passage, namely, that those unprepared for salvation lose their opportunity.

Herodians, to him. Jesus recognized their flattering words (Matt. 22:16b) as malice and called them hypocrites. The controversy with Sadducees over resurrection is only slightly altered from Mark 12:18–27. In Matthew there is an addition to the passage (22:33): "When the crowd heard [this], they were astonished at his teaching."

The episode of the Great Commandment has some minor alterations. In Mark 12:28 scribes ask Jesus, "Which commandment is the *first of all?*" In Matthew 22:34–40 the Pharisees, after having heard Jesus silence the Sadducees, assembled and one of them, a lawyer, tested him with the question, "*Teacher,* which is the *great* commandment in the law?" In Mark 12:29 the reply of Jesus is, "The first is, 'Hear, O Israel: The Lord our God, the Lord is one'" (see Deut. 6:4). Matthew does not reproduce this. Probably by the time of Matthew the "Hear, O Israel . . ."[19] was already what it is today, namely, an affirmation of strict Jewish monotheism; Matthew's omission seems deliberate, for to him Christianity is no longer a Judaism and must not use this Jewish watchword. Matthew calls Deuteronomy 6:5 ("You shall love the Lord your God . . .") "the great and first commandment." He cites Leviticus 19:18 ("love your neighbor as yourself") as "a second like it," summarizing, as Mark does not, "On these two commandments depend all the law and the prophets." In Mark 12:32–34 the scribe praises Jesus for his answer; Jesus replies to the scribe, "You are not far from the kingdom of God." Matthew, however, omits the content of Mark 12:32–34; perhaps he was unwilling to reflect amity and agreement between Jesus and the scribe, being intent on emphasizing controversy and conflict. In the next item, about the Christ as David's son (22:41–46), Matthew tells that the Pharisees were gathered together and Jesus asked them a question; in Mark 12:35 the form is that "as Jesus taught in the temple, he said, 'How can the *scribes* say . . . ?'" Matthew alone has this conclusion: "No one was able to answer him a word, nor from that day did any one dare to ask him any more questions."

There now ensues a long, unified denunciation of the scribes and the Pharisees (23:1–36). A small amount of the material is borrowed from Mark 12:38–44, there an aspersion of scribes alone. There is an indirect parallel here and there in Luke; it is, however,

---

19. *Hear* in Hebrew is *shemá*; the verse Deut. 6:4 is known among Jews as "the Shema." The citation of Deut. 6:5 in both Mark 12:30 and Matt. 22:37 deviates slightly from what is in the Hebrew, probably because they were cited from memory.

essentially unique to Matthew. Apart from the opening words, "The scribes and the Pharisees sit on Moses' seat," the rest of the chapter is an unrelieved denunciation, ascribing not even a nuance of integrity or decency to the scribes and Pharisees. They preach, so we are told, but do not practice. They put burdens on people that they themselves will not lift a finger to move. Their deeds are always for show. Christians should not use their title rabbi, nor call any man father.[20] The scribes and Pharisees shut men out from the kingdom of God but do not themselves enter it. They traverse sea and land to make a single proselyte, thereby making him twice as much a child of hell as they are themselves. They swear not by the Temple but by the gold in it. They are punctilious about trivia but neglect justice, mercy, and faith. They are concerned with external cleanliness, not internal. Like whitewashed tombs, they appear beautiful, but they contain the bones of dead men and all uncleanness. They have built tombs for the prophets, but they are the sons of those who killed them. They will be sentenced to hell. On them will come punishment for the Christians whom they scourge in synagogues and persecute from town to town. The succeeding section is a lament over Jerusalem, blamed for killing the prophets and stoning those sent to her. The house (the Temple) is forsaken. Jerusalem will not see Jesus again until she says, "Blessed is he who comes in the name of the Lord" (23:37–39).

As in Mark 13:1–4, so in Matthew 24:1–2 Jesus predicts the destruction of the Temple. Matthew 24:4–14 reproduces with minor changes the substance of Mark 13:5–13. "The gospel must first be preached to all nations" (Mark 13:10) is moved to the end of the passage (Matt. 24:14), with the addition that after the gospel is so preached "then the end will come." There is an added section that predicts inner Christian distresses, such as apostasy, betrayal, and false prophets who will lead many astray (24:10–13).[21]

Matthew slightly alters the beginning of the passion narrative (26: 1–5) by expanding what is in Mark 14:1–2. While Matthew reproduces the gist of Mark, he puts the content into the mouth of Jesus, portraying Jesus as saying, "After two days the Passover is coming, and the Son of man will be delivered up to be crucified." Mark's statement that the chief priests and scribes sought "how to arrest

20. This title was apparently at one time used affectionately for a Jewish teacher, but it fell into disuse.

21. The remainder of Matt. 24 and all of Matt. 25 are not relevant to our topic.

Jesus by stealth" is altered into "the chief priests *and the elders of the people gathered in the palace of the high priest, who was called Caiaphas,* and took counsel together to arrest Jesus by stealth and kill him." (That is, the allegation of a plot against Jesus is increased in dimension.)

Matthew alters the matter of Judas Iscariot (26:14–16). In Mark, Judas goes to the chief priests in order to betray Jesus, and they are glad and give him money; Judas thereupon seeks his opportunity. In Matthew, Judas, going to the chief priests, asks, "What will you give me if I deliver him to you?" They paid him thirty pieces of silver. Matthew adds, "and from that moment he sought an opportunity." The import of "from that moment" is to increase the sense of the plot.

In the preparation of the Passover (26:17–19) the account in Matthew substantially abbreviates Mark 14:12–16. In place of Mark's words, a question, "Where is my guest room . . . ?" Matthew writes, "My time is at hand; I will keep the passover at your house with my disciples." Matthew omits Mark 14:12b, "when they sacrificed the passover lamb," possibly because sacrificing a lamb was strictly a Temple observance and would not take place in a home, something Mark seems to imply. Neither Mark nor Matthew describes what the preparations for the Passover are or how the preparations were made. (One wonders if the omission of the details of the preparation is deliberate. Did the Gospel writers not know about preparation? Did they know but wish not to describe them so as not to suggest, through depicting Jesus making preparations, that Christians should observe the Passover? The Passover Seder was not carried on as a Christian observance.)

To the brief account of the meal (26:20–25) Matthew adds, "Judas, who betrayed him, said, 'Is it I, Master?' He said to him, 'You have said so.'" This addition is enigmatic. Perhaps it is to prepare for the same words, "You have said so," in 26:64, to suggest that there too they mean yes. Matthew 26:31–32 repeats with only slight changes the prediction in Mark 14:27–28 that the disciples would totally abandon Jesus; the abandonment is related in 26:56.

The arrest of Jesus (26:47–56) has only minor differences from Mark 14:43–52, principally the omission of Mark 14:51–52, which tells of the seizure of a young boy with a linen cloth about his body who left the cloth and ran away naked. One does not know the reason for the omission but notes that Luke too omits this item.

The accounts of Jesus before the Sanhedrin and of Peter's denial (26:57–75) are only slightly different from those in Mark 14:53–72. Mark's words, "They led Jesus to the high priest . . . ," become, "Then those who had seized Jesus led him to Caiaphas the high priest, where the scribes and the elders had gathered." Where Mark 14:56 reads, "Many bore false witness against him, and their witness did not agree," Matthew reads, "many false witnesses came forward." Again, Mark reads: "And some stood up and bore false witness against him, saying, 'We heard him say, "I will destroy this temple that is made with hands, and in three days I will build another not made with hands." ' Yet not even so did their testimony agree."[22] Matthew reads: "At last two came forward and said, 'This fellow said, "I am able to destroy the temple of God, and to build it in three days." ' " Matthew omits the comment that the testimony did not agree. Where Mark reads, "The high priest asked him, 'Are you the Christ, the Son of the Blessed?' " Matthew reads, "The high priest said to him, 'I adjure you by the living God, tell us if you are the Christ, the Son of God.' " Mark reports the reply as, "I am . . ."; Matthew's version is, "You have said so. . . ."

The reaction to the words of Jesus in Matthew is a bit different from that in Mark. Matthew adds to the first words of the high priest, "He has uttered blasphemy." He adds the word *now* to Mark's sentence so that it reads, "You have now heard his blasphemy. What is your judgment?" (Mark reads *decision,* rather than *judgment.*) Mark proceeds, "They all condemned him as deserving death"; Matthew reads, "They answered, 'He deserves death.' " Matthew reproduces the spitting on Jesus, but not the covering of his face. Matthew adds that "some slapped him."[23] The taunt in Mark is a single word, "Prophesy"; in Matthew the reading is, "Prophesy to us, you Christ! Who is it that struck you?"

The Sanhedrin (mentioned in 26:59 and Mark 14:55, both mentions being rather abrupt) introduced is again mentioned in Mark 15:1 about the morning consultation, but this is not the case in Matthew 27:1. In the latter verse the "counsel" is taken by the "chief priests and elders," not the council. The purpose is to proceed against Jesus "to put him to death."

At this point (27:3–10) Matthew tells of the death of Judas,

22. It is to be noted that in John 2:19 there is ascribed to Jesus the words "Destroy this temple, and in three days I will raise it up."

23. Possibly the slapping is in place of the end of Mark 14:65, "The guards received him with blows."

which is completely absent from Mark.   Judas repents and brings back to the chief priests and the elders the thirty pieces of silver. They are not interested.   He throws down the pieces of silver in the Temple, departs, and hangs himself.   The chief priests buy the potter's field as a cemetery, for it was "not lawful to put [the pieces of silver] into the treasury, since they are blood money," this in fulfillment of a prophetic prediction.[24]   The field is known as Field of Blood.[25]   (The narrative contrasts the callousness of the priests with the repentance of Judas, a matter to which we will return.   A different account of the death of Judas is found in Acts 1:15–20.)

Before Pilate (27:11–14; Mark 15:2), in reply to Pilate's question, "Are you the King of the Jews?"   Jesus replies, "You have said so."   Matthew specifies what is only implied in Mark, that Jesus makes no answer to the accusations (in Mark such accusations are termed "many") of the chief priests and the elders.   Mark reads, " 'Have you no answer to make?   See how many charges they bring against you.'   But Jesus made no *further* answer, so that Pilate wondered."   In Matthew, Pilate says, " 'Do you not hear how many things they testify against you?'   But he gave them no answer, not even to a single charge; so that the governor wondered greatly."   (Here too Matthew recasts what is in Mark.)

The sentence of death in Matthew 27:15–26 is longer than the version in Mark 15:6–15.   Among the alterations is the characterization of Barabbas; in Matthew he is a "notorious prisoner," while in Mark he is an imprisoned "rebel" "who had committed murder in the insurrection."   (In some manuscripts of Matthew the name is given as *Jesus* Barabbas.)   Pilate's question in Mark is, "Do you want me to release for you the King of the Jews?"   In Matthew it is, "Whom do you want me to release for you, [Jesus] Barabbas or Jesus who is called Christ?"   Matthew adds that while Pilate was on the judgment seat "his wife sent word to him, 'Have nothing to do with that righteous man, for I have suffered much over him today in a dream.' "   Where Mark reads, "The chief priests stirred up the crowd to have him release for them Barabbas instead," Matthew reads, "The chief priests and the elders persuaded the people to ask for Barabbas *and destroy Jesus*."   In Matthew, Pilate repeats the

24. The quotation is a paraphrase not of Jeremiah but of Zech. 11:12–13. A potter is mentioned in Jer. 18:2–3; a field is bought in Jer. 32:6–15.

25. The name in Aramaic, Akeldama, is given in Acts 1:19.   In Acts, Judas falls headlong and bursts, and his bowels gush out.   There it is not the priests who have bought the field but Judas, this with the money given him.

question as to whom to release. Matthew adds, "So when Pilate saw that he was gaining nothing, but rather that a riot was beginning, he took water and washed his hands before the crowd, saying, 'I am innocent of this man's blood; see to it yourselves.' " (This is the acme of the exculpation of the Romans.)

Matthew 27:25 reads, "And all the people answered, 'His blood be on us and on our children!' " The intent in the verse is that the Jews here have accepted responsibility for the death of Jesus and that their children inherit that responsibility. (When I was a little boy, I was taunted as "Christ-killer" more than once!) Did "all the people" truly say that? Did they truly wish to transmit guilt to succeeding generations? Or do we have in this verse the single item that is the most glaring of New Testament anti-Semitic passages? (The verse has bothered modern Christians very deeply. Some simply disown the passage; others, particularly Roman Catholics, assert that only those Jews present before Pilate, not all Jews and all their children, underwent guilt.)

At the crucifixion (27:33–44; Mark 15:22–32) Matthew alters Mark's statement that the soldiers cast lots for the garments of Jesus, "to decide what each should take," into, "They sat down and kept watch over him." Matthew omits Mark 15:25, "It was the third hour, when they crucified him." He alters matters a bit by some additions: "Over his head they put the charge against him, which read, 'This is Jesus the King of the Jews.' " The taunt in Mark 15:29 is expanded in Matthew 27:40 by the words, "If you are the Son of God, come down from the cross." In Mark the taunts come from chief priests and scribes, in Matthew also from elders. Matthew rewrites the taunt in Mark 15:32, "Let the Christ, the King of Israel, come down now from the cross, that we may see and believe," into, "He is the King of Israel; let him come down now from the cross, and we will believe in him. He trusts in God; let God deliver him now, if he desires him; for he said, 'I am the Son of God.' "

The account of the death of Jesus (27:45–56) has only minor differences from Mark.[26] In Mark a bystander, after offering a sponge full of vinegar, says, "Wait, let us see whether Elijah will come to save him" (Mark 15:36). The words that Jesus "breathed his last" become in Matthew, "yielded up his spirit." Matthew provides miraculous concomitants of the death of Jesus (27:51–53).

26. In Mark the term for God is given as *Eloi,* probably an effort to reflect Aramaic; in Matthew it is Hebrew, *Eli.*

There is an earthquake, and tombs are opened, "and many bodies of the saints who had fallen asleep were raised . . . they went into the holy city and appeared to many." This item is found only in Matthew, who refrains from telling what the ultimate outcome was respecting these risen saints—or, indeed, just who these saints were. In Mark 15:44–45 the Roman centurion seems to be alone; in Matthew, he has soldiers "with him, keeping watch over Jesus." They saw the earthquake and what took place, and "they were filled with awe, and said, 'Truly this was the Son of God.' "

Joseph of Arimathea in Mark 15:43 is "a respected member of the council, who was also himself looking for the kingdom of God"; in Matthew he is a "rich man . . . a disciple of Jesus." Matthew, having stressed that soldiers have been keeping watch over Jesus, omits Mark 15:44, Pilate's inquiry whether Jesus is already dead (see p. 45). Matthew specifies that Joseph departed after laying the body in the tomb, here called Joseph's own. The two Marys here sit opposite the sepulchre (27:61); in Mark 15:47 they see where the body is laid. At this point (27:62–66) Matthew reports, as we said above, that the chief priests and the Pharisees told Pilate that the disciples might come and steal the body.

After telling that the two Marys were sitting opposite the sepulchre, Matthew relates that "after the sabbath, toward the dawn of the first day of the week" the two women went to see the sepulchre. Matthew omits Mark's statement that the two women, and Salome, bought spices to anoint Jesus (Mark 16:1–2). The time in Mark is "very early . . . when the sun had risen"; in Matthew it is "toward the dawn." In Mark 16:3 the women wonder who will roll the stone away from the door of the tomb; in Matthew 28:2 there is a great earthquake and an angel rolls back the stone and sits on it. The guards "for fear of him . . . trembled and became like dead men." In Mark the women see a "young man" dressed in white sitting in the tomb; the words of the angel (Matt. 28:5–7) are changed but not significantly from those of the "young man" in Mark 16:6–7. In Matthew 28:8 the women "departed quickly from the tomb with fear and great joy, and ran to tell his disciples"; in Mark the women "fled from the tomb; for trembling and astonishment had come upon them; and they said nothing to any one, for they were afraid."

In Matthew 28:9–10 (for which there is no parallel in Mark, since the Gospel has already ended) Jesus meets and hails the women, who take hold of his feet and worship him. He tells them not to be afraid but to go and tell his brethren to go to Galilee where

they will see him. With this addition Matthew dissolves the abrupt-
ness of the ending of Mark with its stress on the fear and silence
of the women. The eleven disciples (Judas is dead) went "to the
mountain" in Galilee to which Matthew says Jesus has directed
them, though there is no account of such direction. There they saw
him and worshiped him. Matthew comments, "But some doubted"
—a reflection of currents in his church. Jesus said, "All authority
in heaven and on earth has been given to me. Go therefore and
make disciples of all nations, baptizing them in the name of the
Father and of the Son and of the Holy Spirit, teaching them to
observe all I have commanded you." (One notes the word *commanded.*) "Lo, I am with you always, to the close of the age."

There has been no intention here to present all of Matthew, or to
note some of the sublime passages that are present. Matthew is a
mixture of sublimity and astonishing animosity. The reason for
noting in some detail how freely Matthew rewrites what is in Mark
in matters not relating to Jews is to point out that Matthew rewrites
as freely in matters that do relate to Jews, openly expressing anti-
Semitism that was not explicit in Mark. One senses in reading
Matthew that his anger and hatred of Jews increases as he writes,
especially against the Pharisees, until in chapter 23 it boils over into
a unique, unparalleled specimen of invective. Why is the invective
usually addressed to scribes and Pharisees rather than to "the Jews"?
We can only guess at the answer. One possibility is that it was primarily the Pharisees in Matthew's vicinity who were skeptical about
and critical of Christian habits and contentions, but this is less than
certain.

When Matthew says in passing that at the Resurrection appearance "some doubted" (28:17), it might well be inferred that in the
debates and controversies between Jews and Christians there were
instances in which some Christians were persuaded to doubt and to
leave the movement. It has been a repeated experience in the history of both Christendom and Judaism that there were apostates.
Clear evidence, which we shall see in John, points to the presence
of apostates from the Christian community. The bitterness in
Matthew might rest on the possibility that it was Pharisees who influenced such Christians to have these doubts. Perhaps one should
recall such passages as those found in Mark 13 and Matthew 24:
"Take heed that no one leads you astray"; "Brother will deliver up
brother to death"; "You will be hated by all nations for my name's

sake. And then many will fall away, and betray one another, and hate one another." Matthew's community was scarcely a stable one, neither secure from within nor unassailed from without, and there were Jews who rejected and contended against Christian claims. Apostasy from within was discouraging enough. To encounter it as a result of opposition from pagans was bitter, but to encounter it because of Jews was intolerable.

But, again, why the Pharisees, not "the Jews"? It is possible that Matthew fixes on them because that is how he can handle the situation that his Gospel is about Jesus the Jew, his Jewish disciples, and the Jewish setting; Matthew could not readily call the opponents, presumably of the age of Jesus, "Jews," for Jesus himself was one. (John, as we shall see, does what Matthew is reluctant to do.) Moreover there were Jews, Jewish Christians, in Matthew's church. Another answer suggests itself. Though the new movement by Matthew's time is clearly a separate entity, it had as yet not acquired a name. It still bore the label "Jewish." While Acts 11:26 tells that the members of the new movement came to be called "Christians," there is no more than a passing overtone in Matthew that the movement is anything other than Jewish and that its adherents are other than "Jews." In such circumstances the denunciation would not be of "Jews."

Whether these opponents were Pharisees in a literal sense cannot be determined. Where the line was drawn between Pharisaism and the later rabbinic Judaism (that is, where one ended and the other began) we do not know. The ancient rabbinic literature, set down in writing about A.D. 175–200, never calls itself Pharisaism; its term for itself is religion of "the Sages." The ordinary view, especially among Jewish scholars, is that while it is Pharisees who are denounced, it is Jews who are meant. My own opinion is quite different. It seems to me that for Matthew the scribes and the Pharisees represent what we would today call "the establishment" and that Matthew is appealing, as it were, over the heads of "the establishment" to the ordinary Jews, inviting them into the new movement. They should feel free to abandon the blind scribes and Pharisees; they should come into the new movement and become authentically possessed of a righteousness that exceeds that of the scribes and Pharisees.

Mark had discounted the Jews. Matthew, partisan though he is of a Gentile mission, does not wish to discount the Jews but rather wants them in his movement inaugurated by the new law of a figure greater than Moses. In Matthew, Judas Iscariot repents that he has betrayed Jesus; in this sense Matthew rehabilitates him, but in doing so he further denigrates the "establishment"; for him the priests remain complete rascals. Matthew seems to be saying that were "the Jews" to recognize the moral delinquency of the Jewish leaders they could find reason to come into the movement, for Christianity in Matthew's view is the authentic Judaism.

7. The Gospel According to Luke
The Acts of the Apostles

The Gospel According to Luke is an account of Jesus. The Acts of the Apostles, found in the New Testament after the Gospel According to John, is an account of the church after the time of Jesus. Modern scholarship attributes Acts and the Gospel of Luke to the same author, and in this chapter they will be treated as one work.

One can view the Gospel of Matthew as if one of its main purposes was to try to win Jews to the new movement by indicting the Jewish leadership. Luke-Acts does not participate in this indictment. It is addressed not to Jews but to Gentiles, just as Mark was. But Luke, the author, was much less impulsive than Mark. Luke was thoughtful and, in his skillful writing, concerned not to be misunderstood. He was a writer of unusual skill and artistry and there is evidence of his having done some research on Roman history.

The usual view of scholars ascribes to Luke-Acts the governing thesis that the Christians, rather than the Jews, were the true legatees of the promises made in Scripture to the patriarchs. It emphasizes an unbroken continuity between ancient Judaism and the Christian community. Just as Jews had received certain privileges from governing officials among the Romans, so now, Luke-Acts suggests, Christianity should receive the same privileges. Modern scholars usually interpret the exemplary behavior of the Christian community as portrayed in Luke-Acts (no Christian appearing in its pages is guilty of trespassing any Roman or Jewish law) as intended by the author to reassure the Roman government that though Rome had found it necessary to put Jesus to death because he was a threat to the state, there was no need to distrust his followers.

The view in Luke of an unbroken continuity between Judaism and Christianity seems to be at variance with some major aspects of the Gospel According to Matthew. The conception of Jesus as the giver of a new law was hardly consistent with unbroken continuity;

71

the seven statements in Matthew ("You have heard it said. . . . But I say to you"; Matt. 5:21, 27, 33, 38, 43) are all absent from Luke even though Luke reproduces some of the material in Matthew immediately related to these statements. That Luke did not reproduce these statements, or the Sermon on the Mount as such, seems deliberate. However, material in some ways similar to what is in the Sermon on the Mount is found beginning in Luke 6:20 and is often called the Sermon on the Plain. Those scholars who believe that the material common to Matthew and Luke but absent from Mark came from that now-lost source known as Q note that in Matthew the material is found assembled and arranged but that it is scattered in Luke; they conclude that it was in scattered form in that source.[1] Such scholars state that at least the form, and some or much of the content, of the Sermon on the Mount is to be attributed to Matthew rather than to Jesus.

If it is correct that Luke deliberately avoided and rejected the view that Jesus was a new and greater Moses teaching a new law, it was not the content of the new law that apparently disturbed Luke as much as it was the supposition that Christianity represented something new. It is Luke's repeated insistence that Christianity is very ancient, as implied in his contention of an unbroken continuity with ancient Judaism. Luke also differs from Matthew's view that the church needed protection from inner diversity and chaos by regulation through *law*. Luke proposes instead that the church be regulated through properly designated officials. In Mark and Matthew the terms *apostle* and *disciple* are often used interchangeably, and the result is a possible confusion. There is no confusion in Luke. *Disciple* is the term Luke uses for the great abundance of followers Luke tells that Jesus had. As to *apostle,* Luke 6:13 reads, "When it was day, [Jesus] called his disciples, and chose from them twelve, whom he named apostles." An apostle, then, is in Luke a specially designated disciple whom Jesus chose from out of a great abundance of disciples. In Acts, after the time of Jesus, a new apostle receives his authority from a preceding apostle.

As to the theme of unbroken continuity with ancient Judaism, we

---

1. "Q," from the German word *Quelle* (meaning "source"), is the way New Testament scholars customarily allude to this hypothetical source. I am with the minority of scholars who reject the notion of a Q; in my view Luke knew and used Matthew, and Matthew either inherited or created his special material not found in Mark.

shall see how consistently Luke portrays Christians as undeviatingly faithful to Judaism. The difficulties that Jesus and later Christians came to encounter were with Jews who were faithless to Judaism. In Luke's view the Law grew smoothly and naturally into the gospel; whatever was not smooth was a result of Jewish malevolence. Moreover, no responsible or admirable Jewish leader who possessed legitimate authority ever had a fault to find either with Jesus or with any of the apostles, whether in the time of Jesus or after it. God had indeed turned to the Gentiles, but that was because it was the divine plan; the Jews, malevolent as they were, merited pity rather than hate for the evil things they had done. This pity reflects a residual concern in Luke to win Jews to Christianity, but Luke's main concern is to win Gentiles and to reassure Romans.

With this concern to win Jews and still portray their recurrent malevolence, there is to be found in Luke a frequent subtle, genteel anti-Semitism. We shall find such subtlety primarily in the Gospel; in part the subtlety persists in Acts, but there it recedes and the anti-Semitism becomes overt and direct. In his Gospel, as we have said, Luke reproduces only a portion of Matthew's attack on the Pharisees in Matthew 23; what Luke presents is not in the assembled and relentlessly hostile form of the invective against the scribes and Pharisees in Matthew 23.

We look now at the material in Luke that is relevant to our topic. Luke's birth narrative is completely different from that in Matthew. That a Jewish king, Herod, wished to kill the babe Jesus, as related by Matthew, seems to have implied for Luke a rupture of continuity. Moreover, Herod was a client-king, designated by Rome; a Gospel designed to assure Rome of the law-abiding character of Christians would be weakened by the inclusion of King Herod's wish to have Jesus killed. Luke does not reproduce this material. Indeed, Luke portrays Herod's son Antipas and his great-grandson Agrippa II as royal spokesmen respectively for the innocence of first Jesus and then Paul. Instead of Matthew's violence Luke presents an inordinately beautiful birth narrative, free of the harshness of Matthew's account. The tone (but not the content) of Luke's artistic account can remind one of the peaceful tone and beauty of the Book of Ruth.

Luke, we shall see, writes with full freedom to invent or change what he has encountered in Mark and Matthew in order to emphasize his theme of direct continuity. In Luke's exposition the relationship between Jesus and John the Baptist far antedates the baptism by John of Jesus; it goes back to the womb. Luke begins with a prologue to the Gospel addressed to a patron Theophilus, asserting the reliability of his version of the career of Jesus. He presents an elderly righteous couple, Zechariah and Elizabeth, who walked *"in all the commandments and ordinances of the Lord blameless"* but were childless. While Zechariah was serving "as priest before God," according to the custom of the priesthood, "it fell to him by lot to enter the temple of the Lord and burn incense," when an angel appeared to him, informing him that he and Elizabeth would have a son whom he was to name John.

In the sixth month of Elizabeth's pregnancy the angel Gabriel announced to Mary (in Matthew the angel appears to Joseph) that through the Holy Spirit she would conceive a son to be called Jesus, "the Son of the Most High; and the Lord God will give to him the throne of his father David, and he will reign *over the house of Jacob for ever.*" Mary went from Galilee to Judea to visit Elizabeth, who was a kinswoman. When Mary entered the house and greeted Elizabeth, the babe in Elizabeth's womb "leaped for joy."[2] When John was born,[3] he was circumcised. He "grew and became strong in spirit, and was in the wilderness till the day of his manifestation to Israel" (1:80).

Consistent with his appeal to Rome, Luke recurrently mentions specific Roman officials as the prelude to the birth of Jesus, here naming Caesar Augustus and "Quirinius . . . governor of Syria"; the decree that a census of the empire was to be taken prompted Joseph to go to Bethlehem, the city of David, because Joseph "was of the house and lineage of David." He took Mary with him. Jesus was born in Bethlehem and laid in a manger because there was no place for them in the inn. Shepherds in the neighborhood were told by an angel to go to the manger, and they did so. "At the end of eight days" Jesus was circumcised, *in accordance with the Law.* The parents went to Jerusalem for purification and to offer a sacrifice, *"according to what is said in the law* of the Lord." There a righteous man, Simeon, took Jesus up in his arms and blessed him[4] and

---

2. There follows in 1:46–55 the poem called in Latin from the first word "The Magnificat."

3. It was the instruction of the angel (1:13) that the name be John; hence, the proposed name, Zechariah son of Zechariah, was rejected. The poem (1:68–79) speaks in v. 76 of the role of John; he is to "be called the prophet of the Most High; for you will go before the Lord to prepare his ways. . . ."

4. The blessing of Jesus is in 2:29–30.

then the parents, and spoke to Mary about what was to come.[5]   A prophetess Anna, who "did not depart from the temple, worshiping with fasting and prayer night and day," gave thanks to God for Jesus.   When the parents "had performed everything *according to the law of the Lord*" they returned to Galilee (2:39).   They went to Jerusalem every year at the feast of the Passover; they did so also when Jesus was twelve.[6]   By mistake they left Jesus behind when they set out for home, but they returned to Jerusalem and "after three days they found him in the temple, sitting among the teachers, listening to them and asking them questions."   All "were amazed at his understanding."   He said to his parents, " 'Did you not know that I must be in my Father's house?'   And they did not understand the saying."   They returned to Nazareth, "and Jesus increased in wisdom and in stature."   (The theme of fidelity to Judaism permeates the narrative, Luke 2:39–52.)

The public appearance of John the Baptist is presented by Luke accompanied by mention of "the fifteenth year of the reign of Tiberius Caesar, Pontius Pilate being governor of Judea, and Herod [Antipas] being tetrarch of Galilee."[7]   The preachment of John is like that in Matthew against the Pharisees, but, as if to soften any sense of over-againstness between John and the people, a sentence is appended: "So, with many other exhortations, he preached good news to the people" (3:18).   Luke then moves to this place in his Gospel the mention of Herod Antipas; in Mark 6:14–16 and Matthew 14:1–2 Antipas is mentioned in a context of the fame of Jesus.   Luke ascribes to Antipas only the misdeed of shutting John up in prison; he has no parallel to the accounts of the death of John in Mark 6:17–29 and Matthew 14:3–12.   The mention of Antipas at this point in Luke is a literary device, that of foreshadowing his exonerating role in 23:3–16, a role totally different from that in Mark and Matthew, as we shall see.

---

5. The words to Mary are in 2:34–35: "Behold, this child is set for the fall and rising of many in Israel, and for a sign that is spoken against (and a sword will pierce through your own soul also), that thoughts out of many hearts will be revealed."   That is, the future events of the career of Jesus are here revealed.

6. Sometimes this is viewed as if Jesus was here preparing for bar mitzvah. Bar mitzvah arose about a thousand years later.

7. There is mention also of Herod Philip and Lysanias, and the "high-priesthood of Annas and Caiaphas."

Luke turns from the baptism of Jesus[8] to a mention (such as a good historian would make) of the age of Jesus, "about thirty years"; he then presents a genealogy back from Jesus to Adam. Matthew's genealogy goes forward from Abraham. It is suggested that Luke wishes to stress the universal application of Christianity, something beyond the Jewishness implied in Matthew's genealogy, and hence his list goes to the "pre-Jewish" period before Abraham (3:23–38). Luke closes his version of the temptation in the wilderness with the words that the devil "departed from him until an opportune time."[9]

Luke makes a most significant alteration in both the content and position of the rejection of Jesus at Nazareth. In Mark it occurs after about a third of the Gospel, at 6:1–6; it is just short of halfway into Matthew, at 13:54–58. In Luke's version it occurs at the very beginning of the public ministry (4:16–30). Jesus entered the synagogue *"as his custom was, on the sabbath day."* He stood up to read and "there was given to him the book of the prophet Isaiah"; after reading Isaiah 61:1–2 and 58:6 Jesus closed the book, returned it to the attendant, and was seated. He said, "Today this scripture has been fulfilled in your hearing." All spoke well of him, knowing him as Joseph's son. Jesus said, "Doubtless you will quote to me this proverb, 'Physician, heal yourself; what we have heard you did at Capernaum, do here also in your own country.' "[10] (Luke softens the words of Mark 6:4 and Matt. 13:57. His version reads, "No prophet is acceptable in his own country," thereby omitting Matthew's phrase "in his own house," and Mark's phrase "among his own kin and in his own house.")

The further words ascribed to Jesus in this passage recall that the work of the prophet Elijah (1 Kings 18:1–9) was of benefit to the Gentile widow in Sidon, and that of Elisha (2 Kings 5:1–14) to the Gentile Naaman the Syrian. Now those in the synagogue be-

8. In Matt. 3:13–15 it is set forth that John thinks it improper to baptize Jesus (since baptism implies antecedent sin). Luke puts the baptism in a subordinate clause: "When Jesus also had been baptized, and was praying, the heaven was opened, and the Holy Spirit descended upon him in bodily form. . . ."

9. The point of the temptation episode (Mark 1:12–13; Matt. 4:1–11) appears to be to refute in advance for the reader the accusation made later (Mark 3:22–27; Matt. 12:22–30; Luke 11:14–23) that Jesus is possessed by the devil.

10. In moving the position of the rejection there has as yet been no account of deeds in Capernaum as in Mark 1:21–28; that comes later, in Luke 4:31–47.

came angry. They put Jesus out of the city, wishing to throw him off the brow of the hill on which the city was built, but Jesus was able to get away. The incident as it is presented in Luke (4:28–30) suggests that Jesus was rejected by the Jews right at the start of his career and that already then the Jews tried to kill him; also at that very early time it was publicly announced that the benefit to arise from the activities of Jesus was destined for Gentiles. One needs to notice that Jesus is again seen "customarily" attending the synagogue on the Sabbath. The fidelity to Judaism of Luke's Jesus is in contrast to the imputed Jewish infidelity of the Jews themselves.

In the matter of healing the man with the withered hand (Mark 3:1–6; Matt. 12:9–14), Luke tells that scribes and Pharisees were present; it was they who watched to see if Jesus would heal on the Sabbath. After the healing "they were filled with fury and discussed with one another what they might do to Jesus" (6:6–11). In the words about John the Baptist (7:24–35), Luke reads, "The Pharisees and the lawyers rejected the purpose of God for themselves, not having been baptized by him." So blind were they that they rejected John. John had come "eating no bread and drinking no wine; and you say, 'He has a demon.' The Son of man has come eating and drinking, and you say, 'Behold, a glutton and a drunkard, a friend of tax collectors and sinners!' "

The parable of the Good Samaritan (Luke 10:29–37), tells about the succoring of a man beaten by robbers. Both a priest and a Levite callously passed him by but he was aided by a compassionate Samaritan.[11] The parable is not in itself anti-Jewish but in the total context of Luke it does lend itself to a possible alignment with other anti-Jewish passages.

Luke reproduces in 11:37—12:1 some of the diatribe against the Pharisees found in Matthew 23. In Luke's presentation there comes first (vv. 37–44) a denunciation of the Pharisees; next (vv. 45–48) it is "lawyers" who are denounced. Verse 49 reads, "Therefore also the Wisdom of God said, 'I will send them prophets and *apostles,* some of whom they will kill and persecute,' that the blood of all the prophets . . . may be required of this generation." Verse 11:52 reads, "Woe to you lawyers! For you have taken away the key of knowledge; you did not enter yourselves and you hindered those who were entering." The infidelity of the Jews to Judaism is again the theme here.

11. See Chapter 8, n. 6.

Luke 12:11, a version of Matthew 10:19–20, adds some words (here italicized) to reassure Christians: "When they *bring you before the synagogues and the rulers and the authorities,* do not be anxious how or what you are to . . . say. . . ." The implication here presages future Christian experience: the Holy Spirit will guide them.

Another Sabbath conflict story appears in Luke 13:10–17. The head of a synagogue, rebuking Jesus for healing an infirm woman, said, "There are six days on which work ought to be done; come on those days and be healed, and not on the sabbath day." Luke goes on:

> The Lord answered him, "You hypocrites! Does not each of you on the sabbath untie his ox or his ass from the manger, and lead it away to water it? And ought not this woman, a daughter of Abraham . . . be loosed from [Satan's bond] on the sabbath day?" As he said this, all his adversaries [the Jews unfaithful to Judaism, eventually to be rejected by God] were put to shame; and all the people rejoiced at all the glorious things that were done by him.

Still another Sabbath conflict, like that in 13:10–17, occurs at 14:1–6: "[Jesus said], 'Which of you, having a son or an ox that has fallen into a well, will not immediately pull him out on a sabbath day?' And they could not reply to him."

Luke 13:22–30 speaks of those to be excluded from salvation. Such people will

> knock at the door, saying, "Lord, open to us." He will answer you, "I do not know where you come from." Then you will begin to say, "We ate and drank in your presence, and you taught in our streets." But he will say, "I tell you, I do not know where you come from; depart from me, all you workers of iniquity!" Then you will weep and gnash your teeth, when you see Abraham and Isaac and Jacob and all the prophets in the kingdom of God and you yourselves thrust out. And men will come from east and west, and from north and south, and sit at table in the kingdom of God. And behold, some are last who will be first, and some are first who will be last.[12]

That God has rejected the Jews is the theme here.

Luke's version of the marriage banquet (14:15–24) is different in some details from that in Matthew 22:1–14. Luke omits Matthew

---

12. The departure from Galilee that follows (13:31–33) includes words ascribed to Jesus: "It cannot be that a prophet should perish away from Jerusalem." This is followed by the "lament over Jerusalem" (13:34–35), parallel to Matt. 23:37–39.

22:7, that the king, angry, "sent his troops and destroyed those murderers and burned their city." Instead Luke tells that "the householder in anger said to his servant, 'Go out quickly to the streets and lanes of the city, and bring in the poor and maimed and blind and lame. . . . For I tell you, none of those men who were invited shall taste my banquet.' "[13]   (Again the theme of God's rejection of the Jews.)

The parable of the unjust steward (16:1–13) has as its conclusion the words "You cannot serve God and mammon." There is appended (16:14–15) the statement that the Pharisees "were lovers of money." Jesus said to them, "You are those who justify yourselves before men, but God knows your hearts . . . ; for what is exalted among men is an abomination in the sight of God." The parable of the rich man and Lazarus (16:19–31) has two parts. The first (vv. 19–26) deals with the fate of the rich man and Lazarus in the afterlife. These words are addressed to the rich man by Father Abraham: "Remember that you in your lifetime received your good things, and Lazarus in like manner evil things; but now he is comforted here, and you are in anguish." In the second part the rich man says to Father Abraham,

> "I beg you, father, to send [Lazarus] to my father's house, for I have five brothers, so that he may warn them, lest they also come into this place of torment." But Abraham said, "They [the Jews] have Moses and the prophets; let them hear them." And he said, "No, father Abraham. But if some one goes to them from the dead, they will repent." [Abraham] said to him, "If they do not hear Moses and the prophets, neither will they be convinced if some one should rise from the dead."

(The allusion to the disbelief in the resurrection of Jesus on the part of Jews who, it is alleged, are faithless to Moses and the prophets again repeats the contrast, drawn by Luke, to the faithfulness of the Christians.)

In Mark and Matthew the route of Jesus to Jerusalem is presented as a crossing of the Jordan from west to east at the north, a southward journey, and then a recrossing of the Jordan at Jericho, east to west. A journey straight south from Galilee to Jerusalem would have necessitated traversing Samaria and would have implied

---

13. The next item, the parable of the prodigal son (15:11–32), is at times viewed as if the angry older brother represents the Jews, disaffected at the warm reception given the repentant son, representing the Christians.

that Jesus had some contact with Samaritans. Mark and Matthew seem to shun this, in keeping with the view that Jesus was concerned only with the "lost sheep of the house of Israel." In Luke the route is due south, through Samaria, and there is contact with Samaritans, whom Jews viewed as Gentiles.

In the account of the healing of ten lepers (17:11–19), a Samaritan, "a foreigner," was the only one of these ten who returned to Jesus to praise God for the healing. A parable contrasts the arrogant self-righteousness of a Pharisee with the humble sincerity of a tax collector (18:9–14).[14]

At the entry of Jesus into Jerusalem (19:35–44) "the whole multitude of the disciples" rejoiced and praised God "with a loud voice . . . saying, 'Blessed is the King who comes in the name of the Lord! Peace in heaven and glory in the highest!' " Pharisees present asked Jesus to rebuke his disciples (for the mention of the king?), but he declined to. He then wept over Jerusalem: ". . . Your enemies will cast up a bank about you and surround you . . . and dash you to the ground . . . and they will not leave one stone upon another in you; because you did not know the time of your visitation." (That is, the destruction of the Temple in the year 70 was a disaster that Jews merited because of their blindness about Jesus.)

Luke shortens Mark 11:15b and Matthew 21:12–13, "the cleansing of the Temple," by omitting the overturning of the tables of the money-changers and the seats of those who sold pigeons (Luke 19:45–46). As if to avoid giving the impression that this act of Jesus was one of infidelity to Judaism, Luke gives no response on the part of the witnesses to the act (such as Mark 11:18 does); Luke promptly goes on to add that Jesus "was teaching daily in the temple." It is the teaching of Jesus in Luke, not the cleansing of the Temple, that prompted "the chief priests and the scribes and the principal men of the people" to seek to destroy him; "but they did not find anything they could do, for all the people hung upon his words."[15]

14. See also the incident of Zacchaeus, a tax collector, a "lost son" of Abraham (19:1–10). The parable of the pounds (19:11–27) seems to be in part turned into an allegory. The nobleman in the parable is Jesus, who has gone away (to heaven) to receive kingly power. "His citizens hated him . . . saying, 'We do not want this man to reign over us.' " The parable closes with these words, "But as for these enemies of mine . . . bring them here and slay them before me."

15. Luke omits the cursing of the fig tree (Mark 11:12–14, 20–25; Matt. 21:18–22).

Luke presents versions only slightly different from those in Mark and Matthew of the question of authority (Luke 20:1–8), the parable of the wicked tenants (20:9–19), the tribute to Caesar (20:20–26), and the encounter with the Sadducees concerning resurrection (20:27–47). But his freedom to rewrite is seen in his replacing the Great Commandment. He cites it earlier (10:25–28) so that it does not appear here, the place Mark and Matthew allocate to it. He presents the matter of the descent of the Messiah from David (20:41–44; Mark 12:35–37a; Matt. 22:41–46). He then has a brief denunciation of the scribes (20:46–47), seemingly based on Mark 12:38–40. The incident of a poor widow putting two coins into the treasury (21:1–4; Mark 12:41–44) leads to another prediction of the destruction of the Temple (21:5–7; Mark 13:1–4; Matt. 24:1–3) and in 21:8–33 some additional paraphrases of Mark 13:5–37 and Matthew 24:4–35. Luke gives a summary in 21:37–38 that repeats the already stated theme of fidelity: "And every day [Jesus] was teaching in the temple. . . ."

Luke shortens the intention of the chief priests and the scribes to find a way of putting Jesus to death (22:1–2; Mark 14:1–2; Matt. 26:1–5). Having used the anointing of Jesus earlier (7:36–50), he does not present it here as do Mark 14:3–9 and Matthew 26:6–13. Instead Luke moves directly from the intention to kill Jesus to the statement that Satan (last mentioned at the temptation, 4:13) "entered Judas called Iscariot." Judas conferred with "the chief priests and officers how he might betray [Jesus] to them. They were glad, and engaged to give him money." (The thirty pieces of silver [Matt. 26:14–16, 27:3–10] are not mentioned in Luke.) Judas "sought an opportunity to betray him to them *in the absence of the multitude.*" Next comes the preparation for the Passover (22:7–13) in a version slightly different from that in Mark 14:12–16 and in Matthew 26:17–19.

The account of the Last Supper in Luke (22:14–38) is different from that in Mark and Matthew; like Mark, and unlike Matthew, Judas is not identified as the betrayer. Luke shifts to this point (22:24–30) the rivalry of the disciples for eminence, which comes earlier in the accounts of Mark and Matthew (Mark 10:42–45; Matt. 20:25–28). The Last Supper, as indicated by 22:15–16, seems to be viewed as the Passover Seder, a prelude to a future "eschatological" Seder (22:30); it does not seem to be a Seder in Mark and Matthew. (Eschatological means "the end of the age." Luke seems to expect a Seder in the future age.)

Now Luke adds the view that Peter, though he will soon deny knowing Jesus,[16] "turned again," and at that time he should "strengthen [his] brethren" (22:32). Luke does not have the prediction by Jesus that the disciples will "fall away" (Matt. 26:31; Mark 14:27). The Last Supper in Luke ends with instructions to the Twelve to acquire swords; since two swords were already at hand, Jesus said, "It is enough" (22:35–38).

Luke presents the agony in Gethsemane, though he does not give the name "Gethsemane" (22:40–46). In Mark 14:32–42 and Matthew 26:36–46 Jesus has Peter, James, and John with him as he prays; in Luke he apparently has all the Twelve with him, for in Luke they have not abandoned Jesus by fleeing. Luke adds that an angel appears to Jesus to strengthen him. As he prayed his sweat was "like great drops of blood falling down upon the ground." In Matthew and Mark, Jesus three times finds the three disciples asleep; Luke has them fall asleep only once and explains that they were "sleeping for sorrow." (Luke consistently portrays the disciples and apostles in a light more favorable than that in Mark.)

In the arrest of Jesus (22:47–53) a crowd comes to Jesus, but Luke does not say, as do Mark and Matthew, that they have come from the chief priests and the scribes (Mark 14:43) and the elders (Matt. 26:47). Luke shortens and slightly alters the betrayal through the kiss; here Jesus knows exactly what Judas intends to do. Jesus said, "Judas, would you betray the Son of man with a kiss?" The disciples (one recalls the two swords) asked Jesus if they should strike with them, and one disciple struck the slave of the high priest and cut off an ear (which Luke, writing freely, alone identifies as the right one). Jesus said, "No more of this!" He touched the ear and healed the man. At this point Luke mentions that "chief priests and officers of the temple [police] and elders" are among those who have come out against him (22:52). Luke completely omits that the disciples abandoned Jesus and fled (Mark 14:50–52; Matt. 26:56).

On Jesus' being led to the home of the high priest,[17] Luke does not

16. In Mark 14:29–31 and Matt. 26:33–35 the prediction of the denial by Peter takes place after the Last Supper, not during it as in Luke.

17. In Luke 22:54–62 the account of Peter's denial of Jesus is not intertwined with the questioning of Jesus and the false testimony allegedly given, as in Mark and Matthew. By shortening the evening matters, Luke narrates Peter's denial in his own way; that is, Jesus observes Peter's denial: "The Lord turned and looked at Peter. . . . And he went out and wept bitterly." Luke omits both the curse that Peter invokes on himself and Peter's oath (Matt. 26:74; Mark 14:71).

portray any questioning of Jesus or any testimony of false witnesses (as in Matt. 26:59 ff.; Mark 14:55 ff.). Instead, "the men who were holding Jesus mocked him and beat him. . . ." (Luke by implication is suggesting here, as in the sequel, that Jesus is lynched by the mob, rather than tried and condemned by duly constituted authorities.) The questioning presented in Matthew and Mark as on the previous evening takes place in Luke the next morning when "the elders of the people gathered together, both chief priests and scribes; and they led him away to their council" (22:63–66). The questioning is shorter in Luke (22:67–71), lacking the "false witnesses" of Matthew and Mark (Matt. 26:60–62; Mark 14:57–61). In Matthew and Mark it is the high priest who questions Jesus; in Luke it is "they," presumably the assembly of elders, priests, scribes, and the council (22:66–71). Luke has Jesus answer the question "If you are the Christ, tell us" in these words: "If I tell you, you will not believe; and if I ask you, you will not answer. But from now on the Son of man shall be seated at the right hand of the power of God." Luke then reports that "they all said, 'Are you the Son of God, then?' " The reply in Luke is, "You say that I am." (Luke omits the specific allegation of blasphemy found in Mark 14:64 and Matthew 26:65; it would conflict with the motif of Christian fidelity to Judaism.) The opponents say simply, "What further testimony do we need? We have heard it ourselves from his own lips."[18] Luke does not report that the authorities condemned Jesus as deserving death, as do Matthew 26:66 and Mark 14:64. Rather, those assembled bring Jesus before Pilate (Luke 23:1).

There the charge against Jesus is presented: "We found this man perverting our nation, and forbidding us to give tribute to Caesar, and saying that he himself is Christ a king." (In view of Luke 20:20–26, where Jesus is portrayed as saying, "Render to Caesar the things that are Caesar's," the reader of Luke recognizes the falsity of the accusation.) Pilate in Luke asks Jesus a single question, "Are you the King of the Jews?" As in Mark 15:2 and Matthew 27:11 Jesus replies, "You have said so." Immediately Pilate says to the chief priests and the multitude, "I find no crime in this man." (In Matt. 27:14 and Mark 15:5 Pilate wonders; here, though, he is quickly certain.) The reply of the Jews to Pilate is the charge, "He stirs up the people, teaching throughout all Judea, from Galilee even to this place."

18. The mocking and beating, used earlier (in Luke 22:63–64), come at this point in Matt. 26:67–68 and Mark 14:65.

As if prompted by the mention of Galilee, Luke tells—and this is found only in Luke—that Herod Antipas was in Jerusalem; Pilate sent Jesus to him for questioning as chief priests stand by, vehemently accusing. Antipas and his soldiers treated Jesus with contempt and mocked him and sent him back to Pilate (but without condemnation). Pilate then called together the chief priests, the rulers, and the people, saying, "I do not find this man guilty of any of your charges. . . . Nothing deserving death has been done by him." (Up to this point there has been no mention at all in Luke of Jesus' deserving death.) Pilate proposed to chastise Jesus and to release him. The mob demanded the release of Barabbas. After Pilate's third assertion of the innocence of Jesus, the crowd so demanded with loud cries that Jesus be crucified that "their voices prevailed." So Pilate gave sentence that their demand should be granted. "He released [Barabbas] . . . but Jesus he delivered up to *their will*."

On the way to the crucifixion Luke adds material not found in Matthew and Mark (23:27–32). He tells that a great multitude of the people, and women who bewailed and lamented him, followed Jesus (23:27). To the women Jesus said, "Daughters of Jerusalem, do not weep for me, but weep for yourselves and for your children." Luke tells also that two others, criminals, were led away to be put to death with him. One scorned Jesus; the other rebuked the first one and asserted that Jesus, unlike them, had been innocent (23:39–43).

When Jesus was crucified, according to some manuscripts, he said, "Father, forgive them; for they know not what they do." (Jews deserve pity, not condemnation.) Luke 23:35 tells that people stood by watching but that the Jewish leaders scoffed at him. They and the soldiers taunted him to save himself and so did one of the two criminals crucified with him. The other rebuked him, saying, "We are receiving the due reward of our deeds; but this man has done nothing wrong."[19] (Note the theme of innocence.)

Luke tells that Jesus, "crying with a loud voice, said, 'Father, into thy hands I commit my spirit!' "[20] (23:46). He omits the question "Why hast thou forsaken me?" (Mark 15:34; Matt. 27:46). Whereas in Mark 15:39 and Matthew 27:54 the Roman centurion says, "Truly this man was the Son of God!" in Luke 23:47 the words

19. He added, "Jesus, remember me when you come into your kingdom"; Jesus said, "Today you will be with me in Paradise" (20:42–43).

20. Luke shifts the position of the tearing of the curtain of the Temple in two to precede the death of Jesus (23:45), whereas in Mark and in Matthew it follows his death.

are, "Certainly this man was innocent." Luke now reverts to the multitudes assembled (23:27), who returned home beating their breasts. Since the disciples have not fled, as they have in Matthew 26:56 and Mark 14:50, Luke tells that "all his acquaintances and the women who had followed him from Galilee stood at a distance and saw these things" (23:49). Luke does not include Pilate's uncertainty (Mark 15:44) as to whether Jesus is dead. As to the women who on Friday prepared spices and ointments, "on the Sabbath they rested *according to the commandment*" (23:54–56).

On the first day of the week, at early dawn, the women (they seem to be many; in Mark 16:1 they number three, in Matt. 28:1, two) went to the tomb. The stone was found rolled away. They entered but did not find the body. Two men in dazzling apparel appeared to them (in Mark 16:5 it is a young man, sitting in the tomb; in Matt. 28:2–9 it is an angel). Whereas in Mark 16:7 and Matthew 28:7 the words of the young man or the angel foreshadow a resurrection appearance ("he is going before you") in Galilee, in Luke the words are, "Remember how he told you, *while he was still in Galilee.*" (Luke has no resurrection appearance in Galilee.) The women then told all this "to the eleven and to all the rest." The apostles, on being told, thought this an idle tale and did not believe the women.

In Luke the resurrection appearance is not in Galilee but on the road to "Emmaus, about seven miles from Jerusalem," first to two disciples, and then to the eleven in Jerusalem (24:13–49). Jesus parted from the disciples at Bethany. They all "returned to Jerusalem with great joy, and were continually in the temple blessing God" (24:50–53).

As free as Matthew was in recasting Mark, Luke has been even freer—rewriting, omitting, adding, and relocating materials. Two items are constant: the fidelity of Jesus to Judaism and his innocence of any wrongdoing, as evidenced by his not being condemned by any valid Jewish authority. No charge of blasphemy is leveled against him in Luke; he is simply the victim of unthinking malice, not in any thought or deed disloyal to Judaism. The allegations against Jesus (false ones, in Luke's view) amount only to his stirring people up.

The villainy of the Jews in Luke is not primarily in what Luke says against them, or, as in Matthew, in the terms of denunciation against them ascribed to Jesus. It is rather that the acts and words of the Jews are their own indictment. It is in this sense that the anti-Semitism in Luke is more subtle than that in Mark and Matthew.

The crucifixion did not, in Luke's account, disrupt relations between the disciples and Judaism. Unlike Mark and Matthew, Luke seems to take pains to show that despite what has happened the disciples are always loyal to Judaism, for they are still "continually in the temple." That in due course, as related in Acts of the Apostles, Christianity became largely Gentile was due to the working out of the will of God and also the result of blindness and even stupidity on the part of the Jews. These lamentable traits were what led to the loss by the Jews of their favored position in God's plans. These themes reappear in the Acts of the Apostles.

In the Gospel it is Jesus who is central in the unfolding of Christian events. In Acts, beyond chapter 1, it is instead the church after the time of Jesus that, through the Holy Spirit, is the corporate protagonist in the continued unfolding events. That is, what Jesus was to his time, the church was to its time.

Consistent with the view that the church was from the start destined to be Gentile, Acts sets forth in a progressive, indeed logical way, the circumstances of the transition from a Jewish to the Gentile character, always careful to avoid any nuance of infidelity to Judaism in the process. The opening chapters of Acts present an all-Jewish setting, with Christianity still within Judaism and still centered in Jerusalem; the illegal death of Jesus, by lynching, has caused no rift at all, at least not from the side of the church. In Acts 1 the risen Jesus "presented himself alive after his passion by many proofs, appearing to [the apostles] during forty days." (This is unique to Luke-Acts.) They were enjoined not to depart from Jerusalem until they were baptized by the Holy Spirit; then, in the words ascribed to Jesus, "You shall be my witnesses in Jerusalem and in all Judea and Samaria to the end of the earth" (Acts 1:3–9).

The baptism took place on Pentecost (Acts 2), when the Holy Spirit descended on the entire community of the disciples in Jerusalem. Among this community existed the twelve specially designated apostles, chosen by Jesus. No list of the apostles is given in Acts. We encounter them here presented by name as if they are already known in this capacity. The principal ones are Peter, Philip, James, Barnabas, John, and Paul (Acts 1:13). After the apostle Judas dies (he fell and split open, 1:15–20; contrast Matt. 27:5) two disciples are nominated as replacement for Judas, and Matthias is selected as an apostle, to bring the number back to twelve.

Now the followers are ready for their mission. Their "acts," here to be discussed in their chapter-to-chapter sequence, involve throngs of people, a profusion of ancient place names, and a slow progress, through triumph and suffering, back and forth across the Mediterranean world. I have tried, as elsewhere in this book, to guide the reader through the wealth of necessary detail to a comprehension of the main theme: the spread and solidification of the church, through the efforts of the apostles, into its own character and entity.

The work of the apostles begins with Peter and John healing a lame man (3:1-11). An address in the Temple by Peter (3:12-26) annoyed the priests, the captain of the Temple police, and the Sadducees because the apostles were proclaiming the resurrection of the dead (which at least Sadducees denied). The two, Peter and John, were arrested, warned not to speak again about Jesus, and then released (4:1-22). The Christian community "were of one heart and soul . . . they had everything in common" (4:23—5:11).

The growth of the movement through healing the sick and the demon-possessed led to the arrest and imprisonment of the apostles. They were, however, miraculously released from jail, yet brought before the Sanhedrin. There a Pharisee and honored teacher of the Law, Gamaliel, advised the council to leave the apostles alone. Thereupon the apostles were beaten and charged not to speak in the name of Jesus. They were released, but "every day in the temple and at home they did not cease teaching and preaching Jesus as the Christ" (5:12-42).

Seven disciples were designated as deacons, "to serve tables" (this probably means housing and feeding the apostles). Among them was Stephen, who did great wonders and signs among the people and who spoke with the Spirit and with great wisdom. Diaspora Jews, present in Jerusalem, then "arose and disputed with Stephen." They stirred up people so that he was brought before the Sanhedrin where false witnesses rose up against him. In response to a question of the high priests as to whether testimony of the witnesses was true, Stephen spoke at some length (7:2-53) and enraged his hearers by his words. They stoned him illegally. Present at the stoning was one Saul, who "consented" to the illegal death of Stephen (7:54—8:1). (Introduced here quite abruptly, without specified credentials, Saul is later to become focal in Acts as Paul, a convert and a zealous apostle.) That same day a great persecution arose, and the church "were all scattered throughout the region of Judea and Samaria, except the apostles." Saul, so we read, "was ravaging the church" (8:2-3).

Philip, one of those who had scattered, converted many Gentiles in Samaria. Then Peter and John went to Samaria, where "they laid hands on [the converts] and they received the Holy Spirit" (8:17). (The movement has thus spread from Jerusalem into Samaria.) Philip then converted an Ethiopian eunuch who was in Judea and went on to the Gentile city of Caesarea (8:26–40).

The attention in Acts 9 is on Saul/Paul, who is to emerge as the central proponent of the new movement. Here, still in opposition, he is shown journeying to Damascus to extradite Christians from there to Jerusalem. The chapter narrates his vision of the Christ on the road, his baptism in Damascus, and his confounding the Jews there by proving that Jesus is the Lord. Paul was designated by Jesus (according to 9:15) as "a chosen instrument of mine to carry my name before the Gentiles and kings and the sons of Israel." The Damascus Jews plotted to kill him, but "his disciples took him by night and let him down over the wall." (No explanation is offered about the origin of the Christian community in Damascus or who Paul's disciples were or why the Jews should have wanted to kill Paul.) Paul returned to Jerusalem. Though the apostles were suspicious of him, the apostle Barnabas endorsed him. Paul then disputed with Greek Jews in Jerusalem; these thereupon sought to kill him so that the "brethren . . . sent him off to Tarsus." There comes next a summary sentence: "The church throughout all Judea and Galilee and Samaria had peace and was built up" (9:31).

Peter, through one healing, converted residents of Lydda and Sharon, and, through another, the people of Joppa (9:32–42). He was summoned to come to Gentile Caesarea to a Roman centurion named Cornelius. Hungry, Peter saw a vision of "the heaven opened, and something descending, like a great sheet, let down by four corners upon the earth. In it were all kinds of animals and reptiles and birds of the air." As the account proceeds, the meaning of the vision is clarified, namely, that Jewish food prohibitions and the prohibition of eating improper food with Gentiles were nullified. Peter spoke of his obligation "to preach to the people" (the Gentiles). The Holy Spirit then was "poured out even on the Gentiles," that is, the Gentile mission was divinely approved as a direct sequel to the abolition of Jewish food laws (10:1–48).

When Peter came to Jerusalem, the "circumcision party" (those who believed Christians should observe the Mosaic laws) criticized him for going to the uncircumcised and eating with them. Peter then narrated his experiences. Thereupon the Jerusalem people endorsed the Gentile mission: they "glorified God, saying, 'Then to the Gentiles also God has granted repentance unto life' " (11:1–19).

Next, there came to Antioch in Syria those disciples who had scattered because of the persecution of Stephen and who now preached to Gentiles in Antioch. The Christians in Jerusalem sent the apostle Barnabas to Antioch, and Barnabas was gratified by what he saw there. He summoned Paul to Antioch to further this work among Gentiles. The converts—called Christians for the first time (though we have used the term prematurely in these pages for lack of a better one)—committed themselves to send relief funds for the famine-threatened brethren in Judea (11:20–30), demonstrating that the Gentile converts of the Dispersion were faithful to the Christians in Judea.

The Romans had appointed Herod Agrippa I king of Judea (A.D. 39–44). Before and after Agrippa's reign, Roman procurators ruled Judea. Agrippa persecuted the church, and an angel of God slew him (12:1–23). The church grew and multiplied (12:24). This church-favored miracle does not appear in the accounts by Josephus of the brief reign of Agrippa I.

From Antioch the "brethren," prompted by the Holy Spirit, sent Barnabas and Saul (hereafter called Paul) to other Gentile areas. In Cyprus, after a wondrous deed, the Roman proconsul was converted (the first Roman official to enter the movement). Paul and Barnabas moved on. At Antioch in Pisidia, in the synagogue on a Sabbath, Paul rose and spoke; he was asked to speak again the next Sabbath. Meanwhile, "many Jews and devout converts to Judaism" followed Paul and Barnabas. But on the next Sabbath, when the whole town gathered, the Jews were filled with envy. They contradicted Paul and reviled him and stirred up persecution; but Paul and Barnabas went on to Iconium (13:1–52).

At Iconium, after a great company of Jews and Greeks became believers, the Jews stirred up Gentiles and poisoned their minds. Because Paul and Barnabas were in danger of being stoned, they fled to Lystra and Derbe. At Lystra, Paul healed a cripple, so that the crowds thought that Barnabas was Zeus and Paul was Hermes. But Jews came to Lystra and managed to stone Paul; he was thought to be dead but was still alive. He then went to Derbe with Barnabas. They made many converts at Derbe and also in other places. They then went to Antioch in Syria, remaining there for a long time (14:1–28).

Men from Judea now came to Antioch, demanding that circumcision be imposed on the Christians. Dissension and debate ensued. Paul, Barnabas, and some others were appointed "to go up to

Jerusalem to the apostles and the elders about this question." On their journey they gave great joy to the Gentile converts. While they were welcomed in Jerusalem "some believers who belonged to the party of the Pharisees" arose to insist on circumcision and the observance of the laws of Moses. There was then much debate. Peter recalled his experiences and spoke against "putting a yoke upon the neck of the disciples which neither our fathers nor we have been able to bear." Then Barnabas and Paul spoke of their experiences with Gentiles.

James, the head of the church in Jerusalem, gave the decision that Gentile converts need not be troubled; rather, the leaders "should write to them to abstain from the pollutions of idols and from unchastity and . . . from blood." Those present agreed, and an appropriate letter was composed (15:1–29). Thus, Acts records the council in Jerusalem as approving exemption of converts from circumcision and observance of the Mosaic laws. The cumulative implication in Acts is that of an orderly, divinely sanctioned transition from the ceremonial requirements of Judaism to their nullification in Christianity. The letter from the council in Jerusalem was brought to Antioch and read there. Paul and Barnabas remained in Antioch for a time. Then Barnabas and a companion, John Mark, left for Cyprus while Paul chose Silas to go with him through Syria and Cilicia (15:30–41).

Henceforth it is Paul on whom Acts concentrates. At Derbe, Paul enlisted Timothy to accompany him. Paul circumcised Timothy, son of a Gentile father and a Jewish mother. (Here again is the motif of Jewish fidelity.) Wherever the two went they brought with them "for observance the decisions which had been reached by the apostles and elders who were at Jerusalem." The church was strengthened in the faith and increased in numbers daily (16:1–6).

Deterred by the Holy Spirit from speaking in Asia Minor, Paul, after a vision, crossed into Macedonia, thus indicating the spread of the church into Europe.[21] In 16:10–18 there occurs the first of four "we passages." These passages are written in the first person, as if they were excerpts from a travel diary and incorporated by Luke into his account. There is much scholarly debate over these passages. At stake is the reliability of the information in these passages, whether they are authentic ancient sources or free editorializing by Luke. At

21. But in 28:14 there are already brethren in Rome.

Philippi, Paul exorcised a demon from a slave girl, whose owners dragged Paul and Silas before magistrates, charging, "These men are Jews and they are disturbing our city. They advocate customs which it is not lawful for us Romans to accept or practice." (Apparently, to pagans, Christians appeared to be Jews.) The crowd attacked Paul and Silas; the magistrates had them beaten and jailed. They were released by an earthquake and their jailer became converted, as did his household. Moreover, Paul protested against the magistrate's treatment of him on the basis of its being a violation of his Roman citizenship (this is to prepare for the return of the same theme in 25:11). He received apologies (16:7–40).

At Thessalonica for three weeks Paul argued the Christian message in the synagogue, persuading some Jews, "a great many of the devout Greeks, and not a few of the leading women." The Jews, with some wicked rabble, gathered a crowd before the home of a Jew, Jason, where Paul and other Christians were staying. They brought Jason and some Christians before the city authorities, alleging that "they are all acting against the decrees of Caesar, saying that there is another king, Jesus." Jason and the rest were released on bond, and Paul and Silas were sent away to Beroea. There the Jews were "more noble," for they received the Christian message "with all eagerness, examining the scriptures daily to see if these things were so." Many believed, as did "not a few Greek women of high standing." The Jews of Thessalonica, learning about this, came to Beroea and stirred up the crowds. The Christians sent Paul off to Athens (17:1–15).[22]

At Corinth, Paul argued in the synagogue every Sabbath, persuading Jews and Greeks. When the Jews there opposed and reviled him, he shook out his garments and said, "Your blood be upon your heads! I am innocent. From now on I will go to the Gentiles." (There is no discoverable basis in Luke-Acts either for the curse on the Jews or for this statement of innocence.) Paul went to the house of a devout Gentile, Titius Justus, next door to the synagogue. Paul converted Crispus, the head of the synagogue, and his household (18:1–11).

After a year and a half the Jews brought Paul before Lucius Junius Gallio, the proconsul of Achaia, charging, "This man is persuading men to worship God contrary to the law." The outcome of the allegation was untoward. Not only did Gallio reply that he had no

22. The account of Paul in Athens (17:16–33) is not germane to our topic.

interest in internal Jewish affairs, but "they" (the text does not identify them) seized Sosthenes, the head of the synagogue, and beat him, with Gallio paying no attention (18:12–17).

Paul sailed for Syria. At Cenchreae he cut his hair, having "a vow" (18:18), an indication of Paul's fidelity to Jewish practice respecting vows. (There are no details given either here or in another mention of a vow in 21:23–24.) At Ephesus for a while, Paul argued with the Jews in the synagogue. He landed at Caesarea, went to Antioch, and then traveled about Galatia and Phrygia, "strengthening all the disciples" (18:18–23).

A brief section shifts attention to a convert, Apollos (18:24–28). In Ephesus, Apollos spoke boldly in the synagogue but was corrected by Priscilla and Aquila on the matter of baptism. Apollos went to Corinth where he powerfully confuted the Jews in public, showing by the Scriptures that the Christ is Jesus.

Paul went to Ephesus, where to the work done by Apollos he added the conferring of the Holy Spirit on twelve people. In the synagogue for three months he argued and pleaded "about the kingdom of God." When the Jews were stubborn and disbelieving, he withdrew from them, moving to "the hall of Tyrannus." He continued there for two years, "so that all residents of Asia heard the word of the Lord, both Jews and Greeks" (19:1–10). God worked "extraordinary miracles" through Paul. Then some Jewish exorcists undertook to exorcise demons by pronouncing the name of the Lord Jesus; the exorcists included seven sons of a man named Sceva, "a Jewish high priest."[23] For their presumption, an evil spirit leaped on the seven and overpowered them, and they fled naked. This became known to both Jews and Greeks; out of fear many people, confessing past magical practices, now became believers and burned their valuable magic books (19:11–20).

Now Paul resolved "in the Spirit" to pass "through Macedonia and Achaia and go to Jerusalem"; thereafter he must "also see Rome" (19:21–23). En route an incident occurred in Ephesus. The silversmiths of Ephesus who made pagan images were threatened with economic loss through Paul's conversions, and as another result there was danger that the temple of Artemis might "count for nothing." A

---

23. No such high priest is known. Some Christian commentators explain Luke's animosity and scorn as the origin of this curious exaggeration. There are others who ascribe the claim of priesthood parentage as "part of the self-advertisement of a gang of imposters" (*The Interpreter's Bible*, vol. 9 [New York and Nashville: Abingdon Press, 1954], p. 256).

hostile crowd dragged two companions of Paul into the theater. There a Jew named Alexander, whom the Jews had put forward, wished to make a defense. (It is not clear whom or what Alexander is defending; it is conjectured that he is defending Jews from attack by disassociating them from the antimagic acts of Paul.) The two clerks quieted the crowd, asserting that Paul's companions were "neither sacrilegious nor blasphemers of our goddess." The clerk suggested that the silversmiths seek whatever redress they were entitled to through the courts or the proconsul (19:23–41). (The point seems to be to give another instance of the protection of Christians by Roman officials.)

Paul then left for Macedonia and came to Greece. There the Jews plotted against him; Paul, with companions, returned through Macedonia and sailed from Philippi to Troas (20:1–6). (A second "we passage" is found in 20:5–16.)

At Troas, Paul raised from the dead a young man who, falling asleep during Paul's long speech, toppled down from the third story (21:7–12).[24] On arriving at Miletus, Paul summoned there the elders of the church at Ephesus. He alluded to his serving the Lord "with all humility and with tears and trials which befell me through the plots of the Jews." He was now going to Jerusalem, though "the Holy Spirit testifies to me . . . that imprisonment and afflictions await me." The Ephesians sorrowed "because of the word he had spoken, that they should see his face no more" (20:13–38).

Sailing on, Paul landed at Tyre. There the disciples, "through the Spirit," told Paul not to go on to Jerusalem (21:1–6). When Paul arrived at Caesarea, a prophet from Judea named Agabus symbolically bound his own feet and hands with Paul's girdle, saying, "So shall the Jews at Jerusalem bind the man who owns this girdle and deliver him into the hands of Gentiles." The people begged him not to go to Jerusalem. He replied, "I am ready not only to be imprisoned but even to die at Jerusalem for the name of the Lord Jesus" (21:7–14).

At Jerusalem, Paul related to James and the elders "one by one the things that God had done among the Gentiles through his ministry." They told Paul that there were thousands of Jewish Christians, zealous for the Law. These had been told that Paul taught all the

---

24. The account does not specify that the young man, Eutychus, died, but that seems explicit in that Paul raises him from the dead as Peter had raised Dorcas (9:36–42).

Jews who were among the Gentiles (in Dispersion lands) to forsake Moses and "not to circumcise their children to observe the customs." What Paul should now do was join four men who were under a vow and purify himself with them. By doing so "all will know that there is nothing in what they have been told about you but that you yourself live in observance of the law." Paul acquiesced and did this (21:15–26). (How remote this is from the content of Galatians and Romans, where Paul portrays the Law as obsolete and nullified. How compliantly Paul, who has there spoken against the Law, here observed it! One must note, too, how the Jewish fidelity of Jesus, and the difficulty he encountered from the blindness of the Jews in Luke's Gospel, is paralleled by the experience of Paul in Acts.)

Jews from Asia Minor saw Paul in the Temple and stirred up the crowd against him. He was saved from death at the hands of the vicious mob by Roman soldiers, and then arrested by the tribune. Paul was asked if he was not the Egyptian who had stirred up a recent revolt and led four thousand swordsmen out into the wilderness.[25] Paul replied that he was a Jew (and had the right to be in the Temple) and that he was a citizen of Tarsus. He then spoke in Hebrew.[26] He reviewed his career, saying that he was a Jew, born in Tarsus but brought up in Jerusalem. He had been as zealous for the Law as those standing before him. He had persecuted the church until his vision of the risen Christ on the road to Damascus.[27] In the Temple at Jerusalem the Christ had appeared to him, saying, "Depart; for I will send you far away to the Gentiles." The Jews cried out that Paul should not be allowed to live. The tribune then had Paul brought into the barracks. There Paul asserted that it was not lawful to scourge a Roman citizen without a trial.

The next day the Roman tribune commanded the chief priests and all the council to meet and he brought Paul before them (22:30). There Paul, struck on the mouth at the order of the high priest (see John 18:22 for the similar striking of Jesus), cursed him. Paul now perceived that the council was made up of Sadducees and Pharisees; he described himself as "a Pharisee, a son of Pharisees." He said

25. This Egyptian Jew is told of by Josephus in *Jewish War* 2. 13. 5. Josephus numbers the men thirty thousand, not four thousand; in Josephus the Egyptian led them from the wilderness, not into it.

26. The intent is probably Aramaic.

27. In Acts 9:10 Ananias is a Christian; here (22:14), he is instead "a devout man according to the law. . . ."

that he was on trial "with respect to the hope and the resurrection,"[28] thus shifting matters from the allegations about his speaking against circumcision and the law of Moses to the doctrine of resurrection over which the Pharisees and Sadducees differed. On his saying this, "a dissension arose between the Pharisees and the Sadducees." The author explains the difference over the doctrine; he ascribes to the Sadducees a disbelief in spirits and angels,[29] beliefs held by the Pharisees. A great clamor broke out. Some of the scribes of the Pharisees arose to assert that they could "find nothing wrong in this man. What if a spirit or angel spoke to him?" As the dissension became violent, the Roman tribune ordered his soldiers to take Paul by force from among the disputants and bring him back into the barracks. The next night the Lord appeared to Paul, saying, "As you have testified about me at Jerusalem, so must you bear witness also at Rome" (23:1–11). (Again Romans rescued an endangered Christian; the official Jewish body never condemns Paul, as earlier in Acts it had not condemned Peter and in the Gospel had not condemned Jesus. The illegal mob condemnation of Paul in Acts was like the sad experience of Jesus in the Gospel. Not a syllable about these experiences of Paul narrated in Acts is to be found in the Epistles of Paul.)

The next day the Jews made a plot, taking an oath not to eat or drink until they had killed Paul. The plotters asked the chief priests and elders to give notice to the tribune to have Paul brought before the council as if to be put on trial; they were ready to kill him before he came near the council. A nephew of Paul (both the nephew and his mother, Paul's sister, go unmentioned in the Epistles) informed Paul of the plot. Paul had a centurion bring the nephew to the Roman tribune Lysias; the nephew revealed the Jewish plot to the tribune. Lysias sent Paul to Caesarea, the seat of the Roman governor Felix.[30] He also sent a letter to Felix stating that Paul had been seized by the Jews but was rescued when the tribune learned he was a Roman citizen. The tribune had had Paul brought before the

28. The two words *hope* and *resurrection* are a single idea (see 24:15, 21).

29. Nowhere else is such disbelief ascribed to the Sadducees. That Scripture often mentions spirits and angels, and since the Sadducees are uniformly described as loyal literalists, this motif of disbelief is scarcely reliable.

30. The text seems to specify an escort of two hundred soldiers, seventy horsemen, and "two hundred spearmen"—a total of 470. The word *spearmen* is at times interpreted as meaning auxiliary horses.

council in order to know what the charges against him were; Lysias had learned that Paul was accused "about questions of their law, but charged with nothing deserving death or imprisonment." The governor Felix had Paul put under guard "in Herod's praetorium" to await a hearing when his accusers would arrive (23:1–35).

Five days later the high priest, some elders, and a spokesman, Tertullus, arrived in Caesarea. Through Tertullus the allegation was made that Paul was "a pestilent fellow, an agitator among all the Jews throughout the world, and a ringleader of the sect of the Nazarenes.[31] He even tried to profane the Temple, but we seized him." The Jews affirmed that the charge was proper. The governor Felix let Paul speak. Paul stressed that he had come to the Temple to worship, not disputing "with any one or stirring up a crowd, either in the temple or in the synagogues, or in the city." It was his way to worship God according to "the Way" which his opponents called a "sect." He believed everything "laid down by the law or written in the prophets" and also in the Resurrection. He had been seized in the Temple on the accusation of Jews from Asia Minor, who ought to have been present before Felix if they had any allegations to make. He had done nothing wrong except to say before the council that he was on trial about the Resurrection.

Felix, who had "a rather accurate knowledge of the Way," decided to delay decision until the tribune Lysias could appear before him. Paul was to be kept in further custody, but with some liberty and the right to be visited by his friends. (Again, the Romans are portrayed as always friendly to Christians.) Paul was summoned before Felix and his Jewish wife Drusilla to speak about faith in Christ Jesus. Paul's arguments for justice, self-control, and future judgment alarmed Felix (the arguments apparently stirred guilt feelings). Felix deferred decision, hoping for a bribe from Paul. He heard Paul from time to time for a period of two years. He was to be replaced as governor by Porcius Festus; to please the Jews, Felix kept Paul in prison (24:1–27).

After Festus arrived he went to Jerusalem where chief priests and the Jews informed him against Paul. They asked as a favor that Festus send Paul from Caesarea to Jerusalem, for they planned to kill him by ambush on the way. Festus replied instead that men of authority should come to Caesarea to make whatever accusations

---

31. In Luke-Acts the Christians are consistently not portrayed as a sect; only opponents use this term for the Christians. The use here is to suggest the palpable unfairness.

were appropriate. Before Festus at Caesarea the Jews brought serious charges, which they could not prove. Paul said, "Neither against the law of the Jews, nor against the temple, nor against Caesar have I offended." Festus asked Paul if he wished to stand trial (before the Sanhedrin) in Jerusalem. Paul asserted that he should be tried by Romans; since he had done nothing wrong to the Jews, he should not be given up to them. Rather, "I appeal to Caesar." Festus replied, "To Caesar you shall go" (25:1–12).

Agrippa II (who then ruled Judea in conjunction with the procurators) and his queen Bernice came to Caesarea to welcome Festus. The governor told them about Paul and "certain points of dispute [on the part of Jews] with him about their own superstition and about one Jesus, who was dead, but whom Paul asserted to be alive." Festus added that he intended to send Paul to Caesar. Agrippa wished to hear Paul (25:1–22). The next day Paul was brought before Festus, Agrippa, and Bernice so that Agrippa could examine Paul and inform Festus what definite charges Festus might communicate to Caesar (25:23–27). Paul spoke before Agrippa, reviewing his career (26:1–23). Festus charged him with being mad. In reply, Paul asked Agrippa if he believed in the prophets. Though Agrippa caustically rebuked Paul for seeking to convert him, he informed Festus that Paul "is doing nothing to deserve death or imprisonment." Paul might then have been set free had he not appealed to Caesar (26:24–32). The journey to Rome and its vicissitudes (27:1—28:15) are not germane to our topic.

When Paul came to Rome he was allowed to stay by himself with a soldier to guard him rather than be imprisoned. He sent for the "local leaders of the Jews," explaining that, though he had "done nothing against the people or the customs of our fathers" he had been delivered to the Romans as a prisoner. They replied that they had received no letters from Judea about him, nor had any Jewish visitors to Rome spoken evil of him. However, they wished to know his views, for his "sect"[32] (again the word appears) was everywhere spoken against.

By appointment the Jews in great numbers came to his lodging to hear his exposition; some were convinced, some did not believe. Paul cited Isaiah's condemnation of the blindness and opaqueness of the Jews in the prophet's own time, presenting this as foreordaining the Jewish opaqueness and blindness to the Christian message, which

32. See the previous note.

Paul was now encountering. The salvation of God was therefore sent to Gentiles who would listen.

Acts ends with the statement that Paul lived at his lodging for two whole years, welcoming all who came to him, preaching the kingdom of God and teaching about the Lord Jesus Christ quite openly and unhindered. The outcome of Paul's appeal to Caesar is not narrated.

We must now note patently anti-Jewish passages in certain speeches in Acts. The speech of Peter (2:14–36) includes the following:

> Men of Israel, hear these words: Jesus of Nazareth, a man attested to you by God . . . this Jesus, delivered up according to the definite plan and foreknowledge of God, you crucified and killed by the hands of lawless men. . . . Let all the house of Israel therefore know assuredly that God has made him both Lord and Christ, this Jesus whom you crucified.

In another speech (3:11–26) these words occur:

> The God of Abraham and of Isaac and of Jacob . . . glorified his servant Jesus, whom you delivered up and denied in the presence of Pilate, when he had decided to release him. But you denied the Holy and Righteous One, and asked for a murderer to be granted to you, and killed the Author of life, whom God raised from the dead. . . . I know that you acted in ignorance, as did also your rulers. . . . Repent therefore, and turn again, that your sins may be blotted out. . . .

The theme that Jews had crucified Jesus reappears in another speech ascribed to Peter respecting the healing of the lame man: ". . . by the name of Jesus Christ of Nazareth, whom you crucified . . ." (4:10).

In the speech of Stephen (7:2–53), which begins with a long review of Israelite history, the following occurs (7:51–53):

> You stiff-necked people, uncircumcised in heart and ears, you always resist the Holy Spirit. As your fathers did, so do you. Which of the prophets did not your fathers persecute? And they killed those who announced beforehand the coming of the Righteous One, whom you have now betrayed and murdered, you who received the law as delivered by angels[33] and did not keep it.

This theme of Jewish guilt for the death of Jesus is ascribed not to whatever Jews were present but to all the Jews in Jerusalem. Here

---

33. See Gal. 3:19 on this same theme, which is found in Christian writings but never in Jewish.

and there in Acts it is stated that some Jews became Christians (these are said to number thousands in 21:20); the usual motif, however, is the disbelief of all the Jews. The blindness about Jesus and the unreserved hostility to him of the mobs in the Gospel are in Acts paralleled by the same blindness and hostility to the apostles; the Jews killed Stephen and tried in various ways to kill Paul. Just as Jesus knew in advance what would happen to him at the hands of the Jews, so Paul knew what awaited him; these animosities occurred despite the fidelity to Judaism, first of Jesus and then of the apostles. True, the mission to the Gentiles included steps in which the obligations of the Law were progressively removed, but these steps were both orderly and the result of supernatural visions of the Lord, and did not entail any disloyalty to Judaism. Paul, in Acts, is in no way the preacher of justification by faith (this theme is totally absent from Acts, though it is found in Romans and Galatians), but Paul in Acts is also an undeviatingly faithful observer of Jewish obligations, raised in Jerusalem, and at one time a student of the eminent Gamaliel. The allegations of the Jews of Asia Minor that Paul was disloyal to the Law were totally false.

The Christians were no longer a sect within Jewry but had become the bearers of the true Judaism. It was the Jews, whether in Judea or in the Greek world, who had caused the troubles for the blameless and faithful Christians. The Jews had often beaten the Christians; they had also brought them before Roman authorities who, properly, refused to intervene. As in the Gospel, Herod Antipas had found no crime in Jesus, so Agrippa II in Acts had found none in Paul. Though individuals such as chief priests had denounced Christians, the council had convicted neither Jesus nor Paul of any trespass; indeed, Gamaliel had persuaded the council not to take any action against the apostles.

The question of whether Acts is historically reliable has been raised, especially at some of my lectures. A brief account of the Christian scholarship on Acts, such as that given in *The Interpreter's Bible* by G. H. C. Macgregor,[34] might be helpful to the reader. Macgregor summarizes the work of scholars from 1644 into the twentieth century. Some Christian scholars have expressed the judgment that "Acts as history is thoroughly untrustworthy. . . ." Macgregor himself, however, rejects such views as extreme. He writes:

---

34. *The Interpreter's Bible*, vol. 9 (New York and Nashville: Abingdon Press, 1954), pp. 10–15.

"Though our author's treatment of events may not always be well informed or intelligent, there has been no deliberate falsification of history. . . . Though Luke's accuracy may sometimes be challenged, there is at least no question concerning his good faith."[35]

Whether Acts is historically reliable or not will always remain a matter of subjective interpretation and is not an issue to be settled here. But can it be denied that Acts is written from a Christian viewpoint? Suppose we try to reconstruct matters from a Jewish viewpoint: Itinerants claiming to be Jews arrive in our city, are treated hospitably and welcomed in our synagogue, and are allowed to preach to us. In their preaching they say things that some of us find either incredible or distasteful or both. Why, if they know our beliefs, have they bothered to come to our synagogue? Why did they cause an uproar? Why did they not hire their own hall and leave us Jews alone? Why do they claim to be Jews when in their life-style and in what they advocate they express views about the Law, especially our food laws, that go against what we have always espoused? We would not have had uproars in our synagogue if these people had not intruded. It was only when they violated our hospitality that some of our people were moved to throw them out as unwelcome troublemakers. (In our own time certain Jews who have added a belief in Jesus to their Judaism interrupt worship in Jewish synagogues, as do comparable "charismatic" Gentiles in Christian churches.)

In Acts, "the Jews" are villains and their villainy could not be worse. But are the Jews of Acts real people or puppets of the author? Is Acts an account of what really happened or is it, with respect to Jews, a series of vilifications?

35. Ibid., p. 15.

8. The Gospel According to John

Certain aspects of the Gospel According to John, such as its treatment of John the Baptist[1] and of "Gnostics,"[2] do not directly concern our topic. For our purposes, what is most significant is that while in the Synoptic Gospels (Matthew, Mark, and Luke) the opponents of Jesus are usually Pharisees, scribes, priests, and elders, in this Gospel they are "the Jews." It has been contended with justice that the term "the Jews" does not have a single or restricted import. In some passages it seems to mean Judeans as contrasted with Samaritans and is thereby a regional rather than a religious designation; in other passages it seems to be a shorthand designation for the Jewish leaders rather than for all Jews. Yet, granted that the meaning varies in different passages, the fact that "Jews" is the designation for the opponents of Jesus implies, and indeed creates, such an over-againstness in the total effect that, on the one hand, Jesus in this Gospel often appears not to be a Jew and, on the other hand, John is widely regarded as either the most anti-Semitic or at least the most overtly anti-Semitic of the Gospels.

Not only is the Gospel According to John different in content and structure from the Synoptics, but the nature of the Jewish-Christian controversy there is quite distinctive. As Christian scholars have noted, one encounters in the Synoptics a Jesus for whom early events

1. As scholars have noted, this Gospel reduces the significance by denying that John the Baptist is Elijah. Certain passages, especially those that mean Thomas Didymus, are viewed as anti-Gnostic, but in a context in which the Gospel nevertheless reflects some affinities with gnosticism.

2. Briefly stated, Gnostics were highly individualistic persons who believed they had received illumination directly from God. Characteristic of Gnostics, especially in second-century Christianity, were views that denied the physical reality of Jesus, holding instead that he was an apparition. In addition, Gnostics were extreme "dualists," believing this world was so evil that God himself could not have created it; instead, God created a subordinate creator ("demiurge"), who did the actual creating.

led in time to a climax of death and resurrection. The Jesus of John, though there are a few narrative events, often seems to be conceived of as if he is already the resurrected Christ. The controversies in the Synoptics are primarily over things that Jesus is depicted as doing, such as his repeated healings on the Sabbath. In John the controversies are more usually over what Jesus *is,* not over what he has done or said. It is the conviction of John that Jesus is the divine Word, the Logos,[3] which became incarnate; it is the contention of the opponents in John that Jesus is not that eternal Logos. That is, the dimension of the controversy in John is substantially different and its depth is greatly increased. In the Synoptics it is the Jews of the time of Jesus who serve as the essential target for the animosity (though, as we saw, Matthew alludes to the Jews of "up to this day"). In John the targets are the Jews of that later period when his Gospel was written (between A.D. 100–110) and of the unknown area[4] in which John lived. Also, we shall see two phenomena unique to John, (1) the presence of Jews who had at one time been within the Christian movement but are no longer so and (2) the allegation that Jews who were prepared to come into the movement were deterred by such steps as expulsion from the synagogue. The subtle point is that in the Synoptics the disciples and apostles are all conceived of, whether for praise or dispraise, as Jews; in John it is as if the new movement has few if any Jews within it, and therefore the Jews are outsiders and opponents.

In the Synoptics the settings are Galilee and Judea, as these are known to scholars from some of the Apocrypha and Pseudepigrapha of Judean origin. In John the setting purports to be Galilee and Judea, but the atmosphere seems instead to be that of the Greek Dispersion as it is known from the Wisdom of Solomon and from Philo of Alexandria (25 B.C.–A.D. 42). The Grecian atmosphere in John lends itself to a device that is often repeated, the familiar philosophic contrast derived from Plato. An item arises, leading to a misunderstanding, and thereafter Jesus is portrayed as correcting the misunderstanding. The "issue" in these misunderstandings

3. *Logos* is a Greek word. Its content, however, is a blend of Greek and Jewish ideas that have flowed together. Briefly, the Logos (as in Philo) is that facet of the transcendent God which is in touch with this world. Put another way, God himself is beyond man's capacity to know; Logos is the reflection of God that gifted minds are able to conceive of. In John, the view is that the Logos had come to earth and taken on flesh and become Jesus.

4. Usually regarded as Ephesus, about the year A.D. 100.

is the difference between the "literal" and the "spiritual," between literal rebirth and spiritual rebirth, or literal bread or water and spiritual bread or spiritual water. Often the spiritual water or the spiritual bread is identified with the Christ. The distinction drawn between the literal and the spiritual has seemed to scholars to reflect the world of Greek thought and religion rather than the world of Galilee and Judea. For our study, it is important to note that in John the misunderstanding is usually on the part of "the Jews." This is a set of variations on the theme in the other Gospels: that "the Jews" rejected Jesus out of blindness or a failure to understand his divine nature. In John, this failure eventuates in controversies between the Jews and Jesus with accompanying denunciation of "the Jews"; John 8, as we shall see, is even more extreme in its outspoken anti-Semitism than some of the passages in Matthew. The Jews in John are depicted as lacking all religious insight, as proved by their rejection of Christian contentions about Jesus.

A prologue identifies Jesus as the result of incarnation: the divine Logos "became flesh" and dwelt among men (1:14). Jesus had come "to his own home, and his own people received him not" (1:11). Again, "the law was given through Moses; grace and truth came through Jesus Christ" (1:17).[5]

As the Gospel narrative begins, Jews sent priests out to John the Baptist to ask him who he was. John the Baptist told them that he was neither the Christ nor Elijah nor "the prophet" but rather "the voice of one crying in the wilderness." To the question, "Then why are you baptizing?" the reply was that he baptized with water, but "among you stands one whom you do not know. . . ." The next day, John, seeing Jesus come to him, said, "Behold the Lamb of God, who takes away the sin of the world!" He went on to say that Jesus would baptize not with water but with the Holy Spirit (1:19–34). Two disciples now left John the Baptist and became disciples of Jesus.

One of these disciples, Philip, told Nathanael, "an Israelite in whom there is no guile," that the disciples had "found him of whom Moses in the law and also the prophets wrote, Jesus of Nazareth, the son of Joseph." Jesus "recognized" Nathanael; thereupon Nathanael greeted him: "Rabbi, you are the Son of God! You are the King of Israel." Jesus promised that Nathanael would see even greater things. (These "greater things" are "signs" that now unfold.) The

5. There is no effort in this chapter to present the full content of John, particularly that of the Christology.

first sign was at Cana in Galilee, where Jesus turned water into wine; his disciples believed in him (2:1–11).

Jesus went to Jerusalem for the Passover. There he cleansed the Temple (2:13–16). One notes how early this item is in John; in the Synoptics it occurs near the end of each Gospel (Matt. 21:12–17; Mark 11:15–19; Luke 19:45–48). In Matthew and Mark the cleansing of the Temple spurs the "conspiracy" against Jesus; in John it is the "raising of Lazarus" that spurs the "conspiracy." When the Jews asked for a sign, Jesus answered, "Destroy this temple, and in three days I will raise it up." The Jews did not understand that "he spoke of the temple of his body." Many Jews "believed in his name when they saw the signs which he did, but Jesus did not trust himself to them . . ." (2:18–25).

A Pharisee named Nicodemus misunderstood "rebirth"; "Can [a man] enter a second time into his mother's womb and be born?" Jesus replied, "Unless one is born of water [baptism] and the [Holy] Spirit, he cannot enter the kingdom of God." Though Nicodemus was a "teacher of Israel," he did not understand this. Jesus said, "We speak of what we know, and bear witness to what we have seen; but you do not receive our testimony. . . . The Son of man [must] be lifted up [crucified], that whoever believes in him may have eternal life" (3:1–15). (The import of the passage is that Christianity is the only way to God and that Jews have not understood this.) In the sequel (3:18) there occur these words: "He who does not believe is condemned already. . . ."

A transitional passage tells that Jesus and his disciples, as well as John the Baptist, were baptizing people in Judea (3:22–24). Next, John the Baptist is portrayed a second time as subordinating himself to Jesus (3:25–30). In what follows (3:31–36) there is this passage: "He who believes in the Son has eternal life; he who does not obey the Son shall not see life, but the wrath of God rests upon him."

Jesus, on his way to Galilee, had to pass through Samaria. (The first readers of the Gospel knew of the deep animosity between the Samaritans[6] and the Jews, both of whom claimed the authenticity of

---

6. From the standpoint of Jews, the Samaritans were of Gentile extraction, descendants of Eastern peoples, moved into the northern part of Palestine in replacement of the ten northern tribes whom the Assyrians, after 722 B.C., had exiled to the east (see 2 Kings 17:24–41). The Samaritans, on the other hand, believed themselves to be the authentic people of God. Their sacred mountain was not Mount Zion but Mount Gerizim.

being God's special and chosen people.) Yet "salvation" (in its historical origin) is affirmed as "from the Jews" (4:22). Jesus asked a Samaritan woman for a drink. She asked, "How is it that you, a Jew, ask a drink of me, a woman of Samaria?" He replied, "If you knew . . . who it is that is saying to you, 'Give me a drink,' you would have asked him [for water], and he would have given you living water." She misunderstood about the water; he explained that "the water that I shall give . . . will become . . . a spring of water welling up to eternal life." He went on to tell her, "The hour is coming when neither on this mountain [Gerizim] nor [on Mount Zion] in Jerusalem will you worship the Father . . . I who speak to you am [the Christ, the Messiah]" (4:4–26). (Therefore both the Jewish and the Samaritan claims to being God's "chosen" are superseded.)

The disciples, joining him as the woman left, besought him to eat. He said, "I have food to eat of which you do not know. . . . My food is to do the will of him who sent me" (4:27–38). Now many Samaritans believed in him, recognizing him as "the Savior of the world" (4:39–42). Jesus returned to Galilee (4:43–45). At Cana an official begged Jesus to save his ill son. Jesus healed the son from a distance (4:46–53). This was the second sign (4:54).

There comes now a Sabbath controversy (5:1–47). In Jerusalem at the pool of Bethzatha (also known as Bethesda and Bethsaida) Jesus healed a man sick for thirty-eight years. (This was the third sign.) The man then rose and carried his bed pallet. The Jews reminded him that it was not lawful to carry a burden on the Sabbath. The man informed the Jews that it was Jesus who had healed him; the author adds, "And this was why the Jews persecuted Jesus." Jesus said to them, "My Father is working still, and I am working." The Jews "sought all the more to kill him, because he not only broke the Sabbath but . . . [made] himself equal with God." (The theme that the Jews wished to kill Jesus will be repeated again and again.) In reply, Jesus said:

> The Son can do nothing of his own accord, but only what he sees the Father doing. . . . As the Father raises the dead and gives them life, so also the Son gives life to whom he will. . . . He who does not honor the Son does not honor the Father who sent him. . . . The hour is coming, and now is, when the dead will hear the voice of the Son of God, and those who hear will live. . . . The hour is coming when all who are in the tombs will hear his voice and come forth, those who have done good, to the resurrection of life, and those who have done evil, to the resurrection of judgment. . . . You search the

scriptures, because you think that in them you have eternal life; and it is [the scriptures] that bear witness to me; yet you refuse to come to me that you may have life. . . . Do not think that I shall accuse you to the Father; it is Moses who accuses you. . . . If you believed Moses, you would believe me, for he wrote of me. But if you do not believe his writings, how will you believe my words?

John 6:1–14 is John's version of the feeding of the five thousand (Matt. 14:13–21; Mark 6:32–44; Luke 9:10–17). (This was the fourth sign.) The sequel to the feeding is that the people wished to make Jesus king by force, but Jesus withdrew to a mountain (6:1–15). The point of the episode is to deny that Jesus was in any way a political figure. John now (6:16–21) presents his account of the walking on the water (Matt. 14:22–27; Mark 6:45–51).

The people crossed over to Capernaum. There, after they had been fed the bread and the fishes, Jesus said, "Do not labor for the food which perishes, but for the food which endures to eternal life, which the Son of man will give to you. . . ." They asked, "What must we do, to be doing the works of God?" His reply was, "Believe in him whom he has sent." They asked him what sign he would do that they might believe him, such as the sign to their ancestors, the manna in the wilderness (Exod. 16:4, 15; Num. 11:8). The reply was that it was not Moses who had given them the manna, but God; "the bread of God is that which comes down from heaven, and gives life to the world." They asked, "Lord, give us this bread always." He said, "I am the bread of life; he who comes to me shall not hunger, and he who believes in me shall never thirst. . . ."

The Jews murmured at him for saying that he was "the bread which came down from heaven." Was he not known to them, as were his parents? His reply to them contained the assertion, "Your fathers ate the manna in the wilderness, and they died. . . . I am the living bread which came down from heaven; if any one eats of this bread, he will live for ever; and the bread which I shall give for the life of the world is my flesh." The Jews then disputed among themselves over how this man could give them his flesh to eat. Jesus said, "Unless you eat the flesh of the Son of man and drink his blood, you have no life in you; he who eats my flesh and drinks my blood has eternal life."

His disciples said that the words on eating the flesh and drinking the blood were a "hard saying" (that is, difficult to accept). Jesus said, "There are some of you that do not believe." The author then makes the comment that Jesus "knew from the first who those were that did not believe, and who it was that would betray him" (6:64). Thereafter many of his disciples "drew back and no longer went about with him." Jesus asked his twelve disciples if they too wished to go away from him. Peter replied that they had believed and had come to know that he was the Holy One of God. Jesus replied that he had chosen the Twelve, but that one of them was a devil. It was Judas Iscariot (here called "the son of Simon Iscariot") of whom he spoke (6:22–71).

Jesus now remained in Galilee, not going to Judea because "the Jews" sought to kill him. The Feast of Tabernacles was at hand (marked by the daily ceremony of carrying water in a golden pitcher from the Pool of Siloam to the Temple[7]). The brothers of Jesus urged him to go to Judea so that his disciples could see the works he was doing. Jesus replied, "My time has not yet come, but your time is always here. The world cannot hate you, but it hates me because I testify of it that its works are evil." He remained in Galilee, but then did go,[8] though "not publicly but in private. The Jews were looking for him at the feast. . . . For fear of the Jews no one spoke openly of him."

About the middle of the feast Jesus went up into the Temple and taught. The Jews marveled at his learning, since he had never studied. Jesus replied, "My teaching is not mine, but his who sent me. . . . Did not Moses give you the law? Yet none of you keeps the law. Why do you seek to kill me?" They answered, "You have a demon! Who is seeking to kill you?" (This question is not answered.) Jesus said, "I did one deed[9] and you all marvel at it." He proceeded to assert (scornfully) that Jews practiced circumcision even on the Sabbath: "Are you angry with me because on the sabbath I made a man's whole body well?"

Some of the people of Jerusalem wondered that the authorities did not kill Jesus, for he was speaking openly in the Temple. Did the authorities know that he was the Christ? The Christ was presumably unknown; yet Jesus was known and his home was known. To this wondering Jesus replied to the effect that they knew his literal

---

7. See "Water-Drawing, Feast of," *Jewish Encyclopedia,* vol. 12 (New York: KTAV, 1904), pp. 476–77.

8. The contradictions in the passage have long been noted. See *The Interpreter's Bible,* vol. 8 (New York and Nashville: Abingdon Press, 1952), pp. 579–81.

9. What deed is not explained. Unless something has dropped out of the text, the allusion seems to be to the Sabbath healing in 5:2–16.

home (Nazareth) but not his true home, namely, that with God. Though there was now an effort to arrest him, the arrest did not take place because his "hour had not yet come." Many of the people believed in him, but at the same time they wondered if the Christ, when he appeared, would do more signs than Jesus had done (7:1–31). (Even the Jews who believed did not fully understand Jesus.)

The chief priests and the Pharisees sent officers to arrest Jesus. He said, "I shall be with you a little longer, and then I go to him who sent me; you will seek me and you will not find me; where I am [that is, with God], you cannot come." The Jews, not understanding where they would seek and not find him, wondered if he intended "to go to the Dispersion among the [Gentile] Greeks and teach the Greeks" (7:35–36).

On the last day of the feast (at the time of the water-libation) Jesus arose and said, "If any one thirst, let him come to me and drink. . . ." There was a division among the people as to who Jesus was, whether "the prophet" or the Christ (the Messiah). None of the officers laid hands on Jesus; therefore the chief priests and the Pharisees rebuked them. The officers replied, "No man ever spoke like this man!" The Pharisees replied, "Are you led astray, you also? Have any of the authorities or of the Pharisees believed in him? But this crowd, who do not know the law, are accursed."

Now (7:50–52) Nicodemus protested that Jesus must not be condemned without a hearing (but the context is most obscure). Their reply was that no prophet was to arise from Galilee.[10] (This is surprising in view of 2 Kings 14:25; Jon. 1:1; and Isa. 9:1.) Jesus now said, "I am the light of the world. . . ." The Pharisees replied, "You are bearing witness to yourself; your testimony is not true." Jesus replied that though he was indeed testifying to himself (such testimony was regarded in Jewish courts as invalid) there were available the requisite witnesses who must number at least two, namely, Jesus and God who sent Jesus: "In your law [note *your* law] it is written that the testimony of two men is true [Deut. 19:15]; I bear witness to myself, and the Father who sent me bears witness to me." They replied, misunderstanding, "Where is your Father?" Jesus

---

10. There follows in 8:1–11 the account of the woman taken in adultery; it is usually omitted from modern translations and put into a footnote. The passage is missing from important manuscripts of John and found in some manuscripts in Luke. See *The Interpreter's Bible*, vol. 8, pp. 591–92. The ensuing material seems to hang in midair; scholars have made diverse proposals, none satisfactory.

answered, "If you knew me, you would know my Father also." No one arrested Jesus "because his hour had not yet come" (8:20).

Again Jesus spoke: "I go away, and you will seek me and die in your sin; where I am going you cannot come." The Jews, again misunderstanding, wondered this time if his words meant that he was going to kill himself. Jesus said, "You are from below, I am from above; you are of this world, I am not of this world. . . . You will die in your sins unless you believe that I am he." They asked, "Who are you?" He answered, "What I have told you from the beginning. . . . He who sent me is true, and I declare to the world what I have heard from him." The evangelist commented, "They did not understand that he spoke to them of the Father." Jesus continued, "When you have lifted up [crucified] the Son of man, then you will know that I am he." As a result of his words many believed in him (8:13–30).

Apparently there is something missing between the foregoing and what ensues, for a different audience is now addressed, not that of the many who believed but rather that of Jews who had once believed but now had ceased to. Jesus said, "If you continue in my word, you are truly my disciples, and you will know the truth, and the truth will make you free." They answered that they have never been in bondage and were already free. Moreover, they were descendants of Abraham. He replied, "Every one who commits sin is a slave of sin. . . . I know that you are descendants of Abraham; yet you seek to kill me. . . . You do what you have heard from your father." They answered, "Abraham is our father." He answered, "If you were Abraham's children, you would do what Abraham did. . . . You are of your father the devil, and your will is to do your father's desires. He was a murderer from the beginning. . . ."

The Jews said that they were right in deeming him either a Samaritan or demon-possessed. Jesus denied this and added, "If any one keeps my word, he will never see death." The Jews said that Abraham had died, as had the prophets. (How then could Jesus speak of never seeing death?) Jesus said, "Your father Abraham rejoiced that he was to see my day." (That is, Abraham was still alive, in heaven, as in Luke 16:22.) Misunderstanding, they said that Jesus was not yet fifty years old; how could he have seen Abraham (who lived hundreds of years earlier)? The reply was, "Truly, truly, I say to you, before Abraham was, I am." They thereupon "took up stones to throw at him; but Jesus hid himself, and went out of the temple" (8:31–59).

On a Sabbath, Jesus healed a man born blind (9:1–17). (This was the fifth sign.) The Pharisees disagreed over Jesus, some saying that he was not from God since he violated the Sabbath, others pointing to the signs Jesus had done. But "the Jews" would not believe that the man had actually been blind. They consulted the man's parents who, "because they feared the Jews," wished not to be involved; "the Jews had already agreed that if any one should confess [Jesus] to be Christ, he was to be put out of the synagogue." The healed man was now consulted; he affirmed that Jesus had healed him, adding, "Do you too want to become his disciples?" They reviled the man: "You are his disciple, but we are disciples of Moses. We know that God has spoken to Moses, but as for this man, we do not know where he comes from."[11] The man replied, "Never since the world began has it been heard that any one opened the eyes of a man born blind. If this man were not from God, he could do nothing." They answered that it was presumptuous of a man "born in utter sin" to wish to teach them, and they now cast him out. Jesus, hearing of this, found the man and asked, "Do you believe in the Son of man?" He answered, "Who is he, sir, that I may believe in him?" Jesus said, "You have seen him, and it is he who speaks to you." The man said, "I believe," and he worshiped Jesus. Jesus said, "For judgment I came into this world, that those who do not see may see, and that those who see may become blind." Some nearby Pharisees asked, "Are we also blind?" Jesus said, "If you were blind, you would have no guilt. But [because] you say, 'We see,' your guilt remains" (9:18–41).

Jesus then spoke about entrance into the "sheepfold" (a figure of speech for the true people of God). If one does not enter by the door but climbs in, he is a thief and robber, but if he enters by the door he is the shepherd of the sheep; the gatekeeper opens the gate for him, the sheep hear his voice, and he calls his own sheep by name. The sheep will not follow a stranger. Those who heard him did not understand the figure. Jesus said,

> I am the door of the sheep. All who came before me are thieves and robbers. . . . I am the door; if any one enters by me, he will be saved. . . . The thief comes only to steal and kill and destroy; I came that they may have life. . . . I am the good shepherd. The good shepherd lays down his life for the sheep. . . . I have other sheep [Gentiles], that are not of this fold; I must bring them also, and they will heed my voice. So there shall be one flock, one shepherd.

11. On the surface this seems to contradict 7:27.

Again "there was a division among the Jews because of these words." Some thought he had a demon, others said that a demon could not open the eyes of the blind (10:1–18). At Hanukkah, the Feast of Dedication, Jesus was at the Temple. The Jews said, "How long will you keep us in suspense? If you are the Christ, say so plainly." Jesus answered, "I told you, and you do not believe . . . ; you do not belong to my sheep. . . . My Father, who has given them to me, is greater than all. . . . I and the Father are one."

The Jews again sought to stone him. He asked them for which of his many good works they wished to stone him. They replied, "It is not for a good work that we stone you but for blasphemy; because you, being a man, make yourself God." The reply of Jesus cites a half verse from Psalm 82:6; if those who are mentioned in Psalm 82:6 can be called gods, why is it deemed blasphemy for Jesus, "whom the Father consecrated and sent into the world," to assert he is the Son of God? Again "they tried to arrest him, but he escaped from their hands" (10:19–39).

Jesus retired to Trans-Jordan, the place where John had first baptized. Many affirmed that everything John the Baptist had said about Jesus was true. Many there believed in him (10:40–42). While Jesus was there, a certain Lazarus fell ill in Bethany near Jerusalem, and his sisters Mary and Martha sent word to Jesus. Jesus knew that the illness was not ultimately to culminate in death and that he would be "glorified" through what would ensue respecting Lazarus. Jesus stayed two days longer; he then told his disciples that they were to go to Judea. The disciples said, "The Jews were but now seeking to stone you. Are you going there again?" Jesus spoke to calm their fears. But when he went on to say that he would waken Lazarus from the sleep that Lazarus had fallen into they did not understand. He explained to them that Lazarus was dead; the miracle Jesus would perform would confirm their faith. Arriving at Bethany, it was learned that Lazarus had been dead for four days. Jesus assured Martha that her brother would rise again, not at the final resurrection but soon. He said, "I am the resurrection and the life; he who believes in me, though he die, yet shall he live, and whoever lives and believes in me shall never die." Martha believed.

The other sister, Mary, came to Jesus and fell at his feet, saying that if Jesus had been present Lazarus would not have died. Jesus saw that she and the Jews who were with her to console her were weeping. Some Jews commented on Jesus' great love for Lazarus, but others wondered, "Could not he who opened the eyes of the blind man have kept Lazarus from dying?" At the grave of Lazarus,

Jesus prayed that on his miraculous deed soon to come the people standing by would believe. He now called Lazarus to come from the tomb and Lazarus came. (This was the sixth sign.)

Now many Jews believed in him. But the chief priests and the Pharisees, on learning of the matter, gathered the Sanhedrin, to discuss what to do. "If we let him go on thus, every one will believe in him, and the Romans will come and destroy both our holy place and our nation."[12] The high priest that year[13] Caiaphas, spoke (as if speaking prophetically a Christian message!): "It is expedient for you that one man should die for the people, and that the whole nation should not perish." The author comments that the high priest "did not say this of his own accord," but on this occasion was moved to prophesy that Jesus should die "for the nation, and not for the nation only, but to gather into one the children of God." The purpose here is to give an almost official, though isolated, Jewish affirmation of the role of Jesus; it is followed, in effective contrast, by the statement: "From that day on they [the Pharisees and the council] took counsel how to put him to death. Jesus therefore no longer went about openly among the Jews, but went from there to the country near the wilderness" (11:1–54).

During the period before the Passover many Jews looked for Jesus in the Temple, wondering if he would come. The chief priests had given an order that "if any one knew where [Jesus] was, he should let them know, so that they might arrest him." Six days before the Passover, Jesus came to Bethany. There, in the presence of Lazarus, Mary anointed the feet of Jesus, with Judas Iscariot protesting against the extravagance, though he was a thief and had stolen from the money box.[14] When the great crowd of the Jews learned that Jesus was there, they came to see him and Lazarus. The chief priests "planned to put Lazarus also to death, because on account of him many of the Jews were going away and believing in Jesus." (There is no sequel given to the wish to kill Lazarus.) A great crowd, learning that Jesus was coming to Jerusalem,[15] went out to meet him. The

12. That political overtones were, or appeared to be, attached to Jesus is found also in 6:15, 12:13, 18:33, and esp. 19:12.

13. There is no purpose here in entering into the problem of the phrase "that year"; one may consult a commentary on John 11:49.

14. We are not told which money box.

15. The account in John of the entry into Jerusalem and the ensuing events varies significantly in content and order from the accounts in the Synoptics; commentaries may be consulted. A principal difference is the lack in John of the institution of the Eucharist.

Pharisees said to one another, "You see that you can do nothing; look, the world has gone after him."

Next appears an item that seems to be incomplete (12:20–26). It tells that certain Greeks present for the feast wished to see Jesus. It is not totally clear whether these Greeks are Jews or Gentiles but it is likely that it is Gentiles who are meant.

Jesus was troubled[16] but he would not pray that God save him "from this hour." An angel now spoke, not for the benefit of Jesus but for the crowd. Jesus said, "I, when I am lifted up from the earth, will draw all men to myself." He said this "to show by what death he was to die." The crowd answered him that they "have heard from the law that the Christ remains forever. How can you say that the Son of man must be lifted up? Who is this Son of man?" In reply Jesus spoke of himself as "the light": "The light is with you for a little longer. Walk while you have the light, lest the darkness overtake you." Jesus then hid from them: "Though he had done so many signs before them, yet they did not believe in him" (12:20–41). Nevertheless, "many even of the authorities believed in him, but for fear of the Pharisees they did not confess it, lest they should be put out of the synagogue: for they loved the praise of men more than the praise of God" (12:42–43).

The Last Supper (13:1–30) in John adds an account of a foot-washing by Jesus not found in the Synoptics, accompanied by his words about humility. This leads to the prediction that one of the Twelve will betray him, "he to whom I shall give this morsel when I have dipped it." He gave the morsel to Judas, saying, "What you are going to do, do quickly." The disciples did not understand this. Judas left. After a discourse on the need of the disciples to love each other, Peter said he was ready to lay down his life for Jesus; Jesus replied that "the cock will not crow till you have denied me three times" (13:31–38).

There follow two "farewell discourses" (14:1–31; 15:1–27), the second of which concerns our topic. There these words occur: "He who hates me hates my Father also. If I had not done among them the works which no one else did, they would not have sin; but now they have seen and hated both me and my Father. It is to fulfil the word that is written in their law [note the word *their*] 'They hated me without a cause' [Ps. 35:19]." It continues: "I have said all this to

---

16. The agony in Gethsemane is not directly presented in John; neither is the Transfiguration. Both seem to be indirectly alluded to here.

you to keep you from falling away. They will put you out of the synagogues; indeed, the hour is coming when whoever kills you will think he is offering service to God. And they will do this because they have not known the Father, nor me" (16:1–4).

After the discourses (which end at 17:26) Jesus and his disciples crossed the Kidron valley, "where there was a garden, which [they] entered. Now Judas . . . also knew the place; for Jesus often met there with his disciples" (18:1–2). Judas procured a band of soldiers (these Roman soldiers are unique to John) and "some officers from the chief priests and the Pharisees"; these carried "lanterns and torches and weapons" (this too is unique to John). In John's narration the betraying kiss by Judas is absent; instead, Jesus asked, "Whom do you seek?" They answered, "Jesus of Nazareth." He said, "I am he." They drew back and fell to the ground (as if in worship of him). He asked again whom they sought and again they said Jesus of Nazareth. He replied that he had already told them that it was he; he added, "If you seek me, let these men [the disciples] go." Then Simon Peter, having a sword, struck the high priest's slave, whose name was Malchus, and cut off his ear (18:3–10). (In Mark it is not Simon Peter but a bystander who wields the sword; in Luke, Jesus immediately heals the ear; in the Synoptics the name Malchus does not appear.)

Jesus was now ready "to drink the cup which the Father has given me." The band of Roman soldiers and their captain (unique to John) and the officers of the Jews seized Jesus and led him to Annas, father-in-law of Caiaphas, high priest that year. (The commentaries discuss the problems posed by the mentions of Annas, not found in the Synoptics.) While Peter was in the courtyard,[17] Annas questioned Jesus "about his disciples and his teaching." Jesus replied, "I have spoken openly to the world; I have always taught in synagogues and in the temple, where all Jews come together. I have said nothing secretly. . . . Ask those who have heard me what I said to them." One of the officers struck Jesus, saying, "Is that how you answer the high priest?" Jesus said, "If I have spoken wrongly, bear witness to the wrong; but if I have spoken rightly, why do you strike me?" (This is unique to John.) Annas now sent Jesus bound to Caiaphas the high priest. (It is to be noted that no mention is made of the Sanhedrin.) Apparently, however, nothing took place before Caiaphas, so that one wonders why it is mentioned that Jesus was sent to him (18:12–24).

17. The account of Peter's denial is concluded in 18:25–27.

"They" led Jesus from the house of Caiaphas to the praetorium, the official residence of a Roman official. It was early in the morning. "They . . . did not enter the praetorium, so that they might not be defiled, but might eat the passover." (In John these events, including the crucifixion, are ascribed to the day before the Passover, not to the Passover, as in the Synoptics.) Pilate came out to them. (Except for the motif of Pilate's innocence, which is common to all the Gospels, the details given here respecting Pilate are unique to John.) Pilate asked, "What accusation do you bring against this man?" They replied, "If this man were not an evildoer, we would not have handed him over." Pilate said, "Take him yourselves and judge him by your own law." The Jews then said, "It is not lawful for us to put any man to death." The allusion here is not to Mosaic law. The point seems to be that though the Romans, not the Jews, carried out the subsequent execution, it was only because the Jews, then subject to Rome, were passingly prohibited by Roman rule from doing so themselves! Some scholars debate the historical correctness of the alleged prohibition. Whether they were empowered to execute or not, the responsibility of the Jews for the death of Jesus is clearly indicated by this part of the Gospel. The account proceeds with the comment, "This was to fulfill the word which Jesus had spoken [in 12:32–33] to show by what death [crucifixion] he was to die" (18:32).

Pilate called Jesus into the praetorium (18:33–38). He asked, "Are you the King of the Jews?" (John has not specified what charge "the Jews" have made against Jesus, whether blasphemy or insurrection.) Jesus answered, "Do you say this of your own accord, or did others say it to you about me?" Pilate replied, "Am I a Jew? Your own nation and the chief priests have handed you over to me; what have you done?" Jesus answered, "My kingship is not of this world; if my kingship were of this world, my servants would fight, that I might not be handed over to the Jews." (Why "to the Jews" instead of, as the narrative events lead one to expect, "to the Romans"? Is this not one more instance of directing the blame to the Jews?) Pilate said, "So you are a king?" Jesus said, "You say that I am a king. For this I was born, and for this I have come into the world, to bear witness to the truth." Pilate asked, "What is truth?"

Pilate went out to the Jews, telling them, "I find no crime in him. But you have a custom [in Mark 15:6 and Matt. 27:15 it is *Pilate* who has the custom] that I should release one man for you at the Passover; will you have me release for you the King of the Jews?" They cried out, "Not this man, but Barabbas" (18:38–40). (Barabbas has not yet been mentioned; Mark 15:7 and Matt. 27:17 mention him before Pilate's offer; Luke, like John, has the Jews ask for the release of Barabbas prior to any mention of him.) Barabbas is now identified as a robber (in Mark and Luke he is in prison for insurrection and murder; in Matthew he is a "notorious prisoner"). Then Pilate scourged Jesus. The Roman soldiers plaited a crown of thorns and put it on his head, arrayed him in a purple robe, and, hailing him as "King of the Jews," struck him. Pilate again went out to the Jews, saying, "See, I am bringing him out to you that you may know that I find no crime in him." The chief priests and the officers, seeing him, cried out, "Crucify him, crucify him!" Pilate said, "Take him yourselves and crucify him, for I find no crime in him" (19:1–4).

"The Jews" answer, "We have a law, and by that law he ought to die, because he has made himself the Son of God." (That is, it is a religious not a political trespass that is alleged.) Pilate, "the more afraid," entered the praetorium; he asked Jesus where he was from, but Jesus gave no answer. Pilate said, "You will not speak to me? Do you not know that I have power to release you, and power to crucify you?" Jesus said, "You would have no power over me unless it had been given you from above; therefore he who delivered me to you [that is, the Jews] has the greater sin." Pilate again sought to release Jesus. The Jews cried out, "If you release him you are not Caesar's friend; every one who makes himself a king sets himself against Caesar" (19:7–12).

It was now the sixth hour on the day before Passover. Pilate said, "Behold your King!" They cried out, "Away with him, away with him, crucify him!" Pilate asked, "Shall I crucify your King?" The chief priests answered, "We have no king but Caesar." Then "he handed him over to them [notice *over to them*] to be crucified." (Who are the "them," the Jews or the Roman soldiers? Scholars debate the issue. But does not the text[18] read as if it is the Jews who in John do the crucifying?) "They" took Jesus to Golgotha and there crucified him with two others (19:14–18).

Pilate wrote a "title" to put on the cross, "Jesus of Nazareth, the King of the Jews." Many of the Jews read this title, for it was written in Hebrew, Latin, and Greek. (This matter of three languages is unique to John.) The chief priests asked Pilate to change the title to "This man said, 'I am King of the Jews,'" but Pilate refused

18. It is also stated in some manuscripts of Matthew and Mark that Pilate turned Jesus "over to them"; scholars reject these readings.

(19:19–22). (This is also unique to John.) When the soldiers (do they not seem abruptly mentioned?) have crucified Jesus, they divided his clothes into four parts, one for each soldier. His tunic was without any seam; they cast lots for it instead of tearing it and dividing it (19:23–24). (This too is unique to John.)

John alone narrates that the mother of Jesus (mentioned in the Gospel only once before, 2:1–5) stood at the cross with other women. The "beloved disciple" was present; Jesus entrusted his mother to him. Then, "knowing that all was now finished, [Jesus] said (to fulfill the scripture), 'I thirst.'" (No direct citation of Scripture is given.) He drank a spongeful of sour wine. He said, "It is finished." He bowed his head and gave up his spirit (19:25–30).

"The Jews," in order to prevent the bodies of the three from remaining on the cross into the Sabbath,[19] asked Pilate that their legs be broken. The soldiers broke the legs of the two crucified with Jesus, but finding that Jesus was already dead they did not break his legs (19:31–33). (This is unique to John.)

Joseph of Arimathea—here alone described as a *disciple* of Jesus— asked Pilate for the body of Jesus, "but secretly, for fear of the Jews." He was helped by Nicodemus (see 3:1; 7:50). They laid Jesus in the tomb (19:38–42). (The remainder of the Gospel is not relevant to our topic.)

Earlier it was said that "the Jews" apparently means different things in different passages (p. 101). A related but somewhat different view has at times been advocated, namely, that "Jews" does not really mean Jews but is rather a term for all human opaqueness about Jesus or else for dissent from or opposition to Christianity or, in the interpretation in later centuries, the general evil in the world.

Is this a tenable view? Or is it only a way by which to exculpate the Gospel from its manifest anti-Semitism by those who strongly reject the anti-Semitism but cannot bring themselves to reject the Holy Scripture? Is the contention tenable that it is not Jews but humanity in general who are meant, even in the passages that deal with such specifics as the role of the Jews in the passion narrative or the allegation that they are descended not from Abraham but from the devil or that the Pharisees love money and the approval not of God but of man? Is it "the world" in John who demand the crucifixion of the innocent Jesus whom Pilate wishes to free, or is it the

19. See Deut. 21:23.

Jews who, as villains, are depicted as the ultimate in villainy? Partisanship inevitably enters into the answer, and objectivity is most elusive. It is, however, unmistakable that even if it could be the general human opaqueness or hostility that is meant, it is Jews specifically who were spoken of, scorned, and pilloried.

Again, on the assumption that it is the world and not the Jews who are meant, how shall one characterize the spirit of the Gospel? Are believers alone eligible for love, and nonbelievers eligible for denunciation and hate? Is the spirit of the Gospel in some way elevated if the target of attack is not the Jews but the world? Are only those who share Christian convictions worthy of God's favor and grace? No fair-minded person can deny that Jewish writings include such exclusivist claims concerning God's favor, and Christian scholarship has been zealous in noting these, seemingly unmindful of the motif in the Gospel of John. How many commentaries on John revel in aspersing Jewish exclusivism and denigrating Judaism, even beyond the Gospel itself![20]

That the opponents are "the Jews" is a reflection of the Gospel writer's environment. By his time (A.D. 100–110) the categories in Mark of Sadducees, Pharisees, Scribes, and Herodians are outmoded; these represented Judea in the age of Jesus. The Herodians were never a meaningful group; the scribes have given way to the rabbis; the Sadducees have virtually disappeared. Within the Christian tradition there were memories of these groups, particularly the dominant Pharisees. But the controversies in John over the messianic role of Jesus reflect not Jesus in his age but the ongoing bitterness between Jews and Christians that had accumulated in the intervening decades.

The empty tomb, so important to Mark, is of little consequence to John. His case for what Jesus is rests on four major matters: (1) the sudden single mention (21:24) that the author of the Gospel is an eye-witness;[21] (2) the "signs," that is, the seven miraculous deeds Jesus had performed; (3) the recurrent motif that the events in the career of Jesus were the fulfillment of Scripture; and (4) the identification of Jesus as the Logos incarnate. The wavering belief of some

20. See, e.g., the comment on 19:1–7 in *The Interpreter's Bible*, vol. 8, pp. 771–72.

21. Modern scholars are almost unanimous in rejecting the authenticity of the claim that the Gospel of John is written by an eye-witness. Scholars a generation ago, believing the Gospel to have been written around A.D. 100, thought that John may have been a young boy at the time of the crucifixion in the year 29 or 30.

Jews and the disbelief of others arose from the extreme claims made in the Gospel on behalf of Jesus, that he had in his lifetime performed supernatural wonders and therefore was himself supernatural. John is offering a record not of natural, credible events but of supernatural and, in that sense, incredible[22] deeds. Anyone who was skeptical about the deeds inevitably was skeptical about the supernatural nature of Jesus. The "incredible" nature of the claims was, of course, an issue between Christians and Jews, but it was also an inner Christian issue; hence the so-called anti-Gnostic motif in John, that is, opposition to contentions by some Christians who interpreted Jesus as a symbol rather than as a truly historical, truly human man.

The presence of Samaritans in John is independent of whether they were present in the second-century Greek world from which the Gospel arises. They believe in Jesus, who denies their claim as chosen of God, while the Jews, the authenticity of whose claim Jesus supports, do not believe. Again, by contrast with the Jews, Greeks (12:20–21) came to seek out Jesus, while Jews turned away. On the other hand, pagan incredulity, such as is reflected in the Epistles of Paul, does not appear directly in John. Perhaps such incredulity is meant in the frequent allusions to the disbelieving "world."

The frustration of the Christian expectations respecting the Jews permeates the Gospel of John with its bitterness. Jews of all people should have believed, for Jesus was a Jew (as were his disciples), and he preached in synagogues and in the Temple, and Scripture foretold him. But instead of believing, Jews contended against Christian assertions and harassed their fellow Jews who inclined toward the movement. Worst of all, some Jews had been in the movement and had left it. The Gospel According to John reflects the ultimate in the reflection of one side of a *reciprocal bitterness,* a two-sided animosity. One may accordingly explain the historical circumstances but one cannot deny the existence of a written compilation of clearly expressed anti-Jewish sentiments.

---

22. Incredible means "unbelievable"; it does not mean untrue. There are people who find the astronauts' trip to the moon incredible. That does not make the trip untrue.

9. Other New Testament Literature

THE EPISTLE TO THE HEBREWS

The growth and development of early Christianity appear to have influenced initially what we might call the ordinary person rather than the wealthy or the highly educated.' There are on record studies which purport to show that it was especially the poor and uneducated who were first attracted to the movement. The Epistle to the Hebrews, however, reflects education and culture. Hebrews is an exposition of the conviction that Christianity is the ideal religion, the realization of the Platonic "idea." Though not a profound philosophical treatise, it is philosophical in its manner. Whereas in the usual Platonism there is what one might call a vertical relationship between the idea above and its earthly imitation, Hebrews presents a "horizontal" relationship, this geared to the unfolding of history. In this unfolding, Judaism is viewed as "the imitation," the forerunner of the perfection that came in the form of Christianity, the ideal. My teacher, the late Clarence Tucker Craig, once characterized Hebrews as contending that Christianity is the perfect religion because it is even better than the second best, Judaism.

Judaism is not vilified in Hebrews, nor are Jews aspersed. Though here and there there are echoes of material found in the Gospels and of the views that the Law was revealed by angels[1] rather than by God himself, none of this material is directly focused on Jews. Hebrews seems concerned not with a relationship to the Judaism or the Jews of the age when it was written (as are the Gospels), but with the ancient Judaism of Scripture. Its basic viewpoint is that at the pinnacle of revelation which began in ancient Judaism is the figure of the Christ. This theme is expressed in the first sentence: "In many

1. See Gal. 3:19–20.

120

and various ways God spoke of old to our fathers by the prophets; but in these last days he has spoken to us by a Son."

Consistent with the theme of Christianity as the pinnacle and perfection of Judaism, Hebrews in a variety of ways sets forth the uniqueness of the Christ. Christ is superior to the angels through whom, by inference, the Law came (2:2). Jesus was faithful, as was Moses, but Jesus "has been counted worthy of as much more glory than Moses. . . . Moses was faithful . . . as a servant . . . but Christ was faithful . . . as a son" (3:2–6). Christ had been designated by God as high priest. He was like Melchizedek, king of Salem, priest of the most high God, to whom Abraham gave a tenth of everything (Gen. 14:17–20). Melchizedek[2] blessed Abraham: "it is beyond dispute that the inferior is blessed by the superior" (7:7). (That is, the priest-Melchizedek was superior to Abraham.) The Levites, men descended from Abraham, received tithes from the Israelites but were mortal and died; the Christ, also receiving tithes, is testified to be still alive. Indeed, "Levi himself . . . paid tithes through Abraham, for he was still in the loins of his ancestor when Melchizedek met him" (7:8–10).

Presently there are intertwined two motifs (8:1—9:10), one relating to the "first covenant" with the ancient Hebrews (that is, the ancient Judaism) and its "regulations for worship and an earthly sanctuary," the tabernacle in the wilderness (Exod. 26). This first covenant (Exod. 24:3–8) has now become obsolete and has given way to a "new covenant" (with Christianity), and the earthly tabernacle has given way to the Christ. In the Jewish system of atonement, priests had performed their ritual duties in the outer chamber of the tabernacle; into the inner chamber the high priest alone could go, and he only once a year (on the Day of Atonement). But the Christ, on appearing, entered once for all into the Holy Place, making atonement not through the blood of animals (as did the high priest) but through "his own blood." Indeed,

Christ has entered, not into a sanctuary made with hands . . . but into heaven itself. . . . Christ, having been offered [at his first coming] to

2. In "Myths, Genealogies and Jewish Myths and the Writing of Gospels," in my *Two Living Traditions: Essays on Religion and the Bible* (Detroit: Wayne State University Press, 1972), pp. 158–65, I suggested that Heb. 7:3, which declares that Melchizedek was "without father or mother or genealogy," was a dissent from the manner of Matthew and Luke, both of whom present genealogies (see also 7:6). Hebrews, so I wrote, is an effort to write an "unassailable Gospel."

bear the sins of many, will appear a second time, not to deal with sin but to save those who are eagerly waiting for him. For since the law has but a shadow of the good things to come instead of the true form of these realities, it can never, by the same sacrifices which are continually offered year after year, make perfect those who draw near.

Again, "every [Jewish] priest stands daily at his service, offering repeatedly the same sacrifices, which can never [permanently] take away sins. But when Christ had offered for all time a single sacrifice for sins, he sat down at the right hand of God" (9:11—10:12).

If a person has become a Christian and thereafter sins (10:26), "there no longer remains a sacrifice for sins" (that is, he cannot be forgiven).[3]   Converts to Christianity "endured a hard struggle with sufferings, sometimes being publicly exposed to abuse and affliction, and sometimes being partners with those so treated. . . . You [Christians] joyfully accepted the plundering of your property, since you knew that you yourselves had a better possession and an abiding one. Therefore do not throw away your confidence" (10:32–35).   This passage leads to a long section on faith, defined as "the assurance of things hoped for, the conviction of things not seen."   Such faith was exemplified by Abel, Enoch, Noah, Abraham, Sarah, Moses, and indeed others.   (That is, the Epistle to the Hebrews draws affirmative lessons from the ancient Judaism.)

In summary, it is the ancient Judaism with which Hebrews deals, regarding it as the worthy but imperfect preparation for the perfection which is Christianity.   The Christ has superseded the Law; Christianity has superseded Judaism.

THE REVELATION TO JOHN

In the Revelation to John is a passage in a letter to the "angel" of the church in Smyrna (2:8–11), which expresses sympathy for "your tribulation and your poverty . . . and the slander of those who say that they are Jews and are not, but are a *synagogue of Satan!*"   Again, in a letter to the angel of the church in Philadelphia (3:8–13) there is the following sentence (v. 9): "Behold, I will make those of the *synagogue of Satan* who say that they are Jews and are not, but lie— behold, I will make them come and bow down before your feet. . . ."   Precisely what is meant by those "who say that they are Jews and

---

3. A different view is found in 1 John 2:1–14. In later Christianity a distinction was drawn between "mortal sin," which is unforgivable, and "venial sin," which is forgivable.

are not" is not clear. Perhaps, since the term *Christian* may as yet not have come into universal use, these people are "Jewish Christians." It is more likely though that the intent is to say that *true* Jews would not oppose Christianity, and therefore those Jews who oppose it are not true Jews. The opposite of being true Jews is being descended from Satan, as in John 8:44; hence the expression "synagogue of Satan." Clearly controversy and conflict are here reflected, but on what issue is not clarified; they seem to be inner Christian.

One must notice that Revelation can be quite bitter: There are those in the church "who call themselves apostles and are not." There are the Nicolaitans (who cannot be identified) whom the church of Ephesus and the author join in hating. There are also targets of hatred such as a certain woman, Jezebel, who calls herself a prophetess and who, having refused to repent, will be thrown "on a sickbed, and those who commit adultery with her I will throw into great tribulation . . . and I will strike her children dead, unless they repent of her doings" (2:22–23).

THE EPISTLES OF JOHN, THE PASTORAL EPISTLES (1 AND 2 TIMOTHY, AND TITUS), AND JUDE

Inner Christian controversy and conflict are frequently reflected, especially in the three Epistles of John and in the Pastoral Epistles. Most frequently such controversy or conflict is over matters of proper belief rather than over conduct. The Letter of Jude denounces some people within the church: "Admission has been secretly gained by some who long ago were designated for . . . condemnation, ungodly persons who pervert the grace of our God into licentiousness and deny our only Master and Lord, Jesus Christ" (v. 4). The First Letter of John denounces some who had been in the church but had left it: "As you have heard that antichrist is coming, so now many antichrists have come. . . . They went out from us, but they were not of us, for if they had been of us they would have continued with us." The passage resumes: "Who is the liar but he who denies that Jesus is the Christ? . . . No one who denies the Son has the Father" (2:18–23). Again: "Many false prophets have gone out into the world. By this you know the Spirit of God: every spirit which confesses that Jesus Christ has come *in the flesh* is of God, and every spirit which does not [so] confess Jesus is not of God" (4:1–3).

Within the church, then, there were controversies about the Christ and Jesus. For example, which of two competing views was right, one view that the Christ became the man Jesus or another view that the man Jesus became the Christ? How human was Jesus—fully, or not at all in any way? Was he a descendant of David or, being eternal, was he on the scene in the time of David or even Abraham? If he was born of Mary, and Joseph was not his father, why a genealogy through Joseph (as in Matt. 1:16); why, indeed, any genealogy at all?

It is in the context of inner Christian disputes that there occur some passages with apparent connection to our topic. In 1 Timothy 1:3–4 the author (identified in 1:1 as Paul) reminds Timothy of the injunction to him that at Ephesus he was to "charge certain persons not to teach any different doctrine, nor to occupy themselves with *myths and endless genealogies. . . .*" In Titus 1:13–14, the injunction is for Titus to rebuke certain people sharply, "that they may be sound in the faith, instead of giving heed to *Jewish myths. . . .*" Again, in 3:9 the counsel is given to "avoid stupid controversies, genealogies, dissensions, and quarrels over the law, for they are unprofitable and stupid. . . ." These passages have been joined together by scholarly commentators who attempt to identify them with the myths and genealogies purportedly found in the Talmud. Often the authors of such explanations have never looked into the Talmud. The context should make clear beyond all doubt that under discussion here are inner Christian concerns. There is much in the "sea of the Talmud," but one will look there in vain for explanation of these passages.[4] More recent scholarship has wisely abstained from mentioning the Talmud, speaking instead of some possible Jewish-Gnostic speculation. My own view is that the word *Jewish* here is only an unimportant bit of name-calling; in Christianity in the second century, one way to denounce something was to label it Jewish.

---

4. See n. 2; the essay there mentioned is referred to in n. 17, p. 18, in Martin Dibelius and Hans Conzelmann, *The Pastoral Epistles,* Hermeneia Series (Philadelphia: Fortress Press, 1972). I must comment that the substance of the article is no way reflected, as if it were mentioned only on the basis of the title.

10. The Components of the Jewish-Christian Controversy in the New Testament

We introduce this chapter with a repetition: Christianity was in origin a Jewish movement that was born in Judea and after a short time spread beyond its borders. It became primarily a Gentile movement, drawing its converts from among non-Jews. In keeping with this transition, it needed to come to some understanding of its relationship to the Judaism into which it had been born and which was a significant surviving element in the movement. In its progression to a religion independent of its parent, there were four facets of development.

One facet was the retention of certain Jewish elements without alteration, particularly the use of Scripture (Old Testament) in support of claims and contentions. This has been the case even where the use of Scripture entailed interpretations unique to the new movement. Christians at that early time, and some still today, have cited Old Testament passages as prophesying and thus validating the meaning of Christian events, and have contended that since these "justifying passages" are in literature sacred to the Jews, Jews ought to be persuaded by them, even in such new application. But the objective reality is that such Old Testament passages, though cited in the New Testament without significant alteration, are not clearly and unmistakably related to Christianity in their common-sense meaning. A book of universal import by its very nature lends itself to interpretations, and the Christian interpretations of Old Testament passages are as uniquely Christian as the Jewish interpretations of the Old Testament are uniquely Jewish. Seldom do these sets of inherited interpretations found in Jewish and Christian postbiblical literature match up with each other, and what is found in the one tradition is missing from the other. Hence, though the Old Testament is held in common to be sacred, the respective understandings of the Old Testament are as different as if they derived from totally different writings. Only in

125

the rise of modern critical biblical scholarship, with its goal to recover the pristine meaning of the Old Testament free from both Jewish and Christian interpretation, have scholars, whether Christian or Jewish, read and understood Scripture in any common way.

A second facet was the retention of certain Jewish elements with some alterations. The use of bread and wine is found in pre-Christian Judaism; the significance of the ceremony of the bread and wine became in Christianity far different from that in antecedent (and ongoing) Judaism. Third, some Jewish elements were completely abandoned, such as circumcision and food laws. Fourth, Christianity made innovations unique to itself, creating institutions, rituals, practices, and a new officialdom.

Basic to Judaism was the conviction of its divine origin. God had chosen the Jews as his people and had revealed to them the laws and doctrines that made them and them alone of all peoples his own special treasure. Since he was the only God, he was the deity, even if unacknowledged, of all peoples. His demands on other peoples were less than his demands on Israel, but there were still demands on them, for example, the laws of Noah (Gen. 9:1–17).[1] Mankind consisted of two divisions of humanity, the Jews and the Gentiles. (So, too, the Greeks divided humanity into the Greeks and the Barbarians!)

The conviction of a divine origin was also basic to Christianity. God had chosen the Christians as his people in a revelation more recent and more climactic than the ancient revelation to the Jews. In choosing the Christians as his people, he had turned away from the Jews because of their blindness and waywardness. The Gentiles to whom he had turned became his chosen people. We should note clearly that with respect to divine origin the claims of the Jews and the Christians directly contradict each other, and each of the claims is exclusivist. Judaism and Christianity each maintained that it and it alone was God's chosen.

The Jews could, at least in theory, have disdained or ignored the Christians as merely some minor sect of little significance, one of a variety of dissident movements. The Christians could not ignore the Jews or the Jewish claims, for as the younger and newer movement Christianity could assert its validity only by denying the validity of its parent. Jews responded with a reciprocal denial of Christian assertions.

---

1. Rabbinic literature counted the laws against bloodshed, murder, and the like as seven. The laws of Noah were deemed to be God's obligation required of all men, the laws of Moses his obligation required only of Israel.

The exclusivist claims of the two groups are the nub of the controversies of the New Testament age. If one of the two was the only true religion, then the other was necessarily false. It is against the background of this impasse, aggravated by the undeniable fact that Christianity was Jewish in origin, that the specific components of the intense, often scurrilous animosity, here to be discussed, must be understood. The controversy was not genteel, and the partisans were not generous or sympathetic. This was the case whether the difference embroiled Jew against Jew, or Christian against Christian. How much the more when Jew and Christian were pitted against each other.

THE RESURRECTION OF JESUS

In the age of Jesus there was no single attitude among Jews toward the afterlife. The ancient rabbinic literature, Josephus, and the Gospels all reflect the inner Jewish division; the Pharisees affirmed the doctrine and the Sadducees denied it. The opposition between the Pharisees and the Sadducees rested squarely on two questions: Was resurrection a tenable doctrine, and was it to be found in the Pentateuch? The authority of the Pentateuch was critical.

Resurrection is explicit only in Daniel 12:2; it may be present, but less explicitly so, in Isaiah 26:19; there the words "thy dead shall live" may, like Ezekiel 37, be in reference to national revival rather than personal resurrection. But in the Pentateuch, resurrection is nowhere explicit. The Pharisees accepted and espoused the doctrine, and the rabbinic literature both espoused it and "substantiated" it as if in the Pentateuch by an interpretation[2] of Exodus 15:1. The Gospel account of the debate between Jesus and the Sadducees (Matt. 22:23–33; Mark 12:18–27; Luke 20:27–38) might readily enough have been recorded in rabbinic literature, for it would have fitted congruently; in the Gospel account, as in the rabbinic literature, resurrection is substantiated by citing the Pentateuch, using Exodus 3:6.

Inasmuch as the Sadducees denied resurrection, they would logically have rejected the resurrection of Jesus. For Pharisees and

2. Unfortunately, a knowledge of Hebrew and of subtleties of Hebrew grammar are necessary to understand how the proof was arrived at. The text reads, "Then Moses and the children of Israel sang. . . ." But the Hebrew word for *then, az,* takes a future verb to express the past. The rabbinic interpretation, ignoring the grammatical peculiarity, reads the passage as meaning, "Then Moses and the children of Israel *will sing*. . . ." When will they sing? In the resurrection age.

others in the Jewish community, it was the particular resurrection of Jesus that was denied, not resurrection itself. This Jewish denial among those disposed to believe in resurrection appears to have taken two different forms. One was the assertion that Jesus had not truly died; confronting this assertion is Mark 15:44, wherein Mark tells that Pontius Pilate summoned the Roman centurion and learned from him that Jesus was indeed dead.

The other Jewish denial was over the matter of the significance of the empty tomb. Christians argued for the resurrection on the basis that the tomb of Jesus was empty the Sunday morning after his Friday burial. The Jewish contention was that the emptiness of the tomb was of no significance. The chief priests and Pharisees are portrayed in Matthew 27:62–66 as warning that the disciples would steal the body from the tomb (and hence it would be empty); thereupon Pilate enjoined them to take a guard of soldiers and make the tomb as secure as possible. Matthew is thus refuting a Jewish contention that the body of Jesus was stolen from the tomb. According to Matthew 28:11–15 the chief priests and elders bribed the soldiers to tell people that while they were asleep the disciples came by night and stole the body. The soldiers took the money and did what they were asked to do. The last sentence of the episode reads: "This story has been spread among the Jews to this day." Curiously, Luke 24:11 records that the apostles too regarded the emptiness of the tomb as an idle tale that they did not believe. Quite likely Luke found the emptiness of the tomb unpersuasive *in itself*; while Luke 24:22–23 again mentions the empty tomb, it is rather the "actual" appearance of the risen Christ that in Luke is persuasive.

The motif of the empty tomb goes unmentioned in Paul's Epistles. His argument in substantiation of the resurrection of Jesus rests, instead, on the appearance to him of the resurrected Christ (1 Cor. 9:1). The Christ, he asserts, had appeared to Cephas, then to the Twelve, then to more than five hundred of the brethren, most of whom were still alive; then to James, then to all the apostles, and last of all to Paul (1 Cor. 15:5–8). He says too that the death and resurrection were "in accordance with the scriptures," but Paul does not quote whatever passage or passages he had in mind.

Paul encountered in Corinth those in the Christian community who "say that there is no resurrection of the dead" (1 Cor. 15:12). Did such people deny that Jesus had been resurrected or did they deny a future general resurrection? It is hard to understand why people, having come into a movement based on a singular resurrection, could have denied the doctrine. For Paul everything falls to the ground if resurrection in general is denied; if there is no resurrection, then even Christ could not have been resurrected (1 Cor. 15:13–18). Paul attempts to answer questions that some in the community have raised: "How are the dead raised? With what kind of body do they come?" His answer to the first question rests on a somewhat fallible botany; a seed that is planted dies in order for it to sprout. Thus, resurrection is achieved by dying. To the second, his answer seems to deny physical resurrection; the resurrected body is a spiritual one.

Why these issues from within the Christian community? The explanation that persuades me goes along the following line: In Greek dualism, even short of the extreme dualism found in Gnostics in second-century Christianity, life in this world was viewed as something evil, something undesirable; man should seek to escape from this world. In Greek thought, immortality was congenial, for immortality did not imply a second physical life. Rather, immortality supposes that the physical body dies, but the immaterial part of man (his soul or spirit) does not die, or at least an aspect of the soul, the *nous* ("mind"), survives the death of the body. But resurrection implies a restoration to life in this world and in effect puts a man right back where he has not wanted to be. Paul does not directly espouse immortality. His term "spiritual body" is an oxymoron, for "body" cannot be "spiritual" nor can "spirit" be "bodily." Thus, the term "spiritual body" retains the term "resurrection" but denies physical resurrection. In Luke it is related that the apostles supposed that the risen Jesus whom they were seeing was a spirit. He depicts Jesus as saying to them, "See my hands and my feet, that it is I myself; handle me, and see; for a spirit has not flesh and bones as you see that I have" (Luke 24:39). Luke here seems to deny the validity of tinkering with the doctrine of resurrection. Therefore we can see that the issue of resurrection was not only between Jews and Christians, but was also an inner Christian matter.

In the unfolding of both the Jewish and the Christian traditions of later centuries, resurrection abided as a basic belief, but it became frequent or even usual for the quasi-philosophical explanation of the term to equate it with immortality. In effect, when resurrection is interpreted as immortality physical resurrection is being denied. Perhaps most people of our time who assert that they believe in resurrection really believe in immortality.

THE MESSIAH

There had arisen in Judaism a series of related but at times slightly varying views about the Messiah—who he would be, when he would come, and what he would accomplish. What we might call the normal Jewish view was that the Messiah would be descended from King David (that is, he could not be a Maccabean or a hated Herodian); his advent would be preceded both by the advent of a forerunner, Elijah the prophet returned to earth, and by political and cosmic upheavals. The Messiah would become the proper, independent Jewish king, who would break the power of the usurping Seleucidian Greeks or, later, the cruel Romans. His coming would inaugurate a new age on earth, one of tranquillity and prosperity, in marked contrast to the evils and miseries of the present age. At his advent, the scattered of Israel—who in the age of Jesus were in much greater abundance outside Judea than inside—would be miraculously ingathered to the freed and prosperous Holy Land according to passages in the ancient prophet. There would take place the great day on which judgment would be meted even to those of the past who had been wicked but unpunished or had been righteous but unrewarded. In one view, all men would be resurrected and made to stand judgment; in another, all men would be judged and the innocent and righteous among them would be resurrected.

A significant Christian alteration of the belief in the Messiah was a view of a two-step event, this replacing a Jewish expectation of a single climactic one. Christians spoke of the initial coming of Jesus, of his career on earth in the recent past, which culminated in his death and resurrection. Jesus had returned to heaven to await the time of his return, his second coming. The first coming had been, as it were, preparatory; the second coming would usher in the culmination of the intention of history.

In Paul the second coming was viewed as destined for the very near future. The two Epistles to the Thessalonians deal with problems that arose because of a delay in the second coming. The Thessalonians appear to have pressed Paul for some definite time schedule, which Paul was unwilling to give. Paul speaks of the second coming as impeded by a certain "restrainer," whether a person or not is unclear; he refuses to give a definite time schedule, asserting instead that the second coming would be as unexpected as a home burglary. That is to say, as early as Paul's time there was already felt the need to recognize that a disappointing delay in the second coming had arisen. In many senses the Christian view of the future second coming and the Jewish view of the future first coming are similar. Both "comings" are impeded by some retardation; despite the delay, the coming will assuredly take place some day.

Some passages, particularly in Matthew, reflect an effort to come to terms theologically with the unexpected delay. Such passages play down the second coming by aggrandizing the first and seem to assume that the shift in ages, from this evil age to the "new age," has already taken place. The shift took place at the first coming, which ushered in "the Christian era." In New Testament scholarship such aggrandizement of the first coming is known as "realized eschatology." The term means that what had once been assigned to the future had in actuality already taken place in the past. In a general way, the Gospels as totalities seem to embrace the view, reformulated from Paul's, that the first coming was the decisive event. The Messiah has already come, and man is already living in the messianic age. Yet, except for John, the Gospels do not appear to abandon entirely the expectation of the second coming.

The Jewish denial of the messiahship of Jesus was simply a denial that the messianic age here on earth had come. The career of Jesus had not brought about what Jews expected of the Messiah. The evil power of Rome had not been broken, no Jewish king had risen to an independent throne, the scattered of Israel had not been miraculously restored to the Holy Land, and the expectation of tranquillity and prosperity had not come about.

There are found in the New Testament only dim echoes of those Jewish expectations. Though Christians retained the word *Messiah* (Greek, "Christ"), the content and meaning of the term were significantly altered. The echoes of the Jewish expectations rotate about the word *king*. In John's version the titulus on the cross reads, "Jesus of Nazareth, *king* of the Jews." In Acts 1:6 the risen Christ is asked, "Will you at this time restore the kingdom to Israel?" In Matthew 2:2 the wise men from the east ask, "Where is he who has been born *king* of the Jews?" The chief priests and scribes, in telling Herod about the place where the Christ is to be born, answer, "Bethlehem," and they quote Micah 5:2, that from Bethlehem "shall come *a ruler* who will govern my people Israel" (Matt. 2:3–6). On the other hand, John 18:33–37 takes pains to divert one from associating Jesus as king in the sense in which Jews expected a ruler: "My kingship is not of this world."

The passion narratives in all the Gospels play down the suggestion that the role of Jesus was in some way connected with a royalty that would supplant Roman rule (esp. in Matt. 26:51–53 and Luke 22:49–51), for Jesus rejects the reliance on the sword or swords that his disciples seem intent on using. The question ascribed to Pilate

(Matt. 27:11; Mark 15:2; Luke 23:3), "Are you the King of the Jews?" never elicits an affirmative answer. But the premise in the question is the equation of Messiah and king.

Since there are such dim echoes of the Jewish association of Messiah with king, scholars have inferred recurrently that Jesus in his lifetime was regarded by his Jewish contemporaries as embarked on a religious-political effort to become the independent Messiah-king. Some such scholars contend that the view of Jesus as a man of peace, remote from political events, was deliberately and artificially developed. Respecting the latter, Professor S. G. F. Brandon, in his book *Jesus and the Zealots,* contends that the "Pacific Christ" was a deliberate falsification of the realities about Jesus. Jesus, according to Brandon, was a political rebel.[3]

How seriously is a view such as Brandon's to be taken? Such theories go beyond what is demonstrable. They rest rather on a certain logic: the Messiah was to be the Jewish king who supplanted Roman authority; Jesus was hailed as the Messiah; therefore, Jesus must have aspired, or even expended efforts, to become this Jewish king. The absence of crystal-clear evidence, coupled with the Gospel passages in which Jesus is portrayed as rejecting political intentions, deters most Christians from accepting the view of a Brandon or that of his eighteenth-century predecessor, Samuel Hermann Reimarus. Moreover in Hebrews, Jesus is likened to Melchizedek of Genesis 14:17–20; Melchizedek was from Salem, a word kindred to the Hebrew *shalom* ("peace") so that in Hebrews 7:2 the Christ is termed the "king of peace." In developed Christian lore, "Prince of Peace" is a frequent epithet for Jesus. Consequently Christians ordinarily find distasteful any theory that links Jesus with political-military endeavors, even though they might concede that Pilate did view Jesus in this light. But Pilate was mistaken, or misled by the Jews. The ancient or modern Jewish denial that Jesus was the Messiah rests simply on the observation that the career of Jesus did not bring about what Jews expected the Messiah to accomplish.

On the other hand, what Christians (Paul for example) saw in the Christ is far removed from what the Messiah meant to Jews in general. In Paul there is no clear echo of the Messiah as king or of the Messiah as a national hero-redeemer of the Jews. Instead, a decisive shift in understanding of the Messiah-Christ arose. In Paul, Christ is perceived of as the means by which man is redeemed from

3. S. G. F. Brandon, *Jesus and the Zealots* (New York: Scribner's 1967).

sin. *Messiah* literally means "a person anointed with oil." Such anointment was the ceremony that raised a commoner to royalty; the prophet Samuel had anointed Saul and then David (1 Sam. 10:1; 16:13). Among Greeks, anointment was in no way a ceremony of this kind; anointment was merely a form of cosmetics. Paul uses the term *Christ* almost as if it is a unique name, but never in relation to the rise of a commoner to royalty. Paul associates the Christ Jesus not with Judean independence or the ingathering of the exiles but with sin and atonement. Indeed, Paul views the Christ in ways so changed from the usual Jewish view that in most basic matters there is almost nothing in common but the word. Paul's view of the Christ is so thoroughly different from the one held by the Jews that ordinarily Jews are quite unable to understand it, and ordinarily Christians, not informed on what Jews believed about the Messiah, are equally unable to understand the Jewish denial of the messiahship of Jesus.

The Role of Jesus

Christianity developed an array of terms for Jesus. Some of these terms Jews readily grasp, such as *Son of David*. Others are more difficult for them, for example, *Son of man*.[4] Even more unintelligible to Jews is the term *Lord*. For them *Lord* and *God* are exact synonyms. In the Greek translation of the Hebrew Bible *kyrios* ("lord") renders the Hebrew *YHWH*, as *theos* ("God") renders *elohim*. In Greek the word *kyrios* had a number of diverse meanings: the owner (of a house), a respected person,[5] or a ruler. It was also the term for the Greek deity to whom a cult was dedicated. "Lord" is a frequent New Testament epithet for Jesus. Especially in Luke, Jews become confused by the title *Lord,* wondering if Christians view Jesus as God,[6] as Jews do not. Divine power unmistakably seems to be ascribed to Jesus when the Gospels say that Jesus taught "with authority." This was not a momentary gift but an indication of his supernatural character; that Jesus was born of a

4. There is an immense body of scholarly writing on this phrase from Daniel, frequent in the Gospels. My own "Son of Man in Mark" is reprinted in my *Two Living Traditions: Essays on Religion and the Bible* (Detroit: Wayne State University Press, 1972), pp. 166–77.

5. *Kyrios* appears to be a translation also of the Aramaic *mar*, as in *maran atha* (1 Cor. 16:22, "May our Lord come!"), or, as some prefer, *marana tha* ("O our Lord, come!").

6. In the period after the New Testament there were Christians who did so view Jesus.

virgin—unmentioned in Mark and Paul—reinforces the view of him as a supernatural being.

Though Jews may not have understood precisely what godlike character such extraordinary endowments were meant to imply, they have been unwilling to ascribe any special supernatural character to Jesus beyond what other men possess. Such reservations about the figure of Jesus have not been limited to Jews. A book of essays by seven eminent British Christian theologians entitled *The Myth of God Incarnate* contends that Jesus never "claimed to be the son of God, but was promoted to that status by pagan and other influences on early Christians."[7] In Germany there appeared a work by a born Catholic, Rudolf Augstein, published in an English translation under the title *Jesus, Son of Man,*[8] which repudiates and bitterly attacks the historic Christian assertions of the supernatural nature of Jesus. Thus, on the part of Christians from within the church and ex-Christians from without, there exist questions akin to those of Jews, for the holding of which Jews have been condemned.

In the past century Jews in an abundance of writings have lauded Jesus as a teacher, a "rabbi," a social reformer, or a prophet. This praise, however, has been reserved for the human Jesus, not for the supernatural one. In contrast to the ancient Jewish disparagement of Jesus reflected in the Gospels, such as the allegation that his exorcisms were accomplished through the power of Satan, the literature by Jews on Jesus in the last two centuries is almost entirely adulatory and is often addressed, openly or indirectly, toward "reclaiming" Jesus for Judaism. A characteristic example from the 1920s is found in the last paragraphs of *Jesus of Nazareth* by Joseph Klausner, written originally in modern Hebrew and translated into many languages: "If the time should ever come that the legends and theology would be removed from the figure of Jesus, he would emerge as the true son of the synagogue that he was, a master teacher of ethics and a master teacher of parables."[9] It is clear that the Jesus of Klausner is far removed from the Christian incarnate Son of God whose death brought redemption to mankind.

Jews both in the age of Jesus and today have not accepted or agreed with the substance of the Christian contentions about him;

7. John Hick, ed., *The Myth of God Incarnate* (Philadelphia: Westminster Press, 1977); the quotation is from the *Cincinnati Post,* July 9, 1977, p. 13.

8. Rudolf Augstein, *Jesus, Son of Man,* trans. Hugh Young (New York: Urizen Books, 1977).

9. Joseph Klausner, *Jesus of Nazareth* (New York: Macmillan, 1929), p. 414.

hence the Christian insistence that the Jews of the age of Jesus were blind. Yet in our day many Christians view Jesus in a way little different from that of such Jews as Klausner. That hundreds of millions of Confucians, Buddhists, and Muhammadans have also not accepted the Christian contentions about the unique divinity of Jesus is a matter of public record. In the New Testament literature it is essentially Jews alone who are singled out for disparagement and abuse.

DEICIDE

A theme recurrent in the New Testament is that Jesus voluntarily died a sacrificial death in order to bring atonement to mankind. His death, accordingly, is regarded as part of a divine plan to bring unique benefit to mankind. It is also the view in the Gospels, especially Mark and John, that the death of Jesus was not a surprise, for Jesus knew in advance that it would happen and on a number of occasions so informed his disciples. His death was not a defeat but a working out of preordained Divine Providence. Nevertheless, the term *deicide* arose after the New Testament age in order to put the blame on the Jews for their role in the death of Jesus as presented in the Gospels. The word means "the death of a god," or "the death of a divine being."

In the Gospels, as far as the narration of events is concerned, it is never stated that Jews literally executed Jesus; rather, it is said unmistakably that Roman soldiers did the executing. Those Jewish scholars who have argued that crucifixion was a Roman form of punishment and that, hence, Jews were not guilty of "deicide," have failed to grasp the Gospel emphasis that it was the Jews who plotted against Jesus and insisted that the Roman authorities execute him. The responsibility for the death of Jesus therefore lies with the Jews, and the Romans, who carried out the deed, are in effect innocent. The passion narratives in Mark, Matthew, and John present the Jewish establishment—the Sanhedrin, leading priests, and high priests—as concluding that Jesus merited execution; Luke differs in that he does not portray the Sanhedrin as condemning Jesus. Before Pilate, the Jewish crowds impelled an unwilling Pilate to sentence Jesus to death.

Yet if the Gospels are clear that it was Romans who executed Jesus, the parable of the owner of the vineyard in Mark 12:1–12, Matthew 21:33–46, and Luke 20:9–18, as we saw above, so telescopes matters that the parable sets forth that Jews alone bore the blame, for there is in the parable no overtone at all of Roman participation. Even more forcefully stated is the apocryphal Gospel of Peter, in which the Romans go unmentioned and the execution there is actually carried out by the Jews. Thus, it has been a repeated Christian accusation throughout the ages that the Jews were guilty of deicide. Which Jews? As we saw above (p. 66), the answer in inherited Christian lore has come primarily from Matthew 27:25, where the crowd of Jews says, "His blood be on us and on our children!" That is, Jews of every period and geographical area came to be charged with deicide.

The inconsistency that on the one hand the death of Jesus was divinely ordained and on the other hand the Jews, not God, caused it is never directly confronted in the Gospels. Rather, the Jewish killing of Jesus is presented as the climax to earlier killings, as if indeed "the Jews" (not individual monarchs) had killed their own prophets (and as if "the Americans" killed Lincoln, McKinley, and Kennedy).

The taunts recorded in the Gospels to the effect that Jesus ought to have saved himself (Mark 15:31; Matt. 27:41–43; Luke 23:35) quite likely reflect not the events themselves but a Jewish-Christian controversy of a later period. The Jewish assertion in Jewish-Christian quarrels was to the effect that if Jesus had indeed been divine as Christians were asserting, he should have been able to save himself.

How broadly were "the Jews" responsible? Were Jews in Alexandria in Egypt involved or those in Athens or in Galilee? The Sanhedrin numbered 71. Add leading priests, say 50. Add the crowd in Jerusalem, say 100. Can the total have been more than 250? The Jewish population of the world in the age of Jesus is estimated as between 2 and 4 million. Do the Christian Scriptures intend to convey that the Jews—all the Jews, of every age and region —killed Jesus?

Some Jewish scholars, in noting that crucifixion was a Roman mode of execution, have often suggested that no Jews at all were involved in the death of Jesus. This full innocency does not persuade me; it seems reasonable that some Jews might well have been involved. We can understand an emphatic contention of the fullest Jewish innocency only as an extreme response to the extreme charge of sole Jewish responsibility.

Did the Jewish authorities, the Sanhedrin for example, truly hold a trial and condemn Jesus? In response, one needs to note how very laconic all four Gospel accounts of the trial are. Conceivably the brevity of these possibly telescoped accounts is responsible for the acute and multiple disparities among the Gospels themselves and between these Gospel accounts and recorded Jewish prescriptions for trying a man on a capital charge.[10] At the minimum it can be said objectively that the accounts of the trial are not historically accurate as they are presented, simply because they are so very brief and because they do not accord with each other.

But are they simply over-brief historical reports of what actually took place or are they colored by partisan considerations to the point that they are nonhistory? Let us recall that in the Gospel presentation, especially in Mark and in Matthew, the disciples had fled, abandoning Jesus. Then how could they give a well-founded account of what happened at the trial? Or, is the trial (as some Jewish[11] and Christian[12] scholars have suggested) totally without historical basis and instead an invention of Mark, thereafter repeated by the later evangelists? I know no objective answer to this question.

And what is meant by the theme of the betrayal by Judas Iscariot? Did Judas inform the authorities who an unknown Jesus was? Hardly, for according to Gospel accounts Jesus was openly teaching in the Temple daily. Or is it possible that this depiction of Jesus as publicly known, with many followers and warm response by the Jewish crowds, is a late recasting of something earlier, namely, that Jesus was in secret working with guerrilla followers and it was this unknown Jesus who was betrayed to the authorities?

Did Judas Iscariot, as related in Matthew, feel remorse, as Matthew relates? Or was he never remorseful as is suggested in Luke-Acts? If he was indeed remorseful, does he not compare favorably with Peter, who three times denied Jesus and afterward only wept bitterly without expressed remorse? Is Judas (his name in Greek is the same as the word for *Judean* or for *Jew*) a historical character, or has Christian hostility invented Judas as a symbol to represent the Jews?

10. Parts of the Bible, and particularly the ancient rabbinic treatise the Mishna Sanhedrin.

11. Such as Paul Winter, *On the Trial of Jesus* (Berlin, 1961; 2d ed., Elmsford, N.Y.: DeGruyter, 1973).

12. For example, John R. Donahue, *Are You the Christ?: The Trial Narrative in the Gospel of Mark* (Missoula, Mont.: Scholars Press, 1973); see esp. his citation on pp. 238–39 of my "The Trial of Jesus: Reservations," *Judaism* 20:74.

The Jewish charge against Jesus is repeatedly specified in the Gospels as blasphemy. This blasphemy would appear to consist either in his forgiveness of sins, a capacity in Jewish thought ascribed to God alone, or in his assertion of his special divinity. In the trial the charge of blasphemy ensues not from any incident about the forgiveness of sins but from Jesus' statement that he is "the Christ, the Son of the Blessed" and that the authorities would "see the Son of man sitting at the right hand of Power, and coming with the clouds of heaven." (Luke, we recall, neither mentions a charge of blasphemy nor depicts the council as condemning Jesus.) Is it the Gospel intent to suggest that Jews in protesting blasphemy were thereby themselves guilty of it? It seems so.

In the passion narrative the authorities fear the crowds, who presumably are partial to Jesus; hence, the authorities must resort to stealth. But then the crowds abruptly seem to become hostile to Jesus, with no explanation being offered for this change. Not only is the motif of stealth apparently thereafter forgotten, but the wish of the authorities to avoid confronting Jesus on the Feast of Unleavened Bread is strangely altered in Mark, Matthew, and Luke into a direct confrontation on the feast day.

It can be seen that the charge of deicide, a monolith of accusation that has survived the centuries, is actually composed of a number of items. The trial by the Sanhedrin is in the nature of a first climax of these items, but this in turn is exceeded by the true climax, namely, that the crowd impelled Pilate to condemn Jesus to death, though Pilate was persuaded that Jesus was innocent and he wished to release him.

Vagueness and a curious network of explicit or implicit inconsistencies and contradictions make up the material that exists in Christian Scripture and later Christian lore to persuade the literal-minded of the substance of Jewish guilt. The charge of deicide itself, though, is the historical product of the bitter two-sided controversy raging at the time of the writing.

The "New Covenant"

Scriptural thought had used the figure of the covenant to describe the relationship between God and his people. The covenant, a contract between two parties with each party undertaking responsibilities and obligations to the other, appears in connection with the individuals such as Abraham (Gen. 15:7–18; 17:1–14) and with collective Israel through Moses (Exod. 24:4–8). By the covenant the people were elevated into a unique role of God's Chosen. The reciprocal responsibilities were the obligation of the Deity to protect and defend his people, and that of his people to worship him exclusively and faithfully observe commandments that he had revealed. Just as a covenant could be entered into and faithfully observed, so too could a covenant be violated by one party and thereby nullified.

The theme is found in prophets such as Amos and Isaiah that Israel, through cumulative collective guilt, had violated the covenant to the point of nullification, or just past it. Such nullification implied that Israel was now bereft of God's defense and protection and therefore prey to conquering nations such as the Assyrians. Amos warns that God would not prevent the Assyrians from entering and overrunning Israel; Isaiah says that God was actively bringing in the Assyrians to overrun Israel, this as punishment for the violation and nullification of the covenant. The Assyrian conquest of Israel in 722 B.C. demonstrated the consequence to the Northern Kingdom of the nullification of the covenant.

At least in theory, the conquest of the Southern Kingdom by the Babylonians in 597 B.C. should have implied the further and final nullification of the covenant. In this context, Jeremiah, as if conceding that the earlier covenant had indeed been ruptured, now spoke of a "new covenant" between God and his people (31:26–33). The terms of the old covenant had been recorded on stone (probably an allusion to the stones on which the Decalogue was engraved) but the new covenant would be "written on the hearts of people." The implication of the new covenant was its perpetual character, that it could not and would not ever be annulled.

But whether in the old covenant or in Jeremiah's new one, the contracting parties were God and Israel. It was and is a Jewish view that God and the Jewish people were and are bound together in an eternal covenant. In the Jewish view both the old covenant and the new one spoken of by Jeremiah were tokens of an unbroken and unbreakable relationship between God and the Jews.

When early Christianity became aware of its beginning distinction from Judaism and Jews, the matter of covenant was bound to arise, for it was deeply imbedded in Jewish thought. Christians began to conceive of their relationship to God as necessarily resting on a covenant. Christians came to view the new covenant of Jeremiah not as defining God's continuing relationship with the Jewish people but as an abrogation of that relationship; the parties to the "new covenant" were now God and the Christian community. That is, not only did the new covenant supplant the old, but Christians supplanted Jews as the party contracting with God.

If Christians have supplanted the Jews, what has happened to the Jews? It would appear that God has cast them off. Though Paul in Romans 9 speaks as if he denies that God has rejected the Jews as his people, he thereafter proceeds to affirm this. He exempts from this divine rejection a saved remnant of the Jews—possibly himself and other Jewish Christians—and he holds out the hope that from this remnant would come the ultimate salvation of all Israel. The words that he speaks about Jews being the olive tree and Gentiles branches engrafted onto it do not amount to any modification of or retreat from his basic conviction that Christians have supplanted Jews as the covenant people.

In the Gospels and Acts the Christians have completely and unreservedly supplanted the Jews, the Jews having been cast off by God. In Judaism the new covenant of Jeremiah is never viewed as implying that someone or somebody is cast off; in Judaism the new covenant renews God's relations with his people. In Christianity the new covenant is not such a renewal; it is instead the basis for affirming God's election of Christianity and at the same time his rejection of the Jews. The view that God and Christians had entered into a new covenant, as a result of which the covenant between God and the Jews was annulled, is found exclusively in New Testament and later Christian writings. It is never found in any Jewish writings, whether of the time of Jesus (the so-called intertestamental writings), Josephus, or the slightly later rabbinic literature. The prooftexts that have been offered in support of the view are exclusively Christian interpretations of Scripture, and there are no Jewish counterparts to this idiosyncratic exegesis. If God did indeed cast off the Jews, information about that drastic and decisive action was somehow never divinely conveyed to them.

The Christian view of "new covenant" is a partisan, indeed parochial, view. Christians have often suggested that Christianity is a great universal religion while Judaism is narrow and particularistic, and the suggestion is buttressed by citing Paul's statement that "in Christ there is neither Jew nor Gentile." The key words *in Christ* are frequently overlooked. What these words imply is that, *once within Christianity,* the origin of persons, whether they were by birth Jewish or Gentile, is of no consequence. Yet Christianity is viewed as a new entity, one that is not a whit less particularistic than Judaism. The terminology about the entity varies: Jews had spoken in words that connote an ethnic entity, for example, "the Jewish people," while Christians have spoken of "the church" as the corporate body of the faithful. Granted that overtones of what is ethnic are different from overtones of what is implicit in the term *the church,* there is no substantial difference in the respective conceptions of an entity that constituted God's special people. In the course of time Christianity spoke of itself as the "true Israel."

The respective attitudes toward the reception of converts became noticeably different. There is no direct evidence in Jewish sources for the kind of active, aggressive missionary activity that characterized Christianity. Rather, Jews accepted converts, at times indeed reluctantly,[13] in what might be characterized as a passive way. But whether the reception of converts was passive (as marked the Jews) or active (as marked the Christians), conversion in either case was entrance into a corporate covenant.

THE LAW

The view of Paul about the laws of Moses was extreme, and there is no parallel in any Jewish literature to his stand. Paul's argument that the laws of Moses should be nullified was fivefold: the Laws are an impediment to righteousness; the Laws induce sin; the Laws are incapable of being observed; God's sovereignty is denigrated in any effort on the part of man to observe the Law, which effort is as useless as it is destined to be unsuccessful; salvation is meted out to those whom God chooses and ordains for it because it cannot be "earned" by obedience to the Law.

About a century after Paul this became somewhat tempered into the usual understanding that the nullification of the Laws related

---

13. The reluctance seems to have been based on two aspects of Jewish experience. One aspect was the Roman persecution that ensued on the collapse of the Bar Kochba rebellion and the prohibition of the Jewish cult practices. Apparently converts included those "informers" who let the Romans know about those who observed the prohibited Jewish rituals such as circumcision, with resultant severe punishment. Hence, all converts were suspect. Second, there appear to have been from time to time converts who insisted on their own terms rather than on what the Jewish religion demanded. The classic passages on the admission of converts stresses the requirement of a disinterested and pure motive; conversion in connection with a marriage was regarded as reflecting an impure motive and was therefore prohibited. It should be recalled that not only have Catholics and Protestants on occasion barred intermarriage, but within Protestantism, Lutherans and Calvinists also prohibited Lutheran-Calvinist marriage. Into our time some Christian denominations continue to bar intermarriage unless the Christian outsider goes through conversion to the host denomination.

only to the ceremonial laws; in the Christian view the ethical laws were deemed to be still binding. Moreover, the Gospel According to Matthew portrayed Jesus as inaugurating Christian law. Canon law also developed in the course of time. Nevertheless, to the extent that aspects of Paul's views became the norm in the unfolding Christianity, Judaism and Christianity have espoused attitudes that are antithetical to each other. In Pharisaism and thereafter in rabbinic Judaism, the premise is always the eternal validity and worth of the Laws.

In time, facets of the Jewish sacred calendar prescribed in Mosaic law failed to be perpetuated in Christianity; essentially only Passover (altered into Easter), Pentecost (commemorating not Sinai but the descent of the Holy Spirit on the Christian community in Jerusalem, related in Acts 2), and the Sabbath (altered from Saturday to Sunday) survived in Christendom. A new calendar was developed for Christianity and in time it became a very full calendar. In the New Testament two ceremonies replacing the abandoned Jewish ceremonies are spoken of: baptism and the Eucharist[14] (the sacrifice of the Lord's Supper); they are conceived of as "sacraments," that is, observances that have a supernatural significance transcending the ceremonies themselves. (In Judaism, ceremonies are ordinarily not conceived of as "sacramental" in this way but are either purely commemorative or simply divine injunctions as to what a person must do.) In due course, the two sacraments were increased in number to seven.[15]

Along with such developments away from the Jewish laws, there was a two-step transition in the implication of the term *faith* from its meaning in Paul. For Paul "faith" was an inner, emotional experience through which man felt himself thoroughly united in mystic communion with the Christ or with God. In the first step of transition, faith was altered into an emphasis on the content of belief, a matter of the mind, not the heart. In this sense faith is primarily intellectual assent.

The second step taken was from "faith" into "proper faith." So rapidly did Christianity spread that diversity in beliefs within the corporate body became not only noticeable but also the basis of

14. *Eucharist* does not occur as a noun in the New Testament.

15. The five additional sacraments (marriage, confirmation, extreme unction, penance, and orders) came to be regarded by Protestants as invalid on the premise that they were not explicit in the New Testament. Roman Catholics retain the full seven.

quarrels and deep divisions. Accordingly there were those whose beliefs were uncongenial to others, and factionalism arose. This was countered in the church by an insistence that membership within the corporate body was in itself insufficient; the acceptable member was expected to espouse certain beliefs and to repudiate other beliefs. To say this another way, there arose a distinction between "orthodoxy" and "heresy." The "orthodox" person espoused the proper faith; the heretic espoused an improper one.

Who was to determine what was orthodox and what was heretical? Such determination could become possible only when there developed an officialdom with the capacity to enforce its tenets. Such capacity to enforce was to come from the state. The Council of Nicaea in A.D. 325, convened by the emperor Constantine, gave Christian officials the coercive power of the state to define and command orthodoxy and to define and uproot heresy by exerting actions on heretics.

One can speak in over-simple terms of diverse themes that characterize historic Christianity and historic Judaism. The theme characteristic of Judaism, based on the premise of the eternity of the Laws and the need to apply them to new situations, with new derivative regulations, is that of "proper conduct." Judaism, through *mitzva* ("scriptural commandment") and *halacha* ("derived commandment") has prescribed what the faithful communicant must do (what to eat, when and how to fast, what specific prayers to recite, and the like). Christianity, through its creeds and authoritative "dogmas," has prescribed not what the faithful must do but what he must believe.

The Jewish view of Judaism as the supreme religion predates Christianity, and its formulation and reformulation is independent of any need to assess Christianity in this context. On the other hand, Christianity's view of itself as the supreme religion has always involved a comparison with Judaism. Christian supremacy has been expressed primarily in the context of the superiority of Christianity to Judaism. This is a part of the New Testament legacy. In the usual total Christian view, if Judaism ever had any value it was to prepare the way for Christianity; beyond that it had no great value and indeed continually declined from even its preparatory utility into a mumbo jumbo of meaningless requirements and incantations.

In the period after the New Testament the mutual antagonisms between Judaism and Christianity underwent further amplification and extension along these lines. It is simply not correct to exempt the New Testament from anti-Semitism and to allocate it to later periods of history. It must be said that innumerable Christians have indeed purged themselves of anti-Semitism. But its expression is to be found in Christian Scripture for all to read. To what extent does Christianity in general, and the New Testament in particular, perpetuate and recapitulate the anti-Semitism that so many Christians have come to feel is unworthy of all that is so noble in their tradition?

11. From New Testament Times to the Present

The amity that exists between Christianity and Judaism, Christians and Jews, in our day can obscure much of the unfortunate history that lies between New Testament times and the present. Yet it is necessary to be aware of that history, as a perspective on our subject and on our contemporary lives.

It is of course regrettable that assertions of the superiority of one religion over the other are found in the Holy Scriptures of both Jews and Christians. Such claims, written in the fervor of their own age and circumstances, have not only been persuasive to subsequent generations but because they are biblical have been accepted by so many as sanctions for hatred and prejudice.

On the Jewish side there are specific scriptural passages in which God elected the forefathers to be his special people and which contend that such election, reaffirmed in the ancient rabbinic literature, still endures. Gentiles have ordinarily been excluded from membership in the elect.

The Jewish notion of the exclusion of Gentiles is not all of a piece. There is sanction for some generosity both in Scripture and in the rabbinic literature. This is based on Genesis 9, which relates that after the great flood God blessed Noah and his sons and made a covenant with them that included commandments which were taken to number seven. These commandments, given at a time when Judaism had not yet emerged, were seen in hindsight by the ancient rabbis as God's requirements for Gentiles, and thereby implied to Jews that Gentiles too could be righteous. The later and numerous commandments through Moses, tabulated to be 613, were incumbent only on Israel. A Gentile could be deemed righteous through his observance of the Noachite laws, a Jew through his obedience to the Mosaic law. It is stated in rabbinic literature, "There are righteous persons among the Gentiles and they have a portion in the world to come."

Both Scripture and the rabbinic literature are unreservedly harsh both with respect to "idolaters" and with respect to those idolaters (such as the Romans) who have on historic occasion persecuted the Jews, whether through conquest or through deeds of malevolence or suppressive persecution in situations apart from conquest. The book of Psalms is an especially abundant source for passages that call for divine wrath to befall the unbelievers. In the rabbinic literature there are few mentions of Jesus or Christians, and these mentions, though somewhat hostile, are not nearly as much so as the mentions of Romans (usually spoken of cryptically as "Edomites"). The few mentions of Jesus, based apparently on hearsay of what is in the Gospels, dismiss him as a misguided magician or exorcist whose achievements were made possible by Satan. It is important to note that these mentions of Jesus are scant and scattered and are responsive rather than initiatory. Similar but greater hostility is expressed toward Sadducees and toward a group called the *minim*. The meaning of *minim* is difficult to ascertain precisely. It is probably a general term for a variety of dissident views. The trespass of the *minim,* in the words of their opponents, is that they affirm a belief in "two authorities." Perhaps the "two authorities" alludes to Persian dualism, wherein there are views of a god of light and a god of darkness. Perhaps, though, the *minim* were "Gnostics," among whom there was a belief in a set of two deities, God himself transcendent and in effect out of contact with this evil world, and a vice-regent, a subordinate deity, who was the actual ruler of this world. There is evidence that some second-century Christians regarded Jesus as such a subordinate deity; among Christian Gnostics a similar view existed, and therefore *minim* is taken to allude to such Gnostic thinking. Quite possibly Christians were included within the category of the denounced *minim*. But since heretics are always insiders many interpreters regard *minim* simply as heretical Jews.

The twelfth of the "eighteen benedictions" of the synagogue morning worship denounces certain people. The text of that passage, which praises God for bringing the "arrogant" low, varies as to who these wicked people are. It begins, "May there be no future for the ———." Three different words are found in varying texts for the blank. One version uses *minim*. Another uses "informers" (Hebrew, *malshinĭm*), apparently arising from the period of persecution after the Bar Kochba rebellion when Romans prohibited the practice of Judaism, with the result that informers told Roman soldiers about Jews who observed the practices secretly. The third version uses the word *nōtzrîm,* apparently meaning "Christians," derived from the kindred word "Nazareth." Scholars have debated as to which of the three words is the original. The origin of the twelfth benediction is ascribed to the period of Jamnia, around A.D. 90, when the reconstruction of Judaism was made firm subsequent to the destruction of the Temple in the year 70. It is related in the Talmudic tractate Berakot 28a that it was asked who among the gathered sages could formulate an appropriate prayer in praise of God who brings low the "arrogant," who defy him. A sage, Samuel the Small, responded by doing so. A year later, however, Samuel's formulation had come to be forgotten and a new one had to be devised. Assuming that *nōtzrîm* is the original word (a perilous assumption), one notices that the matter was of such little urgency that the first formulation was forgotten.

There are some other passages in the ancient rabbinic literature reflecting Jewish-Christian conflict. One such passage is not clearly about Christians, though some have interpreted it to be. The passage deals with the abandonment of the recitation of the Ten Commandments as a part of synagogue worship. The cessation seems to be in refutation of the assertion by some Jews that the Decalogue was an all-sufficient set of commandments; by removing the Ten Commandments from the service the importance of all 613 commandments was reaffirmed. Perhaps this matter relates to a somewhat distorted reflection of the teachings of Paul (who is totally unmentioned in the rabbinic literature).

Another kind of passage has nuances clearly related to Christians. Christian writers, in citing the Old Testament, cited it in the Septuagint form, that is, from the Greek translation, which often deviates from the Hebrew. A sentiment is found which laments that Scripture was ever rendered into Greek. Alongside this lament is the injunction that the oral Torah must never be recorded in writing, lest it be "usurped" by outsiders as Scripture had been. By keeping the oral Torah oral, one could keep it safe within the Jewish community so that it could not become a Christian possession as the Old Testament had become.

That is to say, the surviving Jewish side of the two-sided controversy is minor in extent and somewhat vague. If Jews wrote special tracts against Christians with the same abundance and hostility that Christians wrote such tracts against Jews, these Jewish writings have neither survived nor ever been alluded to in either Jewish or Christian literature. The Christian tracts against the Jews have survived. These anti-Jewish tracts, exemplified by the preserved sermons of John Chrysostom, a priest of Antioch in the fourth century A.D., reinforced the anti-Semitism in the New Testament and deeply influenced the climate of the Middle Ages.

There is neither space here nor real need to specify all the ways in which anti-Semitism flowered in later Christendom. A few scattered examples must be taken as epitomizing what took place over the centuries.

Judaism was normally described not as a religion but as either a superstition or a vomit. Jews were barred from the ordinary personal liberties. They were in due course forced to wear "the Jewish badge." They were alleged to use for the Passover Seder not wine but the blood of Christian children whom they kidnapped and killed for that purpose. They were alleged to sneak into churches and stab the holy wafer ("the host"), from which then flowed the "real blood" of Jesus. In the Black Plague they were accused of poisoning the wells of the Christians. It was declared that they could be distinguished by their own "Jewish" smell. The Jews of the Rhineland were massacred in the First Crusade in 1096, for the Crusaders saw no reason to wait until they reached the Holy Land to show their might to the infidels. The art and folk tales of the age before the invention of printing paved the way for later printed art and picture books showing villainous Jews doing dreadful things to Christians. The Jewish rabbinic writings were recurrently either censored or confiscated and burned. Because pawnbroking was prohibited for Christians, Christian rulers would invite Jews into their realm for their own economic gain; since Jews, as *servi camerae* ("wards of the state"), were the property of the ruler, a ruler could confiscate what the Jews had amassed for whatever occasion he decided. Chaucer, in "The Prioress' Tale," told how the Jews had killed Little Hugh of Lincoln. Shakespeare, at a time some two hundred and fifty years after Jews had been expelled from England (in 1290), wrote his *Merchant of Venice,* with Shylock demanding a pound of Christian flesh.[1] When the medieval period turned into

---

1. Unlike Marlowe in *The Jew of Malta,* Shakespeare makes an intelligible human being out of Shylock. One notices the character ascribed to Shylock's daughter; she is a liar and a cheat and as abominable a woman as created by any playwright. At the end of the play she becomes a Christian. Is this the kind of a person whose apostasy from Judaism Jews should lament?

the modern and Jews in European lands sought for the basic rights of man, the opposition to such granting was invariably based on such ingrained Christian teaching.

The above epitomizes Jewish experience. But, true as it is, there is another side to the story. How did those Jews not killed in medieval pogroms manage to survive at all in Christian lands, apart from hiding or fleeing? Outside the occasions of acute local violence, they survived through Christian protection. Though the medieval Catholic church and its influence on state legislation instituted laws against the Jews on theological grounds, by and large it protected Jews in the limited rights granted them. Paradoxically, the papacy imposed limitations on Jews but also abided sturdily by what it permitted Jews.

So too regional or local officials, usually bishops, followed the lead of the papacy in protecting Jews. The acts of violence that took place were seldom directly inaugurated or prompted by church officials. These acts were the work of bigots who incited mobs, often in connection with charges of "ritual" murder or "desecrations of the Host." In a word, it was not the church as an institution that killed off Jews but the effect of the church's teaching on its indoctrinated faithful. Here and there the church, in a given region, imposed indignities (such as convening Jews to listen to conversionist sermons, with a penalty for stuffing the ears); often a local church official so spurred the congregation on Good Friday that it went from the church to the ghetto. But it was the aroused Christian mob, not the church itself, that did the maiming and the raping and the killing.

The New Testament, however, did contain aspects of antidote to the poison. Jesus was a kindly and beneficent figure who healed the sick and sacrificed himself out of his love for mankind. A Christian who wished deeply to imitate the Christ perforce had to imitate his love and thus was stayed from cruelty.

Also, despite the ghetto walls, individual Jews and Christians often came to know each other. Such acquaintance could persuade a Christian that the Jews whom he knew were unlike the generation of vipers he heard about in Sunday worship. Indeed, the lessons taught from the Gospels often altered the Pharisees from being the Jewish opponents of Jesus into the Christian hypocrites in one's own congregation. However unseemly a Jew was deemed, and however unbelievable his oath in a court was (a special oath was sometimes used, with the Jew standing on a pigskin and calling down on himself all the executions of Scripture if he were lying), experience could teach an individual Christian that the Jew whom he had come to trust was trustworthy.

Indeed, a private, tacit dissent on the part of a man in the pew from what was spoken from the pulpit or read from the Sunday lection was also a factor. The man in the pew may have been uneducated or even illiterate, and a sharer in the general atmosphere of his environment, but he could also possess a good measure of common sense and a private judgment of his own. Besides, it was always possible to neutralize the view that Jews were a damned people by recalling that Jews in the Old Testament were the chosen people and, paradoxically, continued to be thought of that way (as one discovers among rural folk in America still today).

When did matters change in the Western world? (They scarcely changed in eastern Europe at all until the Russian Revolution of 1917.) The beginning of the change was the eruption of the Protestant Reformation—not that Protestants suddenly abandoned Catholic anti-Semitism. Indeed, Martin Luther at an early stage hoped and expected Jews to become Protestants. He wrote that on observing how Catholics treated Jews he would, were he a Jew, prefer to be a dog rather than a Christian. But when Jews did not become Protestants, Luther wrote against them with more virulence than early Christians or the author of the Epistle to Barnabas (second century) or the John Chrysostom of Antioch.[2]

The breakdown of the unity of Christianity in the West, especially when Protestantism itself became fragmented, led to Christian being pitted against Christian in a variety of ways: Catholics versus Protestants; Lutherans versus Pietists; the Church of England versus the disestablished sects. More and more Protestant groupings arose. Some formed on a national basis, some on a doctrinal one. These divisions spurred persecution and wars. Such upheavals jeopardized the stability of Europe, especially its commerce. Moreover, the divisiveness in Christendom raised the issue among intellectuals about the relevancy of partisan claims, especially in the light of the growing academic humanism. The beginning challenge to the divine right of kings in time led to the assertion of personal rights and freedom for all men. One milestone, for example, was the British Act of Toleration of 1689, which extended rights beyond the Church of England. The act limited rights to trinitarian Protestants but nevertheless set a

2. In "On the Jews and Their Lies" (1543), in *Luther's Works,* ed. and trans. Theodore G. Tappert (Philadelphia: Fortress Press, 1971), vol. 47, p. 121.

precedent for religious liberty. The atmosphere of the time fostered the denials of older views that truth can be positively known, that heretical ideas were matters of consequence, or that coercion in religious beliefs was effective.

Various solutions to religious conflict came into being. For example, under "territorialism" a certain religion could be the only one permitted in a given area,[3] but dissidents could be permitted peacefully to emigrate. A second kind of solution was "latitudinarianism"; while a single communion was established as official, its doctrinal and other demands could be relatively few, thereby allowing for latitude in convictions. This has been the English solution. The third solution was *pax dissidentium*,[4] "peace among dissidents," wherein divergent groups were prepared to live with each other in amity and freedom from intimidation.

The existence of "toleration" did not imply universal toleration. Catholics and nontrinitarians were not included in the British Act of Toleration of 1689. John Locke (1632–1704) held that it is of no concern to a state of what church a man is a member, though he regarded some forms of religion, and irreligion, as harmful to the state and he viewed Catholics, Jews, and atheists as socially dangerous. On the other hand, the eighteenth-century Enlightenment, especially the French "Encyclopedists," even attacked Christianity as such, this in the interest of what they viewed as a "natural morality."

For the most part the rise of toleration and then of religious liberty in the Western world was directly addressed to the sects within Christendom. At first there was no direct concern about Jews. (An exception was Holland, which granted rights to Jews as early as the mid-eighteenth century.) Where Jews attained political freedom, this was usually indirect, as in the First Article of the American Bill of Rights. In France the "Rights of Man" after the French Revolution was initially not viewed in Parliament as including the Jews, but then was applied to them too. In Britain, Catholics were exempted from legal disabilities in 1829. British Jews were granted rights of naturalization of the "Jew Bill" of 1753, but the Jew Bill was repealed in 1754. In the early 1830s, after the Catholic emancipation, a num-

3. In the United States certain churches were "official churches" in some states into the first third of the nineteenth century. The First Amendment prohibited the federal government from establishing an official religion but did not prohibit state constitutions from doing so.

4. I here follow Roland H. Bainton, "The Struggle for Religious Liberty," *Church History* 10 (1941): 95–124.

ber of efforts for "Jewish emancipation" were introduced into Parliament but did not pass. Some Jews were elected to Parliament, but these were not allowed full rights there until 1858. Complete and unreserved equality was not provided for Roman Catholics and Jews in Britain until 1890.

Though in England and America Jews did achieve and retain "emancipation," it proved to be transient in Germany and failed of attainment in most of eastern Europe. There the Jewish desire for civil rights turned to "self-emancipation," a quest for rights in some hoped-for Jewish entity that led in the course of the nineteenth century to Zionism. The creation of the State of Israel is the result of two distinctive elements. One is the Jewish messianic longing for the "return of the exiles," expressed in the daily prayers of Jews. The other is the failure of Jews to achieve rights of citizenship in nineteenth-century Europe.

The unification of Germany in 1870 brought Jews great measures of rights that they lost under Hitler. "Racial" anti-Semitism culminating in the Nazi destruction of the Jews, which has come to be called the Holocaust, arose in France in the 1870s, at the same time that religious anti-Semitism had abated and was virtually ended. Nazism in the twentieth century would prove to be almost as stridently anti-Christian in ideology as it was anti-Jewish.

Meanwhile the idea of religious freedom, and the rejection by Christians of the validity of persecuting other Christians, had acted in the nineteenth and early twentieth centuries to end the Christian persecution of Jews. Indeed, in the nineteenth century not only did Christians cease actively to persecute (though some individual Christian dignitaries were avowedly hostile to Jews and Judaism), but notable Christians expressed sympathy for or gave aid to Jews in connection with striking events, such as the Damascus persecutions in 1842, the Mortara case[5] in 1858, and the Russian pogroms in the 1880s. The end of the ghetto in western Europe, and its absence from the United States and Canada, had brought Christians and Jews, especially the clergy, into unprecedented forms of contact with each other.

---

5. As a Jew and an infant, Edgar Mortara had been baptized by a Catholic servant girl when he was ill. Four years later she confessed this to a priest, who reported the baptism to Rome. Thereupon the authorities had the child abducted from his parents by Vatican police so that he could be reared as a Christian. He was never returned to his parents and became an Augustinian priest. The Mortara case was a *cause célèbre* throughout Europe.

Why the above review? To enable us to confront the question central to this book. To what extent did Christian anti-Semitism (the ghetto, the recollection of the Jew Badge, the ritual murder charges) provide the seedbed in which racial anti-Semitism could grow? To what extent, in this sense, is Christianity and the Christian community responsible for almost complete annihilation of the Jews in countries such as Germany, Austria, Holland, Belgium, France, and Poland? To what extent did the New Testament, read and preached in Christian worship, prompt or perpetuate the hostility to Jews that made Nazism possible?

12. Anti-Semitism and the New Testament

Within Christendom since the time of Hitler there has existed a widespread reaction of shock and soul-searching concerning the Holocaust. The undeniable fact that the indignity and horror wrought against Jews at that time by at least nominally Christian hands has driven many Christians into a deep sense of shame or a feeling of responsibility far beyond shame itself. Christian individuals and Christian communions in abundance have expressed in a variety of ways their disavowal of anti-Semitism.

Such disavowals, however differently phrased, have had the persistent theme that anti-Semitism and Christianity are inconsistent and that therefore Christians fully repudiate anti-Semitism. In some documents there have been specific statements that have repudiated the charge of deicide. As we have said, this charge that the Jews had killed Jesus was so formulated in the Christian tradition that responsibility for the death of Jesus rested not only on Jews in the age of Jesus but on Jews of all ages and of all times. It is this kind of deicide charge that Christian statements have rejected.[1]

Here and there in Christendom the charge of deicide lingers on. A French attorney, Jacques Isorni, wrote a little book in 1967 entitled *The True Trial of Jesus*. In his opinion Pontius Pilate, not the Jews, had killed Jesus. Some eight years later, Abbot George de Nantes, in reviewing the book, denounced Isorni in such immoderate terms

---

1. Father Gerard Sloyan, in his admirable and high-minded *Jesus on Trial* (Philadelphia: Fortress Press, 1973), has questioned the validity of what he correctly calls my "historical agnosticism," my belief that the "facts" about the trial of Jesus cannot be recovered. In a careful study, without a single sentence that might offend Jews, he seeks to penetrate the anti-Jewish character of the Gospel accounts of the trial to get to a rock-bottom set of historical bases. I regard *Jesus on Trial* as by far the best book on the subject, and I warmly applaud the effort, which I find I cannot agree with *on strictly academic* grounds, at the same time that I deeply appreciate the tone of the book.

that Isorni sued the abbot for libel. The abbot had called Isorni a disloyal Catholic who was guilty of distorting and destroying the veracity of the Gospel and of the Catholic church and had implied that Isorni was a paid advocate of the Jews. The abbot affirmed the historical reliability of the Gospel accounts and contended that the Jews were indeed guilty of deicide. The civil suit took place and the abbot was found guilty of libel and enjoined to publish in the same journal where his review of Isorni's book had appeared a retraction of his libelous charges.[2]

When I was a boy there were stories that circulated among us Jews. One was about a man, emerging from a church service, who began to beat up some Jews. A policeman intervened to stop him. The man protested, saying, "The Jews killed Jesus." The policeman replied, "That was two thousand years ago." The man retorted, "But I only heard about it this morning." Another story told of three Jews who were determined to convert to Christianity. Outside a church they drew lots to choose which of the three should go first and then return to tell the other two what happened. When the one came out of the church, the other two ran to him, asking, "How did it go?" He replied, "Get away from me, you Christ-killers!"

The identification by some Jews of Christians as implacably hating foes persists. The pogroms in eastern Europe from which my parents fled began with the ringing of church bells. I remember as an American boy how my mother used to shiver whenever the bells rang in the church near our home. Indeed, some Jews are no less than obsessed by the combination of anxiety and fear of Christians. Once, in a lecture before a Jewish audience when I spoke of Christians who had rescued Jews from Hitler, a woman arose to interrupt in full earnestness, "How can you speak this way? Don't you know the Christians hate us and want to kill us?" I learned after the lecture that the woman, though she had managed to escape from Germany, had lost all her family there. For insight into this kind of bitterness on the part of Jews, Christians should read Dagobert Runes' *Let My People Live!* This book is a highly emotional response by a Jew to Christian anti-Semitism, an unsurpassed accumulation of bitterness toward Christians, distilled out of personal experience. Its thesis, called "A Word to the Reader," states: "The New Testament contains 102

2. I record my deep gratitude to Isorni. I wrote to him early in 1977 to get as much information as I could about his suit. Most courteously and promptly he sent me both his book (a translation of which may soon appear in English) and a copy of the judicial decision.

references to the Jews of [the] most degrading malevolent and libelous kind, thereby creating in the minds and hearts of the Christian children and adults ineradicable hatred towards the Jewish people."[3]

My personal experience, and hence my basic attitudes, clearly arising from a completely different personal background, could scarcely be more different than that of Runes. I am a native American. Happily, neither anti-Semitism in general nor Christian anti-Semitism in particular has been much of a factor in my adult life. My years as a Hillel Director at the University of North Carolina and at Yale include the warmest relationships with Christian ministers and students. As a chaplain in the Navy (1942–46) I had the same experience, except that Catholic priests entered and broadened my ken. If here and there in the Navy in the South Pacific there was an occasional contretemps, it was with some individual chaplain who succeeded in offending Christian chaplains in a measure far beyond his offense to me. The bonds with fellow chaplains were warm and long-lasting.

Shortly before the outbreak of World War II, I began work on a Ph.D. in New Testament. This came about through the vision of Dr. Harvie Branscomb, a Methodist and my professor of New Testament at Duke University, who saw what apparently no Bible scholar had recognized before: the value of a Jew applying his scholarship and instinctive background in Jewish tradition to the understanding and eventually the teaching of early Christianity in its Jewish setting. I taught at Vanderbilt University; I have taught at the University of Chicago and at the University of Windsor; I have lectured at innumerable universities and at Christian colleges and seminaries. The Society of Biblical Literature, in membership predominantly Christian, honored me by electing me its president. The Christian world to me has been primarily that of Christian biblical scholars. My experience has been blessedly different from that of the suffering woman who interrupted my lecture.

For those unacquainted with biblical scholarship, it can be useful to outline certain facets that relate directly to our topic. Scientific, historical scholarship began in the eighteenth century, based naturally on the accumulated humanism that arose in the Renaissance. This scholarship felt a sense of independence from the legacy of traditional

---

3. Dagobert D. Runes, *Let My People Live!* (New York: Philosophical Library, 1975). I reviewed this book, saying in part: "In terms of academic study, this book has little to commend it. For Christians interested in encountering the bitterness which some Jews feel toward Christianity, it is unsurpassed; it is as outspoken as it is bitter."

study. For example, the issue of the authorship of the Pentateuch, traditionally ascribed to Moses, was raised, and new, even iconoclastic answers were offered (as in the so-called Graf-Wellhausen hypothesis with its suggestion of four major periods and layers of authorship, J, E, D, and P, and the completion of the Pentateuch well over a thousand years after the time of Moses). There arose in New Testament studies the so-called "quest for the historical Jesus" (with the view that Mark, rather than being the youngest of the Gospels as tradition held, was the oldest of them). At the same time the Jewish setting of early Christianity underwent renewed, independent study.

In the development of this latter study there was the felt need to try to fit the figure of Jesus into his Jewish setting. The scholarship that made up this effort was exceedingly abundant. Alas, all too often the procedure in the scholarship, especially in German scholarship (which dominated the field), so arrayed the results as to present Jesus over and against Judaism, and thereafter to present, as if on an academic basis, a noble Jesus and a remarkably deficient Judaism.[4] This Judaism, portrayed, for example, in the five-volume work *Commentary on the New Testament, Based on the Talmud and Midrash,*[5]

---

4. At times this denigration of Judaism was couched in dignified theological language, at times in unacademic slurs.

5. Herman L. Strack and Paul Billerbeck, *Commentary on the New Testament, Based on the Talmud and Midrash,* 5 vols. (München: C. H. Beck, 1922–28). In my "Parallelomania" (Presidential Address, Society of Biblical Literature and Exegesis, December, 1961), in *Two Living Traditions: Essays on Religion and the Bible* (Detroit: Wayne State University Press, 1972), pp. 291–304, I spoke in criticism of Strack-Billerbeck and stated that its pages "invite the imprudent and, one must say, the impudent." Those who read German might consult three items: D. Flusser, "Ulrich Wilckens und die Juden," *Evangelische Theologie* 34 (1974): 236–43; U. Wilckens, "Das Neue Testament und die Juden, Antwort an David Flusser," *Evangelische Theologie* 34 (1974): 602–11; R. Rendtorff, "Die neutestamentliche Wissenschaft und die Juden: Zur Diskussions zwischen David Flusser and Ulrich Wilckens," *Evangelische Theologie* 36 (1976): 191–200. In the first of these articles, David Flusser, of the Hebrew University, reviewing a new translation of the New Testament by Ulrich Wilckens, made the charge of greater anti-Semitism in the translation than in the New Testament. In the second article Wilckens, asserting that he was only reflecting in his translation what was contained in the New Testament, contended that Flusser was assailing not himself but the tradition of New Testament scholarship. In the third, Rolf Rendtorff, an Old Testament scholar of the University of Heidelberg, lamented that Flusser was not without justification for the broader charge. See in this connection my "Leo Baeck on Christianity," The 1975 Leo Baeck Institute Memorial Lecture No. 19 (New York, Leo Baeck Institute). See also E. P. Sanders, *Paul and Palestinian Judaism* (Philadelphia: Fortress Press, 1977), pp. 33–59.

by Herman L. Strack and Paul Billerbeck, was presented as a dry, arid legalism, devoid of heart and emotion and marked by a mechanical system of rewards and punishments. Many of the German scholars, no longer believing in the divine Christ, presented a totally human Jesus whose wondrous human virtues were in marked contrast to the abominable vices inherent in Judaism and in Jews. A long chain of German scholars has denied the historical validity of everything in the Gospels—except the anti-Semitism. In a word, the portrayal of Judaism in this widely influential scholarship of the nineteenth and early twentieth centuries was even more anti-Semitic than that in Christian Scripture itself.

The erudition of the German scholars, their copious citations of scholarship, and their learned footnotes should not conceal the simple fact that their repeated misinterpretations of Judaism rest on condescension. One must ascribe to the succession of German scholars a hostility against Jews and Judaism as extreme as it has been repetitious and a presentation of Judaism that is not a picture but a travesty. These scholars taught the clergy, and the clergy preached to the laity. Not all these people were blatantly anti-Semitic; a few, however, like Bruno Bauer and Paul de Lagarde, were notably so, and later such persons as Gerhard Kittel and Johannes Hempel. Tragically, respected German New Testament scholars saw little connection between their devotion to Christianity and the anti-Semitism that they espoused and propagated.

The change in New Testament scholarship came not in Germany but in the United States as the almost single-handed achievement of a Harvard professor, a Presbyterian, George Foot Moore.[6] After a number of decades of sterling Old Testament scholarship and important publications on world religions, he turned to the ancient rabbinic literature. In 1921 he published a long essay entitled "Christian Writers on Judaism."[7] Moore provided a review of Christian writings in ancient and medieval times and then gave attention to modern academic writing, especially what had been written by leading scholars in Germany. With respect to these he made several telling points: One, their studies used Judaism as a foil for Christianity

---

6. But due acknowledgment should be made of significant writings also by R. Travers Herford (e.g., *The Pharisees* [New York: Macmillan, 1924]) and James Parkes (e.g., *The Conflict of the Church and the Synagogue: A Study in the Origins of Antisemitism* [Philadelphia: Jewish Publication Society of America, 1961]).

7. *Harvard Theological Review* 14 (1921):197–254.

rather than seeing Judaism on its own terms. As a consequence, distortions were frequent. For example, the doctrine of the Messiah is peripheral in Judaism but these scholars made it as central in Judaism as it is in Christianity. Second, the legal tradition in Judaism was viewed from the perspective of the Pauline tradition as outmoded, trivial, and mechanical rather than in terms of its own presuppositions and thrust. As a scholar in world religions, Moore was averse to rendering superficial value judgments on religious systems. Third, in the German scholarship there were repeated instances of the mote and the beam. That is, snide comments were made on such matters as rewards and punishment that were deemed to deface Judaism, yet scholars ignored such passages where they are found also in the Gospels. Fourth, the leading motif in Christian writing before the nineteenth century was that of an unbroken continuity between Judaism and Christianity; in nineteenth-century scholarship Jesus and the apostles were portrayed under a motif of discontinuity.

In 1924 Moore published his two-volume work, *Judaism*; a third volume, with extended notes, came in 1930.[8] Jewish scholars, attuned to denigrations of Judaism in the usual New Testament scholarship, hailed Moore's work for its insight and reliability, and especially for its undoubted mastery of the difficult, complex ancient rabbinic literature. There is, in my recollection, no passage in Moore that *praises* Judaism; rather, as a scholar, he set down what he believed were the proper facts, and it was his academic mastery that elicited from Jewish scholars their unstinting praise for his achievement. It is not possible to overestimate the influence of Moore on American Christian scholars. In New Testament introductions for seminary students the scornful treatment of Judaism gave way to understanding and even recurrent sympathy.

In American cities for well over a century there have existed warm and cordial relations between rabbis and Protestant ministers. Cooperation in civic affairs has been frequent; the exchange of pulpits has become routine enough that it fails to elicit notice; interfaith Thanksgiving worship services have become usual. (In the past decade Roman Catholic and Eastern Orthodox priests and laymen have entered wholeheartedly into these cooperative ventures.) Chaplaincy experiences in World War I and II or on college campuses brought American clergy into those relationships that common en-

8. George Foot Moore, *Judaism,* 3 vols. (Cambridge, Mass.: Harvard University Press, 1924–30).

deavors promote. After World War II there was a spectacular rise in chairs of religious studies in American colleges and universities, significantly including chairs of Jewish studies, and scholarship added its own dimension of common interests and goals and tended to blunt the inherited parochialisms and triumphalisms. Among ordinary citizens there were business interchanges and collaborative efforts in charities and cultural enterprises. Social separatisms after the work day tended to abide, for these are apparently the strongest of resistants to change.

In a word, Jews and Christians in abundance came to know each other as fellow Americans. If perhaps the weakening of religious adherence in metropolitan areas helps to explain matters,[9] religious difference in any case by and large ceased to perpetuate the anxieties, suspicions, and hostilities. Christians came to discover that there were worthy Jews (often described as "the finest Christian I know"), and Jews came to discover admirable Christians (whose devotion to learning and to the public welfare equaled what Jews had once thought was uniquely theirs).

Here then emerges the paradox that many a Christian derives his inspiration to nobility from the New Testament and yet the New Testament is a repository for hostility to Jews and Judaism. Many, perhaps even most, Christians are completely free of anti-Semitism, yet Christian Scripture is permeated by it. How have Christians responded to this paradox? Some, whose ties to organized Christianity are either weak or only nominal, seem to disregard the anti-Semitism as having no binding force on them, any more than the prohibitions of divorce found in the Gospels possess binding force. Such people usually regard the New Testament anti-Semitism as a historical item of a long-ago period, and they regard it as both transient and peripheral to Christianity.

Other Christians, whose bent is theological, alter the New Testament use of the term *covenant*. While in the New Testament the new covenant with the Christian community replaces and annuls the old covenant with the Jews, such Christians reinterpret matters to the end that they affirm the Christian new covenant but also hold that the

---

9. The statement is made repeatedly that in the United States a third of the marriages Jews enter into are with mates not born Jewish. I know of no better clue to the decline of religious anti-Semitism, for if Christians as such continued to hate and despise Jews, such intermarriage would scarcely take place. The frequency of such marriages is viewed by many Jews as the single, most important problem Jews face today, for it seems to threaten the perpetuation of the Jewish community.

new covenant did not replace and annul the old. Hence there coexist two valid ongoing covenants that supplement each other, with the result that both Jews and Christians are partners with God, each one in the respective covenants. There are Jews too who subscribe to the "two covenant" idea. The idea of two covenants rests on the wish of Christians and Jews not to exclude each other from a partnership with God; accordingly, the covenant with the Jews is still valid and validates Judaism, and the covenant with the Christians validates Christianity. The contents of the two covenants are of course somewhat different from each other, with the consequence that Jews are obligated to the Mosaic and rabbinic requirements, Christians to the Christian legacy.[10] In the "two covenant" idea, each side is being generous to the other and the notion of one being superior to the other is lacking.

Perhaps a similar kind of conclusion can arise from an approach that is not "theological," as the above, but more "historical." That is, historically rabbinic Judaism and Christianity arose at roughly the same time, out of a shared background, but each developed in its own different way. As matured religions, congruent in their concern for the poor, the sick, and the unfortunate, they have become marked by basic areas of difference, but a difference that does not imply superior or inferior. Indeed, the objective student of world religions is reluctant to trespass into the value judgments involved in words like *superior* and *inferior*.

Yet a residual problem—the tendency to contrast "other Jews" invidiously with Jesus—seems to remain, although there may be no desire to assign one religion to a superior role over the other. Two opposite tendencies have existed in the scholarship. The one is to be found in a repeated judgment—almost a scholar's slogan—that Paul created a religion about a supernatural Jesus, the Christ, to replace the religion lived and practiced by Jesus. This designation of Paul, not Jesus, as the founder of Christianity in effect negates any influence of Jesus on the emergence of Christianity from Judaism. In opposition to this excessive attribution to Paul by scholars, I have elsewhere said that with Paul Christianity, begun with Jesus, had its *second* beginning. It does not seem reasonable to detach Jesus from the historical origins of Christianity.

10. Franz Rosenzweig (*The Star of Redemption,* trans. William Hallo [Boston: Beacon Press, 1972]), is the most eminent Jewish name with respect to the "two-covenant" theory. James Parkes is the most eminent Christian name, his views on this being found in a variety of his books.

Neither does there seem to be justice in the second scholarly tendency: contrasting Jesus so thoroughly with the "other Jews" that he no longer seems to belong within their tradition. The distinctiveness of Jesus in this trend is exhibited through showing him as different from all other Jews of his time and through ascribing to him virtues that other Jews either lacked or lacked in the same measure that he possessed them. In its most extreme form, this line of scholarship accepts as authentic about Jesus only those passages in which Jesus is in conflict with Jews and Judaism; Gospel passages in which Jesus is like the Jews or sympathetic to Judaism are held to be historically inauthentic. This contrast between the perfect Jesus and the imperfect Jews has been set forth by some contemporary scholars as "the principle of dissimilarity."

In earlier scholarship the teachings of Jesus had been judged to be typical of the Judaism of the time, and whatever originality lay in his teachings was primarily a matter of the combination of the components. This new viewpoint by implication seems to deny the basic and general congruency of the teachings of Jesus with those of the Judaism of the time. The purpose of mentioning this matter is to point to the phenomenon that even among the Christian scholars who reject the historical reliability of the Gospels, the virtues or accomplishments of Jesus seem capable of expression only by some invidious comparison with the Jews and Judaism. Is it possible objectively to characterize Jesus without disparaging Jews and Judaism? Many American scholars have come near to this. Others have seemed unaware of the possibility.

To repeat, Christians—their number is legion!—have risen above anti-Semitism. But the presence of anti-Semitism in the New Testament is what presents the occasion for rising above it. The textbooks used in Christian education have for several decades been carefully scrutinized by concerned Christians to the end that textbooks not recapitulate the basic New Testament hostilities. Most admirably, the Roman Catholic Archdiocese of Los Angeles has issued a pastoral letter concerning the homilies in the observance of Holy Week, lest the observance become distorted into anti-Semitism.[11] A "passion

---

11. I record my thanks to Father Royale M. Vadakin and Father Michael A. Nolin for their numerous courtesies to me. Father Vadakin graciously sent me an archdiocese publication, "Guidelines for Ecumenical and Interreligious Affairs" (September 1, 1976), and both a preliminary draft and the final publication of the "Lenten Homily Material" prepared there. These materials resulted from meetings held over a period of years between fifteen priests and fifteen rabbi's. All too often such dialogue terminates in wondrously noble

narrative" has been composed by an Episcopal priest for liturgical use out of Gospel materials, selected with a view to diminishing or eliminating the hostility of the usual liturgical passages.[12] Additional worthy Christian efforts are on record. The good faith and high resolves are not to be doubted.

But alongside such affirmative Christian efforts there abides among some Christians either an unconcern about New Testament anti-Semitism or at least insufficient concern for translating awareness into action. For Christian church school classes often visiting Jewish worship services and Jewish classes visiting Christian services, there is apt to occur again and again what has taken place in the past, namely, that Jewish youngsters hear as part of church worship readings from the New Testament such as John 8 that will upset them. And Christians will hear passages in Jewish worship, of course much less pointed, that so express the doctrine of the "chosen people" that Christians will feel somewhat affronted. Then where are we?

The Christian will to purge Christianity of anti-Semitism exists both broadly and in many places deeply. This will collides with the authority of Christian Scripture for Christians, their devotion to it, and their use of it. In this sense, Rosemary Ruether, a Catholic, seems fully right in her forceful statement that "anti-Semitism" is the "left hand" of Christian theology. She raises the question "Is it possible to say 'Jesus is Messiah' without implicitly or explicitly saying at the same time 'and the Jews be damned'?"[13] It does not seem to me that she exaggerates the extent to which Judaism appears in Christian theology as that which needs negation and rejection.

A searching critique of Rosemary Ruether contends that anti-Semitism was not an element in earliest Christianity but the result of a development in New Testament theology,[14] as suggested in our previ-

---

sentiments but nothing practical. What distinguishes the Los Angeles activities is the production of material that has been printed and distributed. Almost none of this could have happened without the active endorsement and support of His Eminence Timothy Cardinal Manning and his warm espousal of these efforts.

12. The passion narrative is by John T. Townsend and is found in a pamphlet called "A Liturgical Interpretation of Our Lord's Passion in Narrative Form," The Israel Study Group, Occasional Papers No. 1 (New York: National Conference of Christians and Jews, 1977).

13. Rosemary Ruether, *Faith and Fratricide: The Theological Roots of Anti-Semitism* (New York: Seabury Press, 1974), p. 246.

14. Thomas A. Indinopulos and Roy Bowen Ward, "Is Christology Inherently Anti-Semitic?" *Journal of the American Academy of Religion* 45, no. 2 (June 1977): 193–214.

ous chapter on the Gospels. Since this is the case, the critics insist, Ruether is mistaken in her extreme assertion that Christology is inherently anti-Semitic. The academic theological issue here is that she wishes Christians to move on to a new Christology, which will be free of anti-Semitism, while these critics wish Christians to revert to the oldest Christology, which in their view was free of it. On both sides of the argument, there is admission of the existence of New Testament anti-Semitism and unreserved repudiation of it.

Is anti-Semitism indeed beyond total eradication from Christian minds and hearts? Surely the New Testament material reviewed in this book can be used to so argue, as Rosemary Ruether seems to feel. But Ruether in a sense personifies the refutation of herself. That she could think and write as she did surely points the way. What seems to be needed is precisely that frankness which characterizes both Ruether and her thoughtful critics. True, Rosemary Ruether has been vilified as a disloyal Catholic, but her ideas cannot be readily dismissed. She has expressed eloquently what many a Christian has felt but only a few have put into words.

Rosemary Ruether and other involved Christians are of current interest at this writing, but with all due respect for them they may recede from the forefront of attention as others rise to address the question posed by our study. They are mentioned here because, beyond themselves, they represent the fruit of past decades of thought and a concern that is infinitely more broad and equally more profound than even their own endeavors.

I firmly believe, on the basis of my experience with Christians—colleagues, fellow committee members, my hosts or audiences on lecture tours—that once full recognition takes place and the will exists, the solution will be found. Not all at once, and not in a single step, but surely it will come. An essential first condition for fulfillment is set down by one Christian scholar: "Facing the facts as historical study reveals them, no matter how unpleasant, at least will allow for a decent intellectual understanding of the past and possibly also of the present."[15] If it is true that Christianity has shaped Christians, is it not equally true that Christians in the present, working from this intellectual understanding, can shape and determine what Christianity is or can be?

A book such as this, appearing in the last quarter of the twentieth

---

15. Eldon Jay Epp, "Anti-Semitism and the Popularity of the Fourth Gospel in Christianity," *Central Conference of American Rabbis Journal* 22 (1975):35.

century, could not have been written one hundred years ago or even fifty years ago. Perhaps it could not have been written a generation ago. Is it possible that the tragedy of the Holocaust has begun to move the mountain of past misconceptions? This generation of Jews and Christians, receptive to each other, has an opportunity for reconciliation that is without precedent.

Selected Bibliography

Agus, Jacob B. *Dialogue and Tradition: The Challenges of Contemporary Judeo-Christian Thought.* London: Abelard-Schuman, 1971.

Barth, Markus. *Israel and the Church.* Richmond: John Knox Press, 1969.

Blidstein, Gerald. "Jews and Ecumenical Dialogue." *Tradition* 2, no. 2 (Summer 1970).

Bowler, Maurice G. "Rosenzweig on Judaism and Christianity: The Two Covenant Theory." *Judaism* 22, no. 4 (Fall 1973).

Dalman, Gustav. *Jesus Christ in the Talmud, Midrash, Zohar and the Liturgy of the Synagogue.* New York: Arno Press, 1973.

Davies, Alan T. *Anti-Semitism and the Christian Mind: The Crisis of Conscience After Auschwitz.* New York: Herder and Herder, 1969.

Eckardt, A. Roy. *Elder and Younger Brothers: The Encounter of Jews and Christians.* New York: Schocken Books, 1973.

Eckert, W. P.; Levinson, N. P.; and Stöhr, M., eds. *Antijudaismus im Neuen Testament? Exegetische und systematische Beiträge.* Munich, 1967.

Epp, Eldon J. "Anti-Semitism and the Popularity of the Fourth Gospel in Christianity." *Central Conference of American Rabbis Journal* 22 (1975): 35–57.

Flannery, Edward H. *The Anguish of the Jews: Twenty-three Centuries of Anti-Semitism.* New York: Macmillan Company, 1965.

Glock, Charles Y., and Stark, Rodney. *Christian Beliefs and Anti-Semitism.* New York: Harper and Row, 1969.

Goldstein, Morris. *Jesus in the Jewish Tradition.* New York: Macmillan Company, 1950.

Grant, Frederick C. *Ancient Judaism and the New Testament.* New York: Macmillan Company, 1959.

166

Herford, R. Travers. *Christianity in Talmud and Midrash*. Clifton: Reference Book Publishers, Inc., 1966.

Isaac, Jules. *The Teaching of Contempt: Christian Roots of Anti-Semitism*. New York: McGraw-Hill Company, 1964.

Jacob, Walter. *Christianity Through Jewish Eyes: The Quest for Common Ground*. Cincinnati: Hebrew Union College Press, 1974.

Katz, Jacob. *Exclusiveness and Tolerance: Jewish-Gentile Relations in Medieval and Modern Times*. New York: Schocken Books, 1962.

Krauss, S. "The Jews in the Works of the Church Fathers" in *Judaism and Christianity, Selected Accounts, 1892–1962*. (New York: Arno Press, 1973), pp. 122–261.

Littell, Franklin H. *The Crucifixion of the Jews*. New York: Harper & Row, 1975.

Parkes, James. *The Conflict of the Church and the Synagogue: A Study in the Origins of Antisemitism*. Philadelphia: Jewish Publication Society of America, 1961.

Rankin, Oliver S. *Jewish Religious Polemics of Earlier and Later Centuries,* Edinburgh: University Press, 1969.

Rylaersdam, J. Coert. "Jewish-Christian Relationship: The Two Covenants and the Dilemmas of Christology." *Journal of Ecumenical Studies,* Spring 1972, p. 249.

Sandmel, Samuel. *The First Christian Century in Judaism and Christianity: Certainties and Uncertainties*. New York: Oxford University Press, 1969.

———. *We Jews and Jesus*. New York: Oxford University Press, 1965.

———. *The Genius of Paul: A Study in History*. New York: Schocken Books, 1970.

———. *We Jews and You Christians*. New York: J. P. Lippincott Co., 1967.

Strover, Gerald S. *Portrait of the Elder Brother: Jews and Judaism and Protestant Teaching Materials,* New York: American Jewish Committee, 1972.

Synan, Edward A. *The Popes and the Jews in the Middle Ages*. New York: Macmillan Company, 1965.

Talmage, Frank E., ed. *Disputation and Dialogue: Readings in the Jewish-Christian Encounter*. New York: Ktav Publishing House, Inc. and Anti-Defamation League of B'nai B'rith, 1975.

van Buren, Paul M., "Affirmation of the Jewish People: A Condition of Theological Coherence," *Journal of the American Academy of Religion* XLV, 1977.

Williams, Arthur Lykyn, *Adversus Judaeos,* Cambridge: Cambridge University Press, 1935.

Zeitlin, Solomon, *Who Crucified Jesus?* New York: Bloch Publishing Co., 1964.